Introducing
Microsoft® Silverlight™ 3

Laurence Moroney

PUBLISHED BY
Microsoft Press
A Division of Microsoft Corporation
One Microsoft Way
Redmond, Washington 98052-6399

Library of Congress Control Number: 2009929278

Printed and bound in the United States of America.

1 2 3 4 5 6 7 8 9   QWT   4 3 2 1 0 9

Distributed in Canada by H.B. Fenn and Company Ltd.

A CIP catalogue record for this book is available from the British Library.

Microsoft Press books are available through booksellers and distributors worldwide. For further information about international editions, contact your local Microsoft Corporation office or contact Microsoft Press International directly at fax (425) 936-7329. Visit our Web site at www.microsoft.com/mspress. Send comments to mspinput@microsoft.com.

Microsoft, Microsoft Press, Access, ActiveX, DirectShow, Expression, Expression Blend, IntelliSense, Internet Explorer, MS, Outlook, Photosynth, PlayReady, Silverlight, Virtual Earth, Visual Basic, Visual Studio, Windows, Windows Live, Windows Media, Windows Server, and Windows Vista are either registered trademarks or trademarks of the Microsoft group of companies. Other product and company names mentioned herein may be the trademarks of their respective owners.

The example companies, organizations, products, domain names, e-mail addresses, logos, people, places, and events depicted herein are fictitious. No association with any real company, organization, product, domain name, e-mail address, logo, person, place, or event is intended or should be inferred.

This book expresses the author's views and opinions. The information contained in this book is provided without any express, statutory, or implied warranties. Neither the authors, Microsoft Corporation, nor its resellers, or distributors will be held liable for any damages caused or alleged to be caused either directly or indirectly by this book.

Acquisitions Editor: Ben Ryan
Developmental Editor: Devon Musgrave
Project Editor: Rosemary Caperton
Editorial Production: Waypoint Press
Technical Reviewer: Per Blomqvist. Technical Review services provided by Content Master, a member of CM Group, Ltd.
Cover: Tom Draper Design

Body Part No. X15-88611

It's always hard to know what to say when dedicating a book. You have few words to speak about something that has a huge meaning. So I will use the words that mean the most to the people that mean the most to me: my wife Rebecca and my children Claudia and Christopher. I dedicate this book to you to thank you for being you.

I also want to thank the One who makes it all possible: the God of Abraham, Isaac, Jacob, and Jesus, for giving us life, love, happiness, and hope.

Contents at a Glance

Table of Contents

Part I   Introducing Silverlight 3

What do you think of this book? We want to hear from you!

Microsoft is interested in hearing your feedback so we can continually improve our books and
learning resources for you. To participate in a brief online survey, please visit:

www.microsoft.com/learning/booksurvey

What do you think of this book? We want to hear from you!

Microsoft is interested in hearing your feedback so we can continually improve our books and learning resources for you. To participate in a brief online survey, please visit:

www.microsoft.com/learning/booksurvey

Acknowledgments

Thanks to the entire staff at Microsoft Press and Microsoft Learning for putting this book together. Thank you to Rosemary Caperton and Steve Sagman, in particular, who had to project manage me through this process and to whom I owe a huge debt of gratitude for keeping me honest and on pace. I'd also like to acknowledge the extraordinary talents of Christina Yeager and Per Blomqvist, without whom this book would never have been possible!

Introduction

Why Microsoft Silverlight?

As the Web grows and evolves, so do the expectations of the Web user. When the first Web browser was developed, it was created to provide a relatively simple way to allow hyperlinking between documents. Then these early browsers were coupled with the cross-machine protocols encompassing the Internet, and suddenly documents stored on computer servers anywhere in the world could be hyperlinked to each other.

Over time, the people who were using the Internet changed—the user base expanded from a small group of people associated with universities and computational research to encompass the general population. And what had been an acceptable user interface for experts in the field was greatly lacking for commercial applications. People now want high-quality user interfaces that are simple to use—and as more types of information, including many kinds of media files, are available on the Internet, it becomes more difficult to satisfy users' expectations about how easy it should be to access the information they want.

The need to supply users with sophisticated methods of accessing Internet resources that were easy to use led to advanced application technologies. One type of technology, for example, created "plug-in" browser tools that allowed the browser to use some of the user's local computational horsepower.

ActiveX controls, Java Applets, and Flash applications are examples of plug-in technology. Asynchronous JavaScript and XML (AJAX) is another tool that has been introduced to develop new and exciting user interfaces that benefit from immediate partial updates. Using AJAX, the browser's screen area doesn't flash or lock up since the need for full-page refreshes is reduced.

Although AJAX provides technology to enable developers to build Web sites that contain more complex content and are more dynamic than HTML alone could provide, AJAX does have its limitations. For example, it allows asynchronous communication with the server, which means that applications can update themselves using background threads, eliminating the screen flicker so often seen with complex Web user interfaces. But AJAX is strictly a browser-to-server communications mechanism. It lacks graphics, animation, video, and other capabilities that are necessary to provide for truly multimedia user interfaces.

Microsoft has built a Web user experience (UX) strategy to address these limitations by identifying three levels of desired user experience—"good," "great," and "ultimate," which are mapped to development and run-time technologies. These are combined in this book with a term you may find that I use a lot—"rich" or "richness." When I say "rich," I'm trying to describe a concept that's hard to put into words. It's the feeling you get when you use a traditional Web application, with the limitations built into the browser and HTML, versus a desktop application that has the entire operating system to call on for services and capability. The Web applications of today just don't have the same feeling and capability as desktop applications, and the user generally realizes that they are limited by the technology. With Silverlight (and AJAX), the goal is to create Web applications that are much more like desktop applications, and ultimately, to create applications that are indistinguishable from desktop applications.

The lowest level of user experience, the "good" level, can be achieved with the browser enhanced by AJAX. This level identifies the baseline UX expectation moving forward from today—the type of asynchronous, dynamic, browser application empowered by AJAX.

The top or "ultimate" level is the rich client desktop running Windows Vista and using the Windows Presentation Foundation (WPF) and the .NET Framework. These offer a run time that allows developers to create extremely rich applications that are easily deployed and maintained. Broadcast quality graphics, video, and animation are available at this level, as well as application services such as file-based persistence and integration with other desktop applications. In addition, WPF separates design and development technologies so that user interfaces are designed and expressed in a new language called XML Application Markup Language (XAML). Design tools such as the Microsoft Expression series were aimed at designers who are now able to produce their work as XAML documents. Developers then use the resulting XAML to bring the designers' dreams to reality more easily by activating the XAML with code.

I mentioned that there are three levels in the UX strategy because as AJAX and .NET/WPF evolved, it became obvious that there was room in the middle for a new technology that effectively combines the best of both worlds—the global scalability of the Internet application coupled with the richness of the desktop application. This level was named the "great" experience and represents the browser enhanced by AJAX with a new technology: Silverlight.

Silverlight is a plug-in for the browser that renders XAML and exposes a programming interface. Thus, it allows designers and developers to collaborate when building Internet applications that provide the richness of desktop applications.

The first release of Silverlight exposed a JavaScript-oriented programming model that provided powerful scripting of XAML elements within the browser. Silverlight 2 added to this greatly by including a .NET runtime that allows you to use .NET programming languages to go beyond this, manipulating XAML, providing a control base, networking support, powerful data libraries, extensibility and greatly improved performance.

Now with the release of Silverlight 3, your tools have gotten broader and more powerful.

In this book, you'll be looking at Silverlight and how to use it to enhance Web user experience. You'll take a broad look at the platform, and how to build applications, media experiences, rich imaging and more.

Silverlight 3 can and will change the way you think about building applications for the Web. Instead of Web sites, you will build Web experiences. At the heart of a great experience is great design, and with Silverlight, designers and developers can come together like never before through XAML and the Microsoft Expression line of tools.

In this book, my goal is to help you understand the technologies that work together to develop and deploy Silverlight Web applications, from writing basic code that uses Silverlight to using advanced tools to create and deliver Silverlight content. When you have finished reading this book and have worked the examples, you should be ready to use what you've learned to enhance the Web applications you're developing right now. Imagine what you'll be able to do tomorrow!

Who This Book Is For

This book is written for developers who are already working every day to bring new and better Web applications to Internet users and who are interested in adding this cutting-edge Microsoft technology to their store of knowledge—to find out how it can be applied as a tool to bring users more interesting, more capable, and more effective user interfaces. Development managers may also find the easy-to-read style useful for understanding how Silverlight fits into the bigger Microsoft Web technology picture. With luck, this book will provide managers with the technological background they need so that when their developers come to them to talk about Silverlight—with excited looks on their faces—they will understand what the excitement is about!

What This Book Is About

This book is broken into two parts. Part I, *Introducing Silverlight 3*, takes you through the basics of Silverlight. It looks at what Silverlight is and what tools are used to create and maintain Silverlight experiences, including Microsoft Expression Blend and Microsoft Visual Studio.

Part I also looks into the XAML technology and how it uses XML to define your entire user experience, from layout to controls to animation and more. Finally, this part delves into the Silverlight plug-in itself and how it can be used to interface with the browser so that your applications become first-class browser citizens.

Part II, *Programming Silverlight 3 with .NET*, takes you into some more detail on the high-level concepts of Silverlight. It's not an exhaustive reference by any means, but it is designed as a straightforward, no-nonsense introduction to the major things that you'll be doing as a Silverlight developer. You'll take a two-chapter tour of the built-in controls before looking at how easy it is to build your own controls. You'll then look at data, communications, programming for animation as well as some of the advanced controls for managing media, ink, and the new *DeepZoom* and *Photosynth* components that provide eye-popping presentation of images. The book wraps up with a look at the exciting new Dynamic Languages support in Silverlight.

System Requirements

To develop Silverlight applications as used in this book, you will need the following, available at *http://silverlight.net/GetStarted*:

- Microsoft Visual Studio 2008

- Microsoft Expression Design

- Microsoft Expression Blend

- Microsoft Silverlight Software Development Kit

For Microsoft Silverlight, the recommended system configuration is 128 MB of RAM and 450 MHz or faster processor on Windows and 1 GB of RAM on Intel 1.83 GHz or faster processor on Mac OSX.

For Microsoft Visual Studio 2008, the recommended configuration is 2.2 GHz or higher CPU, 1024 MB or more RAM, 1280 x 1024 display, 7200 RPM or higher hard disk. (The minimum requirements are 1.6 GHz CPU, 384 MB RAM, 1024 x 768 display, 5400 RPM hard disk.) For Windows Vista, the following is recommended: 2.4 GHz CPU, 768 MB RAM.

The Companion Web Site

This book features a companion Web site that makes available to you all the code used in the book. This code is organized by chapter, and you can download it from the companion site at this address:

http://www.microsoft.com/learning/en/us/Books/12578.aspx

Note that this book is based on the Silverlight 3 Beta, so check back later for updates to the code for the final release of Silverlight 3.

Support for This Book

Microsoft Press provides support for books and companion content at the following Web site:

http://www.microsoft.com/learning/support/books/

Find Additional Content Online As new or updated material becomes available that complements your book, it will be posted online on the Microsoft Press Online Developer Tools Web site. The type of material you might find includes updates to book content, articles, links to companion content, errata, sample chapters, and more. This Web site will be available soon at *www.microsoft.com/learning/books/online/developer* and will be updated periodically.

Questions and Comments

If you have comments, questions, or ideas regarding the book or the companion content, or questions that are not answered by visiting the sites just listed, please send them to Microsoft Press to:

mspinput@microsoft.com

Please note that Microsoft software product support is not offered through the above address.

Part I
Introducing Silverlight 3

Chapter 1
Introducing Silverlight 3

Microsoft Silverlight represents the next step toward enriching the user's experience through the technology of the Web. The goal of Silverlight is to bring to Web applications the same fidelity and quality found in the user interfaces (UIs) associated with desktop applications so that Web developers and designers can build applications for their clients' specific needs. It is designed to bridge the technology gap between designers and developers by giving them a common format in which to work. This format is rendered by the browser and is based on Extensible Markup Language (XML), making it easy to template and to generate automatically. The format is XAML—Extensible Application Markup Language.

Before XAML, a Web experience designer would use one set of tools to express a design using familiar technology. The developer would then take what the designer provided and interpret it using the technology of his or her choice. The design would not necessarily transfer into development properly or in a problem-free way, and the developer would need to make many alterations that could compromise the design. With Silverlight, the designer can use tools that express a design as XAML, and the developer can pick up this XAML, activate it with code, and deploy it.

Silverlight is a cross-browser, cross-platform plug-in that was developed to deliver a rich media experience and rich interactive Internet applications over the Web. It offers a full programming model that supports AJAX, the .NET Framework, and dynamic languages such as Python and Ruby. Silverlight 1.0 is programmable by using actual Web technologies including AJAX, JavaScript, and Dynamic HTML (DHTML). Silverlight 2 adds dynamic and .NET language support, as well as a host of new features that are only possible when using the .NET Framework, such as isolated storage, networking, a rich control set, and more.

This book introduces you to what is available in these as well as the newest version of Silverlight—Silverlight 3.

The first part of this book introduces you to the fundamentals of Silverlight by looking at the design and development tools that are available, and the second part examines the programming model more closely.

Silverlight and User Experience

Silverlight is designed to be part of a much larger ecosystem that is used to deliver the best possible end-user experience. There are a number of typical scenarios for accessing information on the Internet:

- Mobile devices
- Digital home products
- Unenhanced browsers (no plug-ins)
- Enhanced browsers (using plug-ins such as Flash, Java, or Silverlight)
- Desktop applications
- Office productivity software

Over the years, users' expectations about how these applications should work have evolved. For example, the *expectation* is that the experience of using an application on a desktop computer should provide more to the user than using the same type of application on a mobile device because, as users, we are accustomed to having much more power on the desktop than we do on a mobile device. In addition, many users assume that because the application is on the Web, it might not have the same capacity as a similar desktop application. For example, users might have lower expectations about a Web-based e-mail application because they don't believe it can offer the same e-mail capability that office productivity software such as Microsoft Office Outlook provides.

However, as platforms converge, user expectations are also increasing—and the term *rich* is now commonly used to describe an experience above the current baseline level of expectation. For example, the term *rich Internet application* was coined in response to the increased level of sophistication that Web users were seeing in applications powered by AJAX to provide a more dynamic experience in scenarios such as e-mail and mapping. This evolution in expectations has led to customers who now demand ever richer experiences that not only meet the needs of the application in terms of functionality and effectiveness but also address the perception of satisfaction that users have with a company's products and services. This can lead to a lasting relationship between the user and the company.

As a result, Microsoft has committed to the User Experience (UX) and ships the tools and technologies that developers can use to implement rich UX applications. Additionally, these tools are designed to be coherent—that is, skills in developing UX-focused applications transfer across the domains of desktop and Web application development. So if you are building a rich desktop application but need a Web version, you will have cross-pollination between the two. Similarly, if you are building a mobile application and need an Internet version, you won't need two sets of skills, two sets of tools, and two sets of developers.

Regarding the Web, Figure 1-1 shows the presentation and programming models for the Web that are available today. As you can see, the typical browser-based development technologies are CSS/DHTML in the presentation model and JavaScript/AJAX/ASP.NET in the development model. On the desktop, with .NET Framework 3.x, XAML provides the presentation model, and the framework itself provides the development model. These models overlap, and this is where the Silverlight-enhanced browser provides a "best of both worlds" approach.

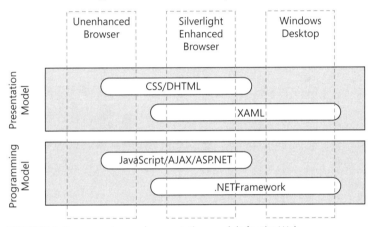

FIGURE 1-1 Programming and presentation models for the Web.

The typical rich interactive application is based on technologies that exist in the unenhanced browser category. The typical desktop application is at the other end of the spectrum, using unrelated technologies. The opportunity to bring these together into a rich application that is lightweight and runs in the browser is realized through the Silverlight-enhanced browser that provides the CSS/DHTML and XAML design model and the JavaScript/AJAX/.NET Framework programming model.

Silverlight achieves this by providing a browser plug-in that enhances the functionality of the browser with the typical technologies that provide rich UIs, such as timeline-based animation, vector graphics, and audiovisual media. These technologies are enabled by the Silverlight browser-based XAML rendering engine. The rich UI can be designed as XAML, and because XAML is an XML-based language and because XML is just text, the application is firewall compatible and (potentially) search engine friendly. The browser receives the XAML and renders it.

When combined with technology such as AJAX and JavaScript, managing your application can be a dynamic process—you can download snippets of XAML and add them to your UI, or you can edit, rearrange, or remove XAML that is currently in the render tree by using simple JavaScript programming.

Silverlight Architecture

As mentioned earlier, the core functionality of Silverlight is provided by a browser plug-in that renders XAML and provides a programming model that can be either JavaScript and browser-based or .NET Framework and common language runtime (CLR)-based. Figure 1-2 shows the architecture that supports this.

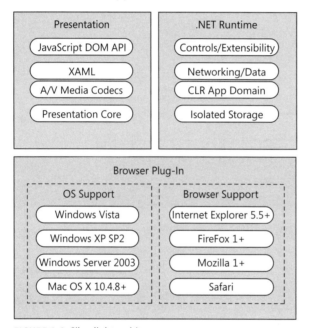

Presentation		.NET Runtime
JavaScript DOM API		Controls/Extensibility
XAML		Networking/Data
A/V Media Codecs		CLR App Domain
Presentation Core		Isolated Storage

Browser Plug-In

OS Support		Browser Support
Windows Vista		Internet Explorer 5.5+
Windows XP SP2		FireFox 1+
Windows Server 2003		Mozilla 1+
Mac OS X 10.4.8+		Safari

FIGURE 1-2 Silverlight architecture

When scripting the control in the browser, the main programming interface that is exposed in Silverlight 1.0 is through the JavaScript Document Object Model (DOM) application pro-gramming interface (API). By using the JavaScript DOM API, you can catch user events that are raised in the application (such as mouse moves or clicks of a specific element) and have code execute in response to them. You can call methods on the JavaScript DOM for XAML elements to manipulate them—allowing, for example, control of media playback or triggering animations.

For a richer and more powerful experience, you can also program an application that is rendered by the control using the new .NET Framework CLR. In addition to what you can do in JavaScript, this capability offers many of the namespaces and controls that come as part of the .NET Framework so that you can do things that are very difficult—or impossible—in JavaScript, such as access data with ADO.NET and Language-Integrated Query (LINQ), communicate with Web Services, build and use custom controls, and so on.

Additionally, the presentation runtime ships with the software necessary to allow technologies such as H264, Windows Media Video (WMV), Windows Media Audio (WMA), and MP3 to be played back in the browser *without* any external dependencies. So, for example, Macintosh users do not need Windows Media Player to play back WMV content—Silverlight is enough. Underpinning the entire presentation runtime is the presentation code, and this manages the overall rendering process. This is all built into the browser plug-in that is designed to support the major browsers available for both Windows and the Macintosh.

The architecture of a simple application running in the browser using Silverlight is shown in Figure 1-3.

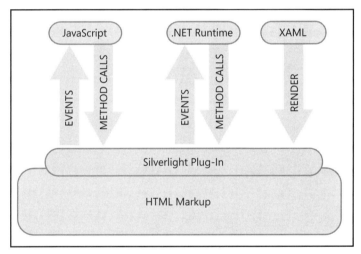

FIGURE 1-3 Application architecture with Silverlight.

Applications that run in the browser typically are made up of HTML. This markup contains the calls to instantiate the Silverlight plug-in. As users interact with the Silverlight application, they raise events that can be captured by either JavaScript or .NET Framework functions. In turn, program code can make method calls against the elements in the Silverlight content to manipulate it, add new content, or remove existing content. Finally, XAML can be read by the plug-in and rendered. The XAML itself can exist inline in the page, externally as a static file, or as dynamic XAML returned from a server.

Silverlight and XAML

Now that we've taken a high-level look at the architecture of Silverlight and how a typical application will look, let's examine the base technology that holds the UX together: XAML.

XAML is an XML-based language that is used to define the visual assets of your application. These include UIs, graphical assets, animations, media, controls, and more. Microsoft introduced XAML for the Windows Presentation Foundation (WPF), formerly Avalon, which is a desktop-oriented technology and part of .NET Framework 3.0 and beyond. It is designed, as discussed earlier, to bridge the gap between designers and developers when creating applications.

The XAML used in Silverlight differs from that in the WPF in that it is a *subset* that is focused on Web-oriented features. So, if you're familiar with XAML from the WPF, you'll notice some missing tags and functionality, such as the *<Window>* element.

XAML uses XML to define the UI using XML elements. At the root of every Silverlight XAML document is a container element, such as *Canvas*, which defines the space on which your UI will be drawn. When building a Silverlight Web application, you have a root *Canvas* that contains the XML namespace declarations that Silverlight requires.

Here's an example:

```
<Canvas
  xmlns="http://schemas.microsoft.com/client/2007"
  xmlns:x="http://schemas.microsoft.com/winfx/2006/xaml"
  Width="640" Height="480"
  Background="White"
  >
</Canvas>
```

Notice that two namespaces are declared. The typical XAML document contains a base set of elements and attributes as well as an extended set, which typically uses the *x:* prefix. An example of an extended namespace attribute is the commonly used *x:Name*, which is used to provide a name for an XAML element so that you can reference it in your code. The root *Canvas* element declares the namespace location for each of these.

The *Canvas* element is a container. This means that it can contain other elements as children. These elements can themselves be containers for other elements, defining a UI as an XML document tree. So, for example, the following is a simple XAML document containing a *Canvas* that contains a number of children, some of which are *Canvas* containers themselves:

```
<Canvas
  xmlns="http://schemas.microsoft.com/client/2007"
  xmlns:x="http://schemas.microsoft.com/winfx/2006/xaml"
  Width="640" Height="480"
```

```
      Background="Black"
    >
      <Rectangle Fill="#FFFFFFFF" Stroke="#FF000000"
          Width="136" Height="80"
          Canvas.Left="120" Canvas.Top="240"/>
      <Canvas>
          <Rectangle Fill="#FFFFFFFF" Stroke="#FF000000"
              Width="104" Height="96"
              Canvas.Left="400" Canvas.Top="320"/>
          <Canvas Width="320" Height="104"
              Canvas.Left="96" Canvas.Top="64">
            <Rectangle Fill="#FFFFFFFF" Stroke="#FF000000"
                  Width="120" Height="96"/>
            <Rectangle Fill="#FFFFFFFF" Stroke="#FF000000"
                  Width="168" Height="96"
                  Canvas.Left="152" Canvas.Top="8"/>
        </Canvas>
      </Canvas>
</Canvas>
```

Here you can see that the root *Canvas* has two children, a *Rectangle* and another *Canvas*. This second *Canvas* also contains a *Rectangle* and a *Canvas*, and the final *Canvas* contains two more *Rectangle*s. This hierarchical structure allows for controls to be grouped together logically and to share common layout and other behaviors.

Silverlight XAML supports a number of shapes that can be combined to form more complex objects. You'll find a lot more details about using XAML in Chapter 4, "Silverlight XAML Basics," but a few of the basic shapes available include the following:

- **Rectangle**   Defines a rectangular shape on the screen

- **Ellipse**   Defines an ellipse or circle

- **Line**   Draws a line connecting two points

- **Polygon**   Draws a many-sided shape

- **Polyline**   Draws many line segments

- **Path**   Allows you to create a nonlinear path (like a scribble)

In addition, XAML supports *brushes*, which define how an object is painted on the screen. The inside area of an object is painted using a *fill* brush, and the outline of an object is drawn using a *stroke*. Brushes come in many types, including solid color, gradient, image, and video.

Following is an example using a *SolidColorBrush* to fill an ellipse:

```
<Ellipse Canvas.Top="10" Canvas.Left="24"
        Width="200" Height="150">
    <Ellipse.Fill>
        <SolidColorBrush Color="Black" />
    </Ellipse.Fill>
</Ellipse>
```

In this case, the brush uses one of the 141 Silverlight-supported named colors, *Black*. You also can use standard hexadecimal RGB color notation for custom colors.

Fills and strokes also might have a gradient fill, using a gradient brush. The gradient is defined by using a number of *gradient stops* across a *normalized space*. So, for example, if you want a linear gradient to move from left to right—phasing from black to white through shades of gray—you would define stops according to a normalized line. In this case, consider the beginning of the normalized line as the 0 point and the end as the 1 point. So, a gradient from left to right in a one-dimensional space has a stop at 0 and another at 1. Should you want a gradient that transitions through more than two colors—from black to red to white, for example—you would define a third stop somewhere between 0 and 1. Keep in mind that when you create a fill, however, you are working in a two-dimensional space, so (0,0) represents the upper-left corner, and (1,1) represents the lower-right corner. Thus, to fill a rectangle with a gradient brush, you would use a *LinearGradientBrush* like this:

```
<Rectangle Width="200" Height="150" >
  <Rectangle.Fill>
    <LinearGradientBrush StartPoint="0,0" EndPoint="1,1">
      <LinearGradientBrush.GradientStops>
        <GradientStop Color="Red" Offset="0" />
        <GradientStop Color="Black" Offset="1" />
      </LinearGradientBrush.GradientStops>
    </LinearGradientBrush>
  </Rectangle.Fill>
</Rectangle>
```

XAML also supports text through the *TextBlock* element. Control over typical text properties such as content, font type, font size, wrapping, and more is available through attributes. Following is a simple example:

```
<TextBlock TextWrapping="Wrap" Width="100">
  Hello there, how are you?
</TextBlock>
```

Objects can be transformed in XAML using a number of transformations. Some transformations include the following:

- **RotationTransform**   Rotates the element through a defined number of degrees
- **ScaleTransform**   Used to stretch or shrink an object

- **SkewTransform** Skews the object in a defined direction by a defined amount

- **TranslateTransform** Moves the object in a direction according to a defined vector

- **MatrixTransform** Used to create a mathematical transform that can combine all of the preceding

You can group existing transformations to provide a complex transformation. That is, you could move an object by translating it, change its size by scaling it, and rotate it simultaneously by grouping the individual transformations together. Here's a transformation example that rotates and scales the canvas:

```
<Canvas.RenderTransform>
    <TransformGroup>
        <RotateTransform Angle="-45" CenterX="50" CenterY="50"/>
        <ScaleTransform ScaleX="1.5" ScaleY="2" />
    </TransformGroup>
</Canvas.RenderTransform>
```

XAML supports animations through defining how their properties are changed over time using a timeline. These timelines are contained within a *storyboard*. Different types of animation include these:

- **DoubleAnimation** Allows numeric properties, such as those used to determine location, to be animated

- **ColorAnimation** Allows colored properties, such as fills, to be transformed

- **PointAnimation** Allows points that define a two-dimensional space to be animated

As you change properties, you can do it in a linear manner so that the property is phased between values over a timeline, or in a "key frame" manner, in which you define a number of milestones along which the animation occurs. You can examine all of this in a lot more detail in Chapter 5, "XAML Transformation and Animation."

Beyond this basic XAML, you define your full UIs using XAML controls and layout, too. You can explore these topics in more detail in Chapter 9, "Silverlight Controls: Advanced Controls," and in the rest of the chapters in Part 2, "Programming Silverlight 3 with .NET."

Silverlight and Expression Studio

Microsoft Expression Studio provides a robust, modern set of tools for designers to express their work using artifacts that developers can include while developing using the Microsoft Visual Studio tool suite.

There are several tools in the Expression suite:

- **Expression Web**   With this Web design tool, you can use HTML, DHTML, CSS, and other Web standard technologies to design, build, and manage Web applications.

- **Expression Media**   With this media asset management tool, you can catalog and organize assets, and encode and change encoding between different formats.

- **Expression Encoder**   This application is designed so that you can manage encoding of media assets. It can also be used to bundle media with the relevant code to have a Silverlight media player for the media.

- **Expression Design**   This is an illustration and graphic design tool that you can use to build graphical elements and assets for Web and desktop application UIs.

- **Expression Blend**   This tool is designed so that you can build XAML-based UIs and applications for the desktop using WPF, or for the Web using Silverlight.

When you use Silverlight, you can use some or all of these applications. The rest of this chapter discusses how Expression Design, Expression Blend, and Expression Encoder enhance your toolkit for designing and building Silverlight applications.

Silverlight and Expression Design

Expression Design is a graphical design tool that you can use to build graphical assets for your applications. It's a huge and sophisticated tool, so this section provides just an overview of how it can be used for Silverlight XAML.

With Expression Design, you can blend vector-based and raster-based (bitmap) images for complete flexibility. Expression Design supports many graphical file formats for import, including the following:

- Adobe Illustrator—PDF Compatible (*.ai)

- Adobe Photoshop (*.psd)

- Graphical Interchange Format (.gif)

- Portable Network Graphics format (.png)

- Bitmaps (.bmp, .dib, .rle)

- JPEG formats (.jpeg, .jpg, .jpe, .jfif, .exif)

- Windows Media Photos (.wdp, .hdp)

- Tagged Image File Format (.tiff, .tif)

- Icons (.ico)

It supports export of the following image types:

- XAML Silverlight Canvas

- XAML WPF Resource Dictionary

- XAML WPF Canvas

- Portable Document Format (.pdf)

- Adobe Photoshop (.psd)

- Tagged Image File Format (.tif, .tiff)

- JPEG formats (.jpeg, .jpg)

- Windows Bitmap (.bmp)

- Portable Network Graphics format (.png)

- Graphical Interchange Format (.gif)

- Windows Media Photos (also known as HD Photo) (.wdp)

As you can see, Expression Design supports export of graphical assets as XAML files. Later in this chapter, you'll see how to use Expression Design to design the graphical elements of a simple application, and you'll export these as XAML, which you can use in Expression Blend and Visual Studio to create an application.

Figure 1-4 shows the Export XAML dialog box in Expression Design. There are several format options, one of which is XAML Silverlight Canvas (shown selected). This option formats your drawing using the subset of XAML elements that is usable by Silverlight so that you can import the resulting XAML into Visual Studio or Expression Blend to build your Silverlight application.

FIGURE 1-4 Exporting XAML from Expression Design.

The content is exported as an XML document containing a *Canvas* element that contains the elements of your design. Here's a (truncated) example:

```xml
<?xml version="1.0" encoding="utf-8"?>
<Canvas xmlns="http://schemas.microsoft.com/winfx/2006/xaml/presentation"
xmlns:x="http://schemas.microsoft.com/winfx/2006/xaml" x:Name="Document">

  <Canvas x:Name="Layer_1" Width="640.219" Height="480.202" Canvas.Left="0" Canvas.Top="0">
    <Ellipse x:Name="Ellipse" Width="135" Height="161" Canvas.Left="0.546544"
      Canvas.Top="20.3998" Stretch="Fill" StrokeLineJoin="Round" Stroke="#FF000000"
      Fill="#FFFFC800"/>
    <Path x:Name="Path" Width="135.103" Height="66.444" Canvas.Left="-0.555986"
      Canvas.Top="-0.389065" Stretch="Fill" StrokeLineJoin="Round" Stroke="#FF000000"
      Fill="#FF000000" Data="..."/>
    <Path x:Name="Path_0" Width="19.4583" Height="23.9019" Canvas.Left="75.8927"
      Canvas.Top="76.1198" Stretch="Fill" StrokeLineJoin="Round" Stroke="#FF000000"
      Fill="#FF000000" Data="..."/>
    <Path x:Name="Path_1" Width="11.0735" Height="24.0564" Canvas.Left="60.473"
      Canvas.Top="106.4" Stretch="Fill" StrokeLineJoin="Round" Stroke="#FF000000"
      Fill="#FF000000" Data="..."/>
    <Path x:Name="Path_2" Width="76" Height="29.8274" Canvas.Left="31.5465"
      Canvas.Top="127.4" Stretch="Fill" StrokeThickness="7" StrokeLineJoin="Round"
      Stroke="#FF000000" Data="..."/>
    <Path x:Name="Path_3" Width="20.3803" Height="27.1204" Canvas.Left="31.2028"
      Canvas.Top="75.306" Stretch="Fill" StrokeLineJoin="Round" Stroke="#FF000000"
      Fill="#FF000000" Data="..."/>
  </Canvas>
</Canvas>
```

You can then cut and paste this XAML into Expression Blend or Visual Studio, and you can use the graphical element in your application.

Silverlight and Expression Blend

Expression Blend has native support for the creation of Silverlight applications. When you start Expression Blend and create a new project, you have two options for creating Silverlight projects:

- **Silverlight Application**   This option creates a boilerplate Silverlight application that contains everything you need to get started with building a Silverlight application. The boilerplate includes the requisite .NET assemblies, a *properties* folder containing the application manifest, the App.xaml with code-behind that defines the application entry points, and a basic page containing an empty canvas, along with code-behind.

- **Silverlight Website**   This is the same as the Silverlight application template but adds a Web project that contains an HTML page that embeds the Silverlight application, along with the required JavaScript files.

Exploring the Silverlight Website Project

When you create a new Silverlight Website project using Expression Blend, your project includes a default HTML file that contains all the requisite JavaScript to instantiate the Silverlight control as well as a copy of the Silverlight.js file that is part of the Silverlight software development kit (SDK). This file manages the instantiation and downloading of the Silverlight plug-in for your users. You can see the project structure in Figure 1-5.

FIGURE 1-5 Project structure for a Silverlight Website project.

The Default Web Page

Listing 1-1 shows some of the code for the basic Web page that is created for you by Expression Blend for Silverlight projects.

LISTING 1-1 Default.html from Silverlight Template

```
<div id="silverlightControlHost">
<object data="data:application/x-silverlight," type="application/x-silverlight-2"
width="100%" height="100%">
  <param name="source" value="ClientBin/SilverlightApplication1.xap"/>
  <param name="onerror" value="onSilverlightError" />
  <param name="background" value="white" />
  <param name="minRuntimeVersion" value="2.0.31005.0" />
  <param name="autoUpgrade" value="true" />
  <a href="http://go.microsoft.com/fwlink/?LinkID=124807"
       style="text-decoration: none;">
    <img src="http://go.microsoft.com/fwlink/?LinkId=108181"
       alt="Get Microsoft Silverlight" style="border-style: none"/>
  </a>
</object>
<iframe style='visibility:hidden;height:0;width:0;border:0px'></iframe>
</div>
</body>
```

The Silverlight control instantiation takes place in the *<object>* tag. This object tags a number of parameters:

- The first parameter is the source that points at a Silverlight-based application package (.xap) file that contains the compiled Silverlight application. This can also be a reference to a static external file, a reference to the URL of a service that can generate XAML, or a reference to a named script block on the page that contains XAML.

- The second parameter is the *onerror* parameter that defines a JavaScript block on the page to call in case the Silverlight application throws an error.

- The third parameter, *background,* defines the background color for the control should it not define one already.

- The fourth parameter, *minRuntimeVersion,* is used by Silverlight to control the version of Silverlight that is, at minimum, needed to execute your application. So, for example, if your application doesn't use any of the features specific to Silverlight 3, you can specify the Silverlight 2 build version here (as in the listing), and users will not be prompted to upgrade to Silverlight 3 upon seeing your content.

- The fifth parameter, *autoUpgrade,* when set to *true*, will automatically upgrade Silverlight to the newest version upon instantiation. When set to *false* nothing will happen.

Using Expression Blend to Build and Run a Silverlight Application

Chapter 2, "Using Expression Blend with Silverlight," explores Expression Blend in more detail. In this section, you can take a quick look at how Expression Blend is used to build and run a simple Silverlight application.

Use the New Project Wizard to create a Silverlight 3 Web site called Chapter1HelloWorld. Open Page.xaml in the editor, and add a new text block to the design surface. Select the text block, and then click the Properties tab.

You can use the options in the Properties tab to change how the text block appears, for example, by changing the text and font size. You can see an example of how it should look in Figure 1-6.

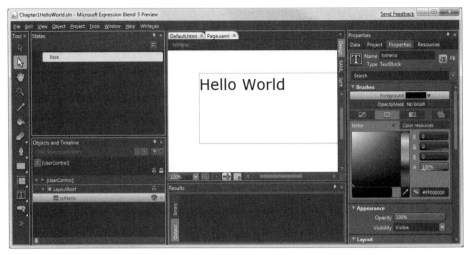

FIGURE 1-6 Editing a Silverlight project using Expression Blend.

You can also edit the code-behind with Expression Blend 3, a new feature that wasn't available in previous versions.

So, for example, originally the text block in Figure 1-6 had no name set (the *Name* property was set to <No Name>). You can change this to txtHello, and then open the Page.xaml.cs file. You'll see some C# code that looks like this:

```
public Page(){
  // Required to initialize variables
  InitializeComponent();
}
```

Add the following line under *InitializeComponent()*:

```
txtHello.Text += " from Expression Blend";
```

Now, if you press F5, you will see that Expression Blend will compile and package the .NET code and open the browser. The browser will render the Silverlight content, which reads, 'Hello World from Expression Blend'.

The content from the designer 'Hello World' has been augmented by the text ' from Expression Blend' by the .NET code.

Although this is a super simple example, hopefully it whets your appetite for some of the many and varied possibilities that you can implement with Silverlight!

Silverlight and Expression Encoder

You can use Expression Encoder to encode, enhance, and publish your video content using Silverlight. Expression Encoder comes with a UI that is consistent with the rest of the

Expression Studio suite or with a command-line interface that can be used for batch work. Figure 1-7 shows Expression Encoder.

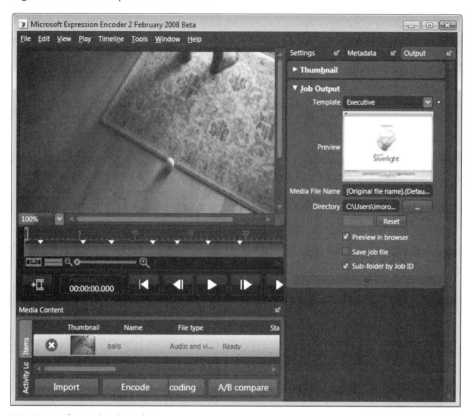

FIGURE 1-7 Expression Encoder.

With Expression Encoder, you can import video from any format for which a DirectShow filter is available and installed on your system. Expression Encoder will then reencode the video into a VC-1–capable WMV using one of a number of preset profiles optimized for the delivery client. The preset profiles include settings for devices as well as for streaming or on-demand content delivered over the Internet.

You aren't limited to what the preset profiles give you—you can override any of the video and audio encoding settings. Figure 1-8 shows an example of how a video encoding might be tweaked.

FIGURE 1-8 Configuring a video encoding profile.

Expression Encoder includes a number of preset media player applications for Silverlight. These applications "wrap up" your video with a Silverlight JavaScript-based application that can be used on any Web server to provide a complete Silverlight-based viewing experience.

In addition to encoding, you can add metadata to your video. A classic metadata experience is when tags are encoded into the video and the application then reacts to these tags. Inserting tags with Expression Encoder is very simple. Simply drag the playhead to the desired point, select Add Marker, and enter the appropriate information for the marker.

You can see an example of this in Figure 1-9 on the right side of the screen, where the marker time and type of ball that is shown on the screen at that time have been configured.

In the Output tab, you can select the template player that you want to use. Figure 1-10 shows the template that matches the Expression product line. To create a video player with this template, simply import a video, and then click the Encode button with the template selected.

FIGURE 1-9 Adding markers to a stream.

FIGURE 1-10 Using Expression Encoder to build a Silverlight media player.

After you select the template player, you'll get a full-featured media player in Silverlight for your video content. You can see an example of a Silverlight media player in Figure 1-11.

FIGURE 1-11 Media player generated by Expression Encoder.

This section just scratches the surface of what is possible with Expression Encoder and how it can be used with Silverlight. For more details, please refer to *www.microsoft.com/expression*.

Summary

This chapter introduces Silverlight 3 and describes how it fits into the overall Web and UX landscape. It discusses how technology from Microsoft is applied to current UX scenarios and provides an overview of the Silverlight architecture, including XAML and how it is used to implement rich UIs.

Additionally, this chapter covers how the Microsoft Expression Suite is designed to complement traditional development tools such as Visual Studio for creating Silverlight applications. It specifically discusses how you can use Expression Design to build graphical assets, how you can use Expression Blend to link assets together into an interactive application, and how you can use Expression Encoder to manage your video assets.

Now it's time to go deeper. The next few chapters discuss the Silverlight API. Chapter 2 starts with a more detailed examination of Expression Blend and how it is used by Silverlight.

Chapter 2
Using Expression Blend with Silverlight

Microsoft Expression Blend is a professional design tool intended to help you create engaging experiences for Windows users and the Web. With Expression Blend, you can blend all the necessary design elements for your Web experiences, including video, vector art, text, animation, images, and other content such as controls, using one set of tools. Expression Blend is designed to help you build Windows-based as well as Web-based applications. This chapter introduces this tool, offering a tour of what you can do with it. Expression Blend has far too many aspects to cover in one chapter, but by the end of this chapter, you should have a good grasp of the basics and be ready to delve further into the features of this wonderful tool on your own.

Getting Started with Expression Blend

Expression Blend is available as part of the Microsoft Expression suite. Details are available at *http://www.microsoft.com/expression*.

After you've downloaded and installed Expression Blend, start it from the Start menu. You'll see the Expression Blend integrated development environment (IDE), as shown in Figure 2-1.

FIGURE 2-1 Expression Blend IDE.

To create a new application, select New Project from the File menu. This opens the)New Project dialog box, as shown in Figure 2-2.

FIGURE 2-2 New Project dialog box in Expression Blend.

The following options are available:

- **Silverlight 3 Application + Website**   Use this option to create a Silverlight application along with the requisite files for hosting it on a Web page for you to deploy to your site.

- **WPF Application**   Use this option to create a Microsoft .NET Framework client application using the Windows Presentation Foundation (WPF).

- **Silverlight 3 SketchFlow Prototype**   SketchFlow is a new technology in Expression Blend 3 that you can use to develop prototype applications that can be quickly reskinned into real ones. You see more on SketchFlow later in this chapter.

- **WPF SketchFlow Prototype**   As with the Silverlight SketchFlow template, with this option you can rapidly develop prototypes of client applications using WPF.

Creating a Silverlight Application

To create a Silverlight application, in the New Project dialog box, select the Silverlight 3 Application + Website template option, and name your new project TestApp. Expression Blend creates a new project for you that contains everything you need for a Silverlight .NET application.

You can see the project structure that Silverlight creates in Figure 2-3. This is identical to the project structure that Microsoft Visual Studio builds, which is discussed in more detail in Chapter 3, "Using Visual Studio with Silverlight."

FIGURE 2-3 Silverlight project structure.

Note that two Extensible Application Markup Language (XAML) files are created. The App.xaml file is used for application-specific (that is, global) variables, functions, and settings, whereas the MainControl.xaml is the default opening page for your application.

The Default *MainControl*

Silverlight deals with your XAML as a *UserControl*. Thus, the template creates your default application XAML content as a file named MainControl.xaml. You can see that the root of this, not surprisingly, is a *UserControl* and not a *Canvas*, as you might expect.

Following is the XAML for the default Page.xaml:

```
<UserControl
  xmlns="http://schemas.microsoft.com/winfx/2006/xaml/presentation"
  xmlns:x="http://schemas.microsoft.com/winfx/2006/xaml"
  x:Class="TestApp.MainControl"
  Width="640" Height="480">
  <Grid x:Name="LayoutRoot" Background="White"/>
</UserControl>
```

Note the use of *<UserControl>* to host the content.

Silverlight generates a code-behind file for *MainControl* for you. This file is named MainControl.xaml.cs or MainControl.xaml.vb, depending on which language you selected when creating the project. The file contains the basic code required to construct the *UserControl*. You can see it here:

```
using System;
using System.Windows;
using System.Windows.Controls;
using System.Windows.Documents;
using System.Windows.Ink;
using System.Windows.Input;
using System.Windows.Media;
using System.Windows.Media.Animation;
using System.Windows.Shapes;

namespace TestApp
{
  public partial class MainControl : UserControl
  {
    public MainControl()
    {
      // Required to initialize variables
      InitializeComponent();
    }
  }
}
```

You aren't *restricted* to using this file for your application logic. You can, of course, create other .cs (or .vb) files that contain shared logic, but this one will be opened whenever the control is instantiated by the Silverlight runtime. The reason for this is in the XAML: You can see that the *x:Class* setting is *TestApp.MainControl*, pointing at the class that this code would compile into.

The Default App.xaml and Code-Behind Files

App.xaml and App.xaml.cs define the startup conditions for your application. These are the first files loaded and executed by Silverlight on startup and the last files closed when the application is shut down.

Silverlight opens and closes these files by using the *OnStartup* and *OnExit* events, which are set up for you by the project template. Note that *MainControl* does not render by default—it has to be instructed to render as part of the application startup. The *OnStartup* event handler accomplishes this, where the *RootVisual* for the application is set to an instance of *MainControl*:

```
public App()
{
  this.Startup += this.OnStartup;
  this.Exit += this.OnExit;
  InitializeComponent();
}
```

```
private void OnStartup(object sender, StartupEventArgs e)
{
  // Load the main control here
  this.RootVisual = new MainControl();
}

private void OnExit(object sender, EventArgs e)
{
}
```

App.xaml does not support visual elements directly, so you cannot add controls or other visual elements directly. Just because it is XAML, don't think of it as a design surface. In this case, XAML is used for definition purposes only. For example, you can define application-specific resources for your application using XAML.

App.xaml.cs is useful for initialization of data that you want to use across several user controls. Keep this in mind as you design your application. For example, you could store some text that could be used across your application by declaring it as a resource in App.xaml:

```
<Application
  xmlns="http://schemas.microsoft.com/client/2007"
  xmlns:x="http://schemas.microsoft.com/winfx/2006/xaml"
  x:Class="TestApp.App">
    <Application.Resources>
        <TextBlock x:Key="txtResource" Text="Hello"></TextBlock>
    </Application.Resources>
</Application>
```

You can now easily access this content from any control in your application as follows:

```
TextBlock t = (TextBlock)Application.Current.Resources["txtResource"];
string strTest = t.Text;
```

Executing the Application

One thing that you might notice is *missing* if you are sharp-eyed is a page to host the Silverlight control. Don't worry! Expression Blend automatically generates one for you. You can see it when you start the application.

Before going any further, add a simple *TextBlock* to the *UserControl* to render some text. Here's an example:

```
<UserControl
  xmlns="http://schemas.microsoft.com/client/2007"
  xmlns:x="http://schemas.microsoft.com/winfx/2006/xaml"
  xmlns:d="http://schemas.microsoft.com/expression/blend/2008"
  xmlns:mc="http://schemas.openxmlformats.org/markup-compatibility/2006"
  mc:Ignorable="d"
  x:Class="TestApp.MainControl"
  d:DesignWidth="640" d:DesignHeight="480">

  <Grid x:Name="LayoutRoot" Background="White" >
```

```
    <TextBlock Text="Hello"/>
  </Grid>
</UserControl>
```

Now if you execute the application, you'll see something like the output shown in Figure 2-4.

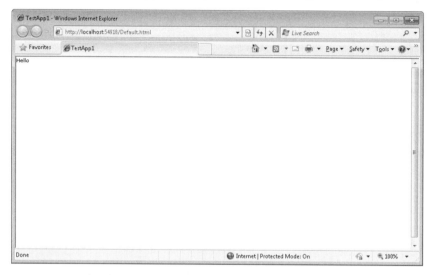

FIGURE 2-4 Running the Silverlight application from Expression Blend.

This simple application runs using the lightweight built-in Web server (sometimes called Cassini). The Web server assigns a random port at run time—hence the random port number 49578 that you can see in the address box in Figure 2-4—by generating an HTML page to host the Silverlight content.

Look at the source code for this page by using the browser command View Source. Do take note of the *<object>* tag. This attempts to instantiate Silverlight, and should it fail, it renders an image with a hypertext reference (HREF) to the Silverlight download in its place.

```
<div id="silverlightControlHost">
    <object data="data:application/x-silverlight,"
            type="application/x-silverlight-2" width="100%" height="100%">
      <param name="source" value="ClientBin/TestApp.xap"/>
      <param name="onerror" value="onSilverlightError" />
      <param name="background" value="white" />
      <param name="minRuntimeVersion" value="3.0.40128.0" />
      <param name="autoUpgrade" value="true" />
        <a href="http://go.microsoft.com/fwlink/?LinkID=141205"
           style="text-decoration: none;">
          <img src="http://go.microsoft.com/fwlink/?LinkId=108181"
               alt="Get Microsoft Silverlight" style="border-style: none"/>
        </a>
    </object>
    <iframe style='visibility:hidden;height:0;width:0;border:0px'></iframe>
</div>
```

You see more about this and other ways of instantiating the Silverlight object in Chapter 6, "The Silverlight Browser Object."

The Expression Blend IDE

Expression Blend offers a flexible IDE that is designed to maximize the amount of information on the screen while keeping it easy for the user to understand what is going on and not be overwhelmed.

The IDE has two main application workspace layouts: the Design workspace, which you use primarily for constructing and customizing the user interface (UI), and the Application workspace, which you use primarily for designing timeline-based animations. You can switch between the workspaces using the F6 key or by selecting the workspace you want from the Active Workspace options on the Window menu.

The screen is divided into *panes* in the Expression Blend IDE, and each of the panes has a fixed purpose, as you'll discover in the following sections.

The Tools Pane

The tools pane is on the far left side of the screen. It contains *tools*, such as Paint or Clip, that can be used to manipulate any object; *visual elements*, such as a *Rectangle* or *Ellipse*; *layout elements*, such as the *StackPanel* or *Canvas;* and *controls*, such as *Button* or *TextBox*. You can see the tools pane in Figure 2-5.

FIGURE 2-5 Expression Blend tools pane.

In Expression Blend, similar tools can be collected and grouped under a single icon in the tools pane. In Figure 2-6, you can see how to view a set of similar tools by clicking the small triangle in the lower-right corner of the tool. When this triangle is present, you can click and hold down the mouse button on a tool to find more members in the same "family" as the selected object. So, for example, if you click and hold down the mouse button on the *Rectangle* tool, a pop-up box shows you the other available shapes, as shown in Figure 2-6.

FIGURE 2-6 Grouped tools.

One nice shortcut that Expression Blend provides is the way it creates a default tool on the toolbar when you have used a tool from the family of tools. That is, the tool that you just used is displayed on the toolbar so that you don't need to hold down the mouse button, wait for the menu to appear, and then select the tool again to use it the next time.

So, for example, in Figure 2-6, the *Rectangle* is displayed on the toolbar, and when you click it and hold down the mouse button, you see a box displaying the other visual element tools of this type that are available. If you then select the *Ellipse* and draw with it on the design surface, the toolbar changes to display the *Ellipse* instead of the *Rectangle*.

The Objects And Timeline Pane

The Objects And Timeline pane, shown in Figure 2-7 and usually located just to the right of the tools pane, is designed to help you with the following tasks:

- View all of the objects on your design surface, including their hierarchy when you are using container objects.

- Select objects so that you can modify them. This isn't always possible on the design surface because objects can be placed off screen or behind other objects.

- Create and modify animation timelines. You learn more about how to do this in the section titled "Using Expression Blend to Design Animations" later in this chapter.

This pane is designed to have two separate highlights. The currently selected object is highlighted by inverting its colors on the list. This is the object that you can currently amend on its properties page or by dragging it around the design surface.

Although it appears gray in Figure 2-7, you can see that the *LayoutRoot* control has a colored border around it. On the design surface, you also can see this border, which indicates that *LayoutRoot* is the currently selected container.

In addition to manipulating objects, you also use the Objects and Timeline pane to create animations and storyboards. You do this by clicking the plus sign (+) button at the top of the Objects And Timeline pane. You explore the ways you can use this pane to create animations in the section titled "Using Expression Blend to Design Animations" later in this chapter.

FIGURE 2-7 Objects And Timeline pane.

The Design Surface

The design surface is the main pane in the Expression Blend IDE. This is where you can manipulate all the objects visually or by amending their underlying XAML code directly.

On the right side of the design pane, you can see three tabs:

- The Design tab gives you the pure design surface.

- The XAML tab gives you the XAML editing window.

- The Split tab provides you with a split window—one half in design view and the other half in XAML view.

You can see the design pane in split view in Figure 2-8.

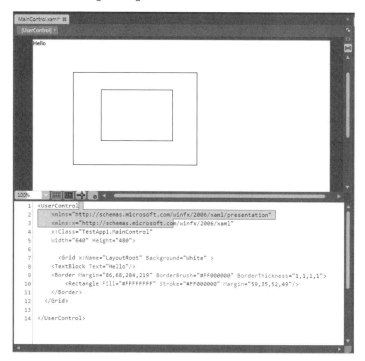

FIGURE 2-8 Design pane in split view.

Note that you can use the Zoom feature in design view so that when you are working on sophisticated interfaces, you can zoom in for a detailed view and zoom out for an overview. You do this by using the Zoom tool at the lower-left corner of the design pane. You can use the drop-down menu to select preset zoom settings, type the specific value you want in the box provided, or drag the mouse within the box to set the desired zoom level.

The Projects Pane

You can use the Projects pane, as shown in Figure 2-9, to manage the files in your project. The important thing to note in this pane is the use of context menus. Depending on *where* you right-click in this pane, you'll get a different (and appropriate) context menu. You might be familiar with context menus that provide commands for a specific pane, but in this case, you see different menus when you right-click the solution, the project, the References folder, and so on in the Projects pane.

FIGURE 2-9 Projects pane.

A *solution* is a collection of one or more projects. When you edit a solution, you can manage everything to do with the solution itself, including building, debugging, cleaning, and managing individual projects. In Figure 2-9, you can see the solution TestApp listed at the top of the Projects pane, and the pane indicates that there are two projects in the solution.

A *project* is a collection of items that, when combined, make up an application that contains one or more Silverlight *pages*. The project definition contains all the references to external components that this application needs in the References folder. When you right-click the project, the context menu that opens for the project offers options that you can use to manipulate the contents of the project, such as adding new items based on a template, adding existing items from other projects, or deleting items from the project.

The *References* folder in the project is used to manage references to precompiled assemblies that contain information that you want to use in the project. For example, if you want to use a custom control, it is compiled into an assembly. If you reference that assembly in the references, you can then use it in your application.

The *Properties* folder contains the application manifest file that describes all the properties of the project, including the list of references, so that the application can understand from where they are loaded at run time. Do not confuse the Properties folder with the Properties pane, indicated by the Properties tab at the top of the window shown in Figure 2-9 and explained in more detail in the following section.

The Properties Pane

You can use the Properties pane to manage all the visual aspects of a particular element. Because XAML elements have many configurable properties, this pane gives you two very useful shortcuts.

The first shortcut is provided by the division of the Properties pane into several classifications that typically provide access to the following visual aspects of elements:

- **Brushes** With brushes, you can set fill and stroke options as well as use an opacity mask on an element. Chapter 4, "Silverlight XAML Basics," describes in a lot more detail how brushes are used.

- **Appearance** In the Appearance section, you can set extended appearance properties for your object. Note that the available appearance properties change drastically based on the object that you are currently editing. So, for example, if you are editing a *Rectangle* element, in the Appearance section of the Properties pane you can set characteristics such as the corner radii, but if you are editing a *Button* element that doesn't have corner radii, this option is not available.

- **Layout** In the Layout section, you can edit the various layout options for your object, such as Width, Height, and Alignment options. You can also use layout options to change the position of an object in a grid—if the layout is on a grid.

- **Common Properties** The Common Properties section effectively contains the properties that are common across a *type* of object. So, for example, typically you edit the common properties for controls that are distinct from shapes here. These options can be very difficult to use, depending on the object that you are editing. For example, if you are editing a control, a common property is its tab index, but if you are editing a shape, the tab index is not available.

- **Transform** In the Transform section, you can edit the *RenderTransform* of your object. This defines how the object can be manipulated by the rendering system. Transformations are covered in detail in Chapter 5, "XAML Transformation and Animation."

- **Miscellaneous** The Miscellaneous section is a catch-all location for properties that aren't available under any of the other classifications.

Do note that these classification panes are further subdivided. You'll notice that many of them have an arrow at the bottom of the pane that you can use to expand and contract the properties view. With this feature, you can hide lesser-used properties until you need them.

The second shortcut in the Properties pane is its Search feature, which you can use to search for a particular property. For example, if you know you want to edit some features of a font but don't know the name of the property itself, you can type **font** into the search engine, and the classifications and available properties will be filtered so that only those that have to do with fonts are displayed. This is done immediately upon a keystroke, so if you are searching for a font property—in this example, as soon as you type **fo**—you will see available properties displayed such as *fo*reground and *rendertransfo*rm as well as the font properties, as shown in the list of properties displayed in Figure 2-10.

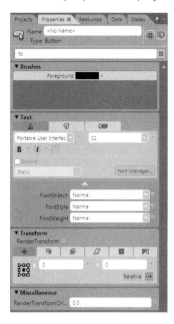

FIGURE 2-10 Using the Properties pane.

The next section looks at how you can use all these tools to build Silverlight applications.

Using Expression Blend to Build Silverlight Applications

You can use Expression Blend to accomplish the following main design-oriented functions as you put together your application:

- Organizing the layout

- Placing and customizing visual elements

- Placing and customizing controls

- Designing animations

You explore each of these functions of Expression Blend throughout the rest of this chapter.

Layout

In Silverlight, you use special tools to create and organize the layout of your application. Several options are available, and the following subsections look at each of them in turn.

Using a Grid

With the *Grid* layout element, you can lay out elements in a structure that looks like a table. (Do not confuse the *Grid* layout element with a *Grid* control that gives you functionality similar to a spreadsheet application.) When using a *Grid* layout tool, you can specify how your elements are placed by indicating their coordinates with virtual row and column designations in the *Grid* layout. For example, consider the following XAML:

```
<Grid x:Name="LayoutRoot" Background="White" >
  <Button Height="38" Margin="104,72,0,0" Width="58" Content="Button"/>
  <Button Height="24" Margin="210,72,0,0" Width="54" Content="Button"/>
  <Button Height="49" Margin="0,96,158,0" Width="80" Content="Button"/>
  <Button Height="54" Margin="297,185,270,0" Width="67" Content="Button"/>
  <Button Height="33" Margin="104,217,0,213" Width="87" Content="Button"/>
</Grid>
```

When rendered, this XAML appears as shown in Figure 2-11.

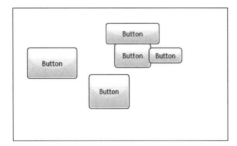

FIGURE 2-11 Random buttons.

Now, if you want to organize these buttons, you could carefully set their positions by dragging them around the design surface to place them at roughly the positions where you want them. But if you position them this way, you will need to zoom in to make sure pixels are aligned.

Alternatively, you could use the *Grid* layout, where you can use the layout properties of the button to determine its location in the grid. If you start with a new Silverlight project, you'll see that it has a *Grid* layout element on it called *LayoutRoot*. Select this element in your project, and look at the layout properties associated with it. Expand the properties viewer until you see the settings for the *ColumnDefinitions* and *RowDefinitions*, as shown in Figure 2-12.

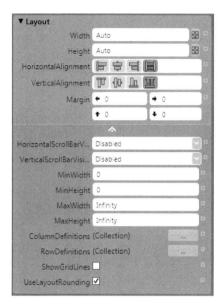

FIGURE 2-12 Layout editor for a grid.

Because *ColumnDefinitions* and *RowDefinitions* are collections, each one has an ellipsis (...) button to the right of the setting name. This indicates that another dialog box will open when you click the button. Select the button next to the *ColumnDefinitions* property setting, and the ColumnDefinition Collection Editor opens, as shown in Figure 2-13.

FIGURE 2-13 ColumnDefinition Collection Editor.

Use this dialog box to add, remove, and manage columns. Click the Add Another Item button three times to add three columns. Repeat this for the *RowDefinitions* property setting so that you have a grid that is made up of three rows and three columns. After you have made these changes to *ColumnDefinitions* and *RowDefinitions*, the designer pane displays a 3 × 3 layout grid, as shown in Figure 2-14.

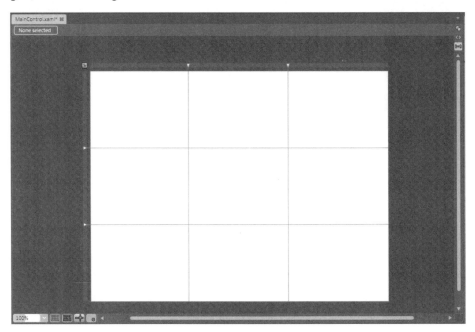

FIGURE 2-14 The 3 × 3 layout grid.

Now, whenever you place an element on the screen, pink guidelines show you how you can snap to a particular grid element, as shown in Figure 2-15. (The guidelines appear as wider gray lines in the figure.) Snapping the button to the grid and column layout like this ensures that the button is always at that relative position and size in the grid.

Place another button in the central square on the grid, as shown in Figure 2-15. This time, do not snap it to the grid. Then, run the application and experiment with resizing the window. You'll see that the first button always remains at the same relative position and the same size, but the second button changes its width and/or height to stay relative to the size of the screen.

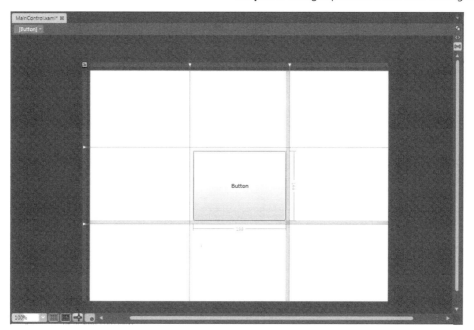

FIGURE 2-15 Using the *Grid* layout.

Using *Canvas*

The *Canvas* layout is a completely free-format drawing surface. You can specify the desired location for a control by setting its *Canvas.Top* and *Canvas.Left* properties or by using its *Margin* property.

So, for example, consider the following XAML:

```
<Canvas Height="261" Width="439">
  <Button Height="101" Width="110" Canvas.Left="101" Canvas.Top="82.5" Content="Button"/>
</Canvas>
```

You can see that the *Canvas.Top* and *Canvas.Left* properties for the button have been set. These indicate that the button will always be at those values *relative* to the parent *Canvas*, so as the *Canvas* moves, the button moves also. The *Canvas* layout is covered in more detail in Chapter 4.

Using *StackPanel*

The *StackPanel* layout always orients its child controls either horizontally or vertically, stacking them (hence the name) based on the *Orientation* property. Note that the panel overrides the positioning of the controls. For example, look at the following XAML:

```
<StackPanel Height="337" Width="224" Orientation="Vertical" >
  <Button Canvas.Top="100" Height="64" Width="98" Content="Button"/>
```

```
  <Button Height="85" Width="92" Content="Button"/>
  <Button Height="48" Width="205" Content="Button"/>
</StackPanel>
```

You can see that the first button has its *Canvas.Top* property set to 100. You would expect that this means that the control is drawn at that position, but as Figure 2-16 shows, this is not the case. The control is stacked by the *StackPanel* layout at the top of the *StackPanel* (because the *StackPanel* has its *Orientation* property set to *Vertical)*.

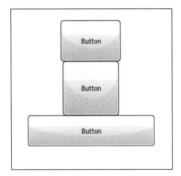

FIGURE 2-16 Buttons in a *StackPanel.*

When you have many controls in a *StackPanel*, you might go beyond the bounds of the *Panel* control itself, in which case the controls are clipped to the bounds of the *StackPanel*. To get around this problem, you can use a *ScrollViewer*, which is explained in the next section.

Using the *ScrollViewer*

The *ScrollViewer* provides scroll bars so that the user can pan around the contents of a layout if the contents exceed the bounds of the *ScrollViewer*. A *ScrollViewer* can contain only one child control, so unless you are using a control that needs a large view area (such as an *Image*), you use a *ScrollViewer* typically only to contain other containers.

For example, following is a *StackPanel* in which the contents exceed the vertical space available to it:

```
<StackPanel Height="300" Width="199">
  <Button Height="44" Width="86" Content="Button"/>
  <Button Height="57" Width="75" Content="Button"/>
  <Button Height="70" Width="59" Content="Button"/>
  <Button Height="109" Width="95" Content="Button"/>
  <Button Height="104" Width="88" Content="Button"/>
</StackPanel>
```

The *StackPanel* in this example is 300 pixels high, but the total height of all the buttons is 384 pixels, so the bottom button is cropped, as you can see in Figure 2-17.

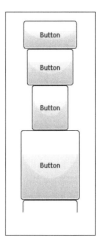

FIGURE 2-17 Cropped elements in a *StackPanel*.

Now, if you contain this *StackPanel* in a *ScrollViewer*, you'll get better results. Note that the *StackPanel* still crops the buttons if you do not change its height, so if you need to have an area of height 300, you can set the *ScrollViewer* to have this height, and then set the *StackPanel* to have a different height. Here's the XAML to do this:

```
<ScrollViewer Height="300" Width="300">
  <StackPanel Height="400" Width="199">
    <Button Height="44" Width="86" Content="Button"/>
    <Button Height="57" Width="75" Content="Button"/>
    <Button Height="70" Width="59" Content="Button"/>
    <Button Height="109" Width="95" Content="Button"/>
    <Button Height="104" Width="88" Content="Button"/>
  </StackPanel>
</ScrollViewer>
```

You can see how the *ScrollViewer* created here appears in Figure 2-18.

FIGURE 2-18 Using the *ScrollViewer*.

Now you can scroll up and down the button list and the buttons all are available; none are unavailable because of cropping if you use the *ScrollViewer*. Note that the button at the bottom in Figure 2-18 can be revealed by dragging the scroll bar down.

The *Border* Control

Not to be confused with the Border Patrol—part of the Department of Homeland Security— you use the *Border* control simply to draw a border, background, or both around another element. For example, consider the following XAML:

```
<Border Height="318" Width="405" Background="#FFFF0000">
  <Button Height="234"
    HorizontalAlignment="Center"
    VerticalAlignment="Center"
    Width="239"
    RenderTransformOrigin="0.5,0.5"
    Content="Button">
  </Button>
</Border>
```

This XAML creates a red background behind the button.

Placing and Customizing Visual Elements

The visual elements available are defined in the XAML specification, and you learn about each of them in detail in Chapter 4. Right now, take a look at the basic shapes and tools that are available on the toolbar. These include the following shapes:

- **Rectangle**   Select this shape to draw a straight-sided quadrilateral with 90-degree angles at each corner. You can make a square by creating a *Rectangle* with equal width and height properties.

- **Ellipse**   Use this shape to draw an elliptical figure, an oval. You can make it a *Circle* by making the width and height properties equal.

- **Line**   The *Line* shape simply draws a straight line between two end points.

You can use the following tools available on the toolbar to create free-form shapes:

- **Pen**   Use this tool to draw a set of connected line segments represented by an underlying *Path* element.

- **Pencil**   Use this tool to draw a set of connected elements, which can be lines or curves. Expression Blend represents the strokes that the user draws with an underlying *Path* element.

Each of these visual elements, including those created with the Pen and Pencil tools, are represented by a single element, and this element can then be treated as any other object; that is, you can modify it in many ways, including setting its properties or animating it. For example, consider Figure 2-19 in which the Pencil tool has been used to draw a set of connected curves to create a representation of the word *Hello* in script. Look on the Objects And Timeline view, and you'll see the object represented as a *Path*.

FIGURE 2-19 Editing a *Path* object.

Now, this pencil "drawing" of the word *Hello* is treated as a single object, so you can edit its properties, including *Fill*, *Brush*, and so forth, simply by selecting it from the Objects And Timeline view and then editing the properties in the Properties pane, as you do with any other object.

Placing and Customizing Controls

Expression Blend treats controls in exactly the same way as it treats visual elements. You simply select controls from the toolbar and draw them on the design surface. After you create them on the design surface, you can edit their properties. Controls are discussed in detail in Chapter 8, "Silverlight Core Controls."

One thing to note is that Expression Blend offers two families of controls on the toolbar. The first includes the text controls: *TextBlock* and *TextBox*. The second includes the set of basic user interface controls: *Button, CheckBox, ListBox, RadioButton, ScrollBar, Slider,* and *GridSplitter.*

Finally, the toolbar gives you the option to add controls that aren't part of this set. You can add controls by clicking the Asset Library link at the bottom of the toolbar, which opens the Asset Library dialog box, as shown in Figure 2-20.

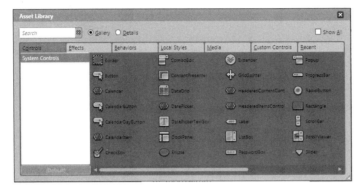

FIGURE 2-20 Asset Library dialog box.

You can select controls in the Asset Library dialog box to add them to the toolbar. You also can search for specific controls by entering the name in the search box. So, for example, if you want to use a *MediaElement* control, start typing the letters of the control's name in the search box. When you see the control you want (in this case, the *MediaElement*), you can select it, and it is then available to you on the toolbar.

Then, you can draw the control on the design surface and manipulate its properties with the properties editor, as you have done with the visual elements and layout controls.

Using Expression Blend to Design Animations

Chapter 5 examines how to create animations in detail, but to put it succinctly, animations occur in Silverlight whenever a property of an object changes its value over time. You can design these kinds of animations visually in a very straightforward manner by using Expression Blend and the timeline editor.

One form of animation that Silverlight supports is *DoubleAnimation*, which is used to change numeric properties, such as the width of an *Ellipse* visual element. Another is *ColorAnimation*, which is used to change the color of the *Brush* property.

For example, consider the *Ellipse* shown in Figure 2-21 (which appears as a circle because its height and width properties are equal). To visually design an animation that changes the width of this *Ellipse* element, add a new *Storyboard* that contains the animation.

FIGURE 2-21 Drawing a circle.

On the Objects And Timeline view, select the *Ellipse*, and then press the + button next to the *Storyboard* list at the top of the pane. Accept the defaults in the Create Storyboard dialog box that opens. The Timeline editor opens. You can also see the message Timeline Recording Is On at the top of the Expression Blend window. You can drag the Objects And Timeline view to below the design pane to make it easier to work with the timeline. Your screen should look something like the one shown in Figure 2-22.

Look for the yellow line in the timeline view. This denotes the *current* position on the timeline. Drag it to the 2-second mark, and then click the Record Keyframe tool at the top of the timeline. The Record Keyframe tool looks like a blob with a little green plus sign (+) at its lower-right side. You'll see a little oval appear in the timeline at the 2-second mark, as shown in Figure 2-23.

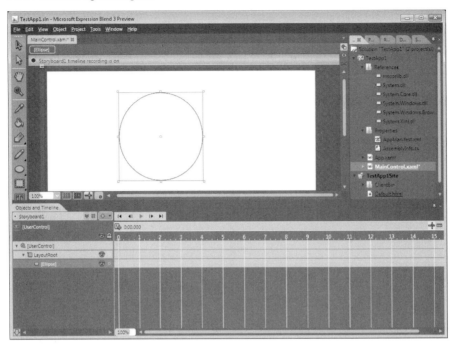

FIGURE 2-22 Editing the timeline.

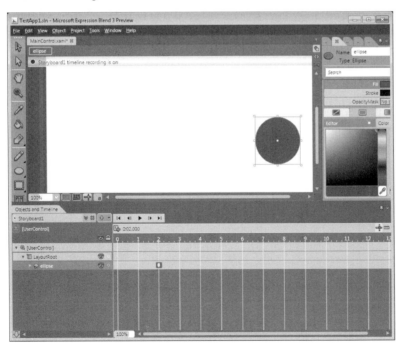

FIGURE 2-23 Adding a keyframe.

Now that you have defined a keyframe, any changes that you make to the properties of the object are recorded at that keyframe, so go ahead and change the width of the *Ellipse* while the yellow line is still at the 2-second mark, indicating the current position of the timeline. For example, change the width to **200** and the *Fill* color to **Red**.

Now drag the playhead (the top of the vertical yellow line on the timeline) left and right, and you'll see a preview of the animation, with the width and color of the circle shape changing over time.

You can see the XAML that is generated by your visual creation of the animation here:

```
<UserControl.Resources>
  <Storyboard x:Name="Storyboard1">
    <DoubleAnimationUsingKeyFrames Storyboard.TargetName="ellipse"
      Storyboard.TargetProperty="(FrameworkElement.Width)"
      BeginTime="00:00:00">
      <SplineDoubleKeyFrame KeyTime="00:00:02" Value="200"/>
    </DoubleAnimationUsingKeyFrames>
    <ColorAnimationUsingKeyFrames Storyboard.TargetName="ellipse"
      Storyboard.TargetProperty="(Shape.Fill).(SolidColorBrush.Color)"
      BeginTime="00:00:00">
      <SplineColorKeyFrame KeyTime="00:00:02" Value="#FFFF2200"/>
    </ColorAnimationUsingKeyFrames>
  </Storyboard>
</UserControl.Resources>
<Ellipse Height="100" Width="100" Fill="#FFFFF500" Stroke="#FF000000" x:Name="ellipse"/>
```

You delve into the structure of this XAML in much more detail in Chapter 5, but the important elements to note here are the *Storyboard.TargetName* instances that indicate for which element the animation is being defined, and the *Storyboard.TargetProperty* that indicates the property that is going to be changed. As you can see in this XAML, there are two animations, one that changes the width of the target and the other that changes its color. Silverlight then takes this definition and uses it to calculate the values required for each frame at the time the animation is rendered.

Using SketchFlow

SketchFlow is a new technology in Expression Blend 3. With SketchFlow, you can sketch and prototype an application, including all interactivity, using Expression Blend. This tool is designed to make it easier for you to experiment with different ideas for dynamic user interaction.

Think of SketchFlow as an electronic version of "paper napkin" prototyping, where you build the look and feel of the UI and present it in a way that is obviously a rough prototype. However, the prototype need not be completely throwaway because you can easily reskin it to form the basis of the final application.

Here is a look at how to build a simple application prototype using SketchFlow.

Create a new application using Expression Blend, and in the New Project dialog box (see Figure 2-2 earlier), select Silverlight 3 SketchFlow Prototype. Name the project SFDemo.

When you're finished, you should see a new pane below the design pane called Application Flow. If you cannot see it, make sure Application Flow is selected on the Window menu, or press Shift+F12.

You can see what the Application Flow pane looks like in Figure 2-24.

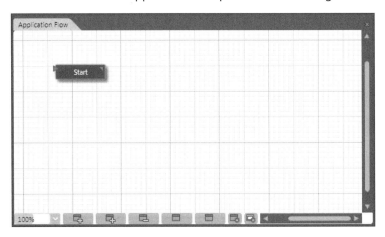

FIGURE 2-24 The SketchFlow Application Flow pane.

Your application contains a single XAML document called Start.XAML, and this is visually represented by the Start box in the Application Flow pane. If you hover the mouse pointer over this, you can see that a small tool window opens underneath it. This window contains options that you can use to set the color tag for the box and to drag out a new window. Use the latter to drag a line out on the design surface, and you'll see a New Navigation Screen box that you can drag around. Drop it, and you'll get a new screen, called Screen 1 on the design surface *and* a new Screen1.xaml code file in your project. See Figure 2-25.

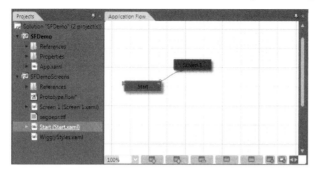

FIGURE 2-25 Adding a new screen with SketchFlow.

Repeat this process to drag another screen linked to Start. It will be called Screen 2. Next, create another two screens linked to Screen 1. They'll be called Screen 3 and Screen 4.

By the time you're finished, your screen should look something like the one shown in Figure 2-26.

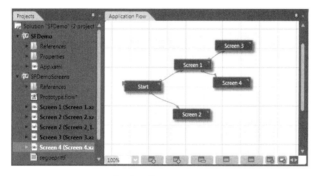

FIGURE 2-26 Your application flow.

Now, double-click Start to open the XAML Designer window.

If you are sharp-eyed, you might have noticed an XAML file in your project called WigglyStyles. With this file, you can reskin your controls so that they look like they were roughly hand-drawn using a pencil.

The point is to make it absolutely clear that this is a prototype application that you can use to test and demonstrate the different interactions, while managing customer expectations that it's just a prototype.

In the Asset Library, you can see the various controls that offer Wiggly styles. Add a couple of Wiggly buttons to the Start screen, and give them the captions Paper and Plastic. Add a text block above them and use it to render text asking the user which choice they'd like to make.

When you're finished, your screen should look something like the one shown in Figure 2-27.

FIGURE 2-27 Your Start page.

If you right-click any of the Wiggly buttons, you'll see a Navigate To option at the bottom of the menu. If you select this, you'll get all of the screens listed plus Back and Forward options.

If you use Back or Forward, SketchFlow remembers your place in the flow and moves you back or forward to the appropriate screen. However, in this case you want Paper to lead you to Screen 1 and Plastic to lead you to Screen 2, so set the properties accordingly.

Open Screen 2 and add some text to the effect of "Sorry, you can't recycle that" and a Wiggly button called Back that navigates back.

Next, open Screen 1 and add some text to the effect of "How would you like to recycle?" Add two more Wiggly buttons called Compost and Burn, and link these to Screen 3 and Screen 4, respectively.

Finally, on these screens, thank the user for recycling in the appropriate style, and add an OK Wiggly button that links back to Start. Note that when you do this, a link is drawn on the Application Flow surface from the screen to Start.

After you've built this basic flow, press F5 to execute your application.

You'll see the SketchFlow Player running in your browser, as shown in Figure 2-28.

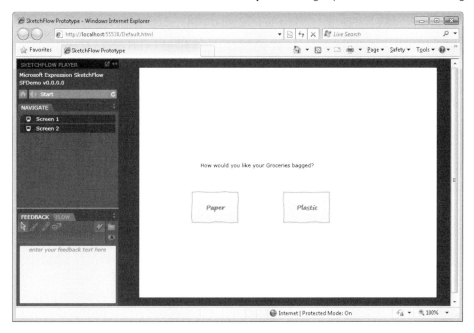

FIGURE 2-28 Testing your application in the SketchFlow Player.

The right-hand side of the screen hosts your application so that you can see how it flows when you select the various options, such as Paper and Plastic.

Additionally, you can jump directly to any screen that is connected to this one from the Navigation pane, as well as give feedback and investigate the flow.

This brief tutorial shows you just the tip of the iceberg of what is possible with SketchFlow. Feel free to experiment and see how you can use SketchFlow to help you work with your customers on prototyping applications.

Summary

In this chapter, you learned the basics of working with Expression Blend by taking a quick tour of what it offers you as a designer or developer for creating and implementing your own Silverlight applications. You saw how to use Expression Blend to create Silverlight solutions and projects, and then you saw what tools the Expression Blend IDE offers you to add and manage visual elements, layout, controls, and animations in your application. You also looked at the new SketchFlow functionality in Expression Blend and how it can be used to rapidly build prototype applications.

This chapter only just begins to investigate what you can do with Expression Blend, but this introduction might well inspire you to want to learn more.

The other half of the designer/developer workflow tool package is found in Visual Studio. Chapter 3 looks at how you can use Visual Studio, what it has in common with Expression Blend, and what powerful features it provides for developers. You will have the chance to use Visual Studio to build your first Silverlight application—a sliding picture puzzle game.

Chapter 3
Using Visual Studio with Silverlight

Chapter 1, "Introducing Silverlight 3," introduces Microsoft Silverlight and the architecture that enables Silverlight and the Microsoft .NET Framework to work together. That chapter shows how Extensible Application Markup Language (XAML) is used as a model for representing your user interface (UI) elements, interactions, and animations. In addition, it demonstrates how the programming model for Silverlight can be hosted in the browser and programmed with JavaScript, and how it can be hosted in a .NET runtime for the browser and programmed using C# or other .NET languages.

Then, Chapter 2, "Using Expression Blend with Silverlight," looks more closely at Microsoft Expression Blend, the design tool that you can use to build Silverlight experiences.

In this chapter, you take a developer's view of this process, getting some hands-on experience as you use Microsoft Visual Studio 2008 to build a simple sliding picture puzzle game. You build on this example in later chapters. By the end of this chapter, you'll have a good understanding of how to use C# and Visual Studio 2008 to build .NET-based applications for Silverlight.

Installing the Visual Studio Tools for Silverlight

Microsoft Tools for Visual Studio includes a "chained" installer that installs the runtime (for the Windows operating system), the Silverlight 3 Software Development Kit (SDK), and the Visual Studio tools themselves. You can download the tools at *http://silverlight.net/GetStarted/*.

Note that this book is written based on the beta of Silverlight 3. I will keep this book up-to-date on my blog at *http://blogs.msdn.com/webnext*. Check there if you have any problems.

Please note the following prerequisites for installing the tools:

- You must be using a release version of Visual Studio 2008. The tools do not work with a beta version. You can use any edition of Visual Studio 2008.

- You must install the Web Authoring feature of Visual Studio.

- You must uninstall any previous versions of the Silverlight runtime before continuing.

- You must uninstall any previous versions of the Silverlight SDK before continuing.

- You must uninstall any previous versions of the Silverlight Tools for Visual Studio before continuing.

If you meet the criteria and start the installer, the Silverlight Tools Installation Wizard appears, as shown in Figure 3-1.

FIGURE 3-1 Starting the Silverlight 3 tools installer.

Click Next, and you'll see a screen where you can read and accept the license agreement. After you do so, the installation will begin immediately. You can see what the installation process should look like in Figure 3-2.

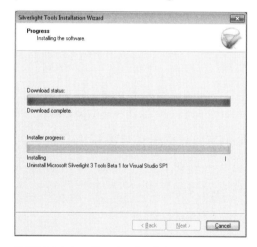

FIGURE 3-2 Installing the Silverlight tools.

When the installer finishes downloading and installing, you have the Silverlight runtime, the SDK, and the Visual Studio tools all ready to go.

Using Visual Studio to Build a Silverlight Application

Now that you have installed the Silverlight Tools for Visual Studio, you are ready to learn how to use them to design and build an application. Figure 3-3 shows the Silverlight sliding picture puzzle game in action. This application is written entirely in C# and XAML and is hosted in the browser.

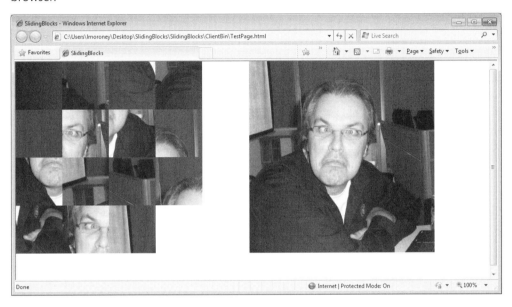

FIGURE 3-3 Sliding picture puzzle game.

In the following sections, you'll see how to use Visual Studio 2008 and Silverlight to build this application in the C# language.

Creating a Silverlight Application in Visual Studio 2008

After you've installed Visual Studio and all of the necessary tools and templates for Silverlight, you will be able to create Silverlight applications. To do this, select New Project from the File menu. This opens the New Project dialog box, as shown in Figure 3-4.

Make sure that the .NET Framework 3.5 filter is selected from the drop-down list at the upper right in this dialog box, as shown in Figure 3-4, and select Silverlight from the Project Types list. You'll see that the Silverlight Application, Silverlight Navigation Application, and Silverlight Class Library templates are available.

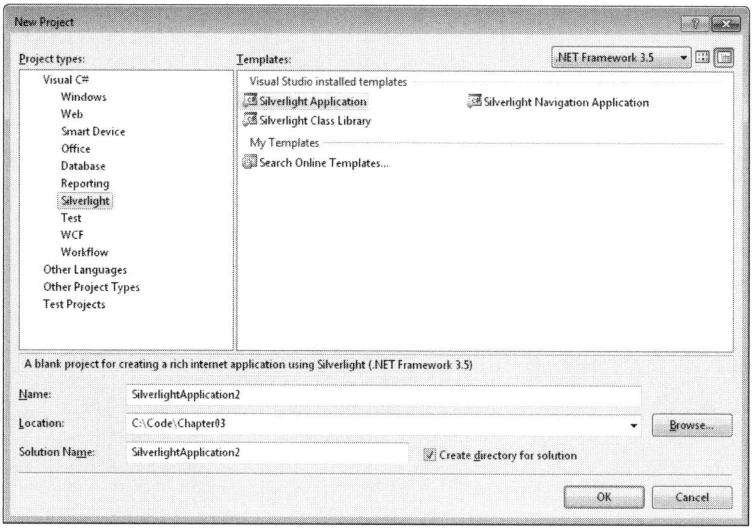

FIGURE 3-4 Visual Studio 2008 New Project dialog box.

Select the Silverlight Application template type, and give your project a name and location. Click OK, and Visual Studio will start the New Silverlight Application Wizard, as shown in Figure 3-5.

In this wizard, you have several options for creating and managing your Silverlight application. All Silverlight applications are built as user controls that can then be instantiated and hosted on a page. Thus, this discussion concentrates on how you will do this.

FIGURE 3-5 New Silverlight Application Wizard.

If you select the check box at the top, the wizard adds a new Web project to the solution. This Web project can be either an ASP.NET Web Application project or an ASP.NET Web Site. The former contains everything for deploying an application to an ASP.NET Web server. The latter is a simpler, lighter structure where your pages can be run from any server or even the file system.

Accept the defaults, as shown in Figure 3-5, and the wizard creates a new Visual Studio solution that contains a Silverlight control and a Web site that hosts the control. You can see the project structure for this in Figure 3-6.

FIGURE 3-6 Default Silverlight project setup.

As you can see in Figure 3-6, two solutions have been created for you: the basic Silverlight control (*SlidingBlocks3*) and a Web Application (*SlidingBlocks3.Web*). In the next section, you examine these projects and learn what each one contains. Following that, you start building the application.

The Silverlight Control Project

The basic project that the template creates for you contains a number of files, including the application manifest, the application XAML file with its code-behind, a sample page with its code-behind, the assembly information file, and some references. Later, you can explore each of these files in turn. This section introduces some of the complexities of a Silverlight project. You might want to skip this part if you just want to start coding, but I recommend that you come back and read this information so that you can understand how everything hangs together.

Understanding the Silverlight Project Properties

The best way to get started is to look at the project properties. To do this, right-click the SlidingBlocks3 project in Solution Explorer and click Properties. The Project Properties page opens, as shown in Figure 3-7.

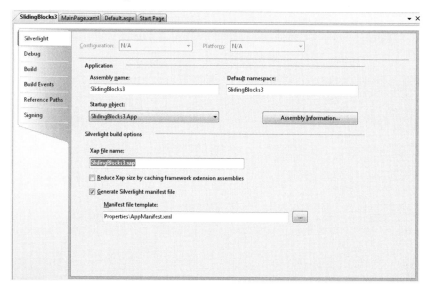

FIGURE 3-7   Silverlight Project Properties page.

If you are familiar with this page, you'll notice that there is an extra tab for Silverlight. This is selected in Figure 3-7 and shows the Silverlight options.

The Assembly Name defaults to the project name. When the application is compiled into a DLL, this is the name that is used.

The Default Namespace also defaults to the project name. If you reference classes in the project, they are prefixed by this namespace.

The Startup Object defaults to the name of the project followed by *.App* (that is, SilverlightBlocks.App). This is a class in your application that will execute first. The template defines this class in App.xaml and its associated code-behind App.xaml.cs, which you look at later in this chapter.

Click the Assembly Information button to open the Assembly Information dialog box, shown in Figure 3-8. In this dialog box, you can define the metadata for your assembly, including Title, Description, Copyright, and Trademark information. This is stored in the AssemblyInfo.cs file and compiled into your Silverlight application.

The other available options are to cache some of the framework extension assemblies so that you can reduce application size by not building them into the application, and the option to generate an application manifest file. You use the application manifest later in this book, in Chapter 6, "The Silverlight Browser Object," in the discussion of out-of-browser scenarios.

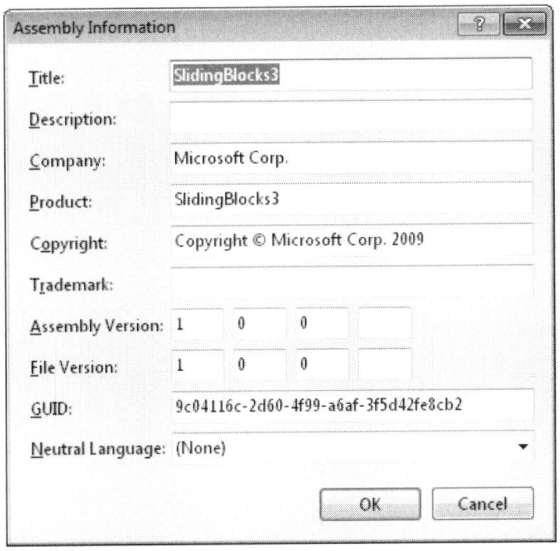

FIGURE 3-8 Defining the assembly information.

> **Tip**   The XAP file is just a ZIP file with a different extension. If you want to investigate its contents, just rename it with a .zip extension and open it with your favorite ZIP utility. Don't forget to change the extension back to .xap when you're finished!

Finally, you are given the option to generate the Silverlight manifest file itself. This file contains details on everything in the package that the Silverlight application will use, such as additional components or controls that are necessary for your application to execute. You'll be seeing more of this as you progress through this book.

The Properties Files

The first folder in your project is the Properties folder that contains the properties files: AppManifest.xml and Assemblyinfo.cs.

AppManifest.xml is generated for you as you compile your project. If your project has any dependencies at run time, such as external controls, references to them are placed here.

Assemblyinfo.cs contains the metadata to be compiled into your DLL that was configured in the Assembly Information dialog box shown in Figure 3-8. You can manually change the information by editing this code file if you wish, but the recommended approach is to use the dialog box.

References

The References folder contains references to a number of assemblies. These are the core Silverlight assemblies that are needed to make your application run:

- **mscorlib**   The *mscorlib* assembly contains the basic core types that are used by Silverlight applications.

- **system**   The *system* assembly contains many of the high-level types used for developing and debugging Silverlight applications, such as the compiler and the debugging and diagnostics classes.

- **System.core**   The *System.core* assembly contains the core Silverlight controls and classes.

- **System.Net** The *System.net* assembly contains the .NET libraries for network communications.

- **System.Xml**   The *System.Xml* assembly contains the Silverlight XML processing libraries.

- **System.Windows**   The *System.Windows* assembly contains the core Windows and Silverlight functionality, including the Silverlight controls.

- **System.Windows.Browser**   The *System.Windows.Browser* assembly contains the libraries used for interacting with the browser.

Silverlight also has a number of nondefault assemblies that you can add to provide plug-in functionality, some of which you'll look at through the course of this book. An example of this is the Dynamic Language Runtime functionality.

The App.xaml and App.xaml.cs Files

The integrated development environment (IDE) creates App.xaml for you when you create a Silverlight project using the template. This file is generally used to store application-global information.

App.xaml contains the declarations for the application's behavior. Here's an example of the default App.xaml that is created by the template:

```
<Application xmlns="http://schemas.microsoft.com/client/2007"
            xmlns:x="http://schemas.microsoft.com/winfx/2006/xaml"
            x:Class="SlidingBlocks3.App">
  <Application.Resources>
  </Application.Resources>
</Application>
```

The first thing to note is the *x:Class* attribute, which specifies the name of the class into which this XAML and its associated code-behind will be compiled. As you can see, in this case it is SlidingBlocks3.App, which you might remember from the Project Properties page shown in Figure 3-7 is defined as the startup object for this application. Thus, when the Silverlight project is run, this class contains the startup functionality.

You can specify a function to execute upon application startup using the *Startup* attribute. This attribute simply contains the name of the code function in the code-behind that will execute when the application starts. You can also specify the function to execute when the application finishes by using the *Exit* attribute, which contains the name of the function in the code-behind that will execute when the application closes.

The code for the default code-behind that is generated by the template is shown here:

```
using System.Windows;
using System;

namespace SlidingBlocks
{
    public partial class App : Application
    {

        public App()
        {
            this.Startup += this.Application_Startup;
            this.Exit += this.Application_Exit;
```

```
            this.UnhandledException += this.Application_UnhandledException;
            InitializeComponent();
        }

        private void Application_Startup(object sender, EventArgs e)
        {
            // Load the main control
            this.RootVisual = new MainPage();
        }

        private void Application_Exit(object sender, EventArgs e)
        {

        }
        private void Application_UnhandledException(
            object sender, ApplicationUnhandledExceptionEventArgs e)
        {

        }

    }
}
```

First, take a look at the constructor (which is the function with the same name as the code module, in this case *App()*). It uses the code method to wire up the *Startup* and *Exit* functions. This was already done in the XAML file, so it isn't necessary to do this in code—but it does show some of the nice flexibility of the XAML/code-behind model that allows you to wire up events at design time (by specifying them in the XAML) or at run time (by declaring them in code).

Next, you can inspect the *Application_Startup* and *Application_Exit* functions. Notice that they take two parameters—the object that raised the event and an arguments object. You'll be seeing this function signature often as you program your Silverlight applications.

The *Application_Startup* function contains code that sets the *RootVisual* property of the application to a new *MainPage* object, declaring that the UI of the *Page* object is the first UI screen that this application should render. If you are going to use other UI screens declared in XAML, these will be started from within the *MainPage* object.

The *MainPage* object is the default XAML object that the template creates to host your application UI.

The MainPage.xaml and MainPage.xaml.cs Files

The MainPage.xaml file provides the default UI for your application. When compiled along with its associated code-behind, it forms the *MainPage* class, from which a *MainPage* object can be created. If you recall from the previous section, the *RootVisual* property of the application was set to a new instance of a *Page* object, thus allowing this class to provide the default UI.

You can see the default XAML for Page.xaml here:

```
<UserControl x:Class="SlidingBlocks3.MainPage"
        xmlns="http://schemas.microsoft.com/client/2007"
        xmlns:x="http://schemas.microsoft.com/winfx/2006/xaml"
        Width="400"
        Height="300">

    <Grid x:Name="LayoutRoot" Background="White" >

    </Grid>
</UserControl>
```

First, notice that the container for the XAML is a *UserControl*, which is something you might not be familiar with if you are coming from Silverlight 1, which didn't have the .NET programming model. As mentioned earlier, when building Silverlight .NET applications in Visual Studio, you actually build controls that compile into a DLL in an XAP that Silverlight opens and renders.

In this case, you can see that this *UserControl* instance is called *SlidingBlocks3.MainPage*. *SlidingBlocks* is the namespace (look back at the project properties to see this), and *Page* is the name of the class in that namespace.

The *xmlns* and *xmlns:x* declarations configure the default namespace and the extended namespace, respectively, to be used to validate the XAML. Earlier you saw the *x:Class* attribute used to define the class for this control, and this is an example of using the extended namespace, which is prefixed by *x:*.

Finally, the width and height are set to the default 400 × 300.

Next comes the root *Grid*. In Silverlight 3, your root element must be a *Container*, which in this case is a *Grid* called *LayoutRoot*. All elements of your UI design ultimately are children of this node.

The code-behind for this XAML is shown here:

```
using System;
using System.Collections.Generic;
using System.Linq;
using System.Net;
using System.Windows;
using System.Windows.Controls;
using System.Windows.Documents;
using System.Windows.Input;
using System.Windows.Media;
using System.Windows.Media.Animation;
using System.Windows.Shapes;

namespace SlidingBlocks3
{
```

```
    public partial class MainPage : UserControl
    {
        public Page()
        {
            // Required to initialize variables
            InitializeComponent();
        }
    }
}
```

If you are familiar with C#, this will look very similar to code you might have used before. Basically, it is a boilerplate class file named *Page* that inherits from the *UserControl* type. In the class constructor, the special *InitializeComponent()* call is used to set everything up. You add your page-specific code to this module, as you'll see in the section titled "Building a Silverlight Game" later in this chapter, where you create the sliding picture puzzle.

The Web Project

In addition to the control project, the template also creates a Web project that hosts your Silverlight application. This Web project contains two ASPX files: Default.aspx, which is an empty Web Form on which you can build an application; and a test page called *<ApplicationName>*TestPage.aspx (for example, SlidingBlocks3TestPage.aspx), which contains everything necessary to run Silverlight from ASP.NET.

Although Silverlight does not have any server-side dependencies, ASP.NET offers some controls that allow the generation of the client-side JavaScript and HTML necessary to host Silverlight in the browser.

The TestPage file includes references to these controls. Following is some of the markup for the ASPX file:

```
<%@ Page Language="C#" AutoEventWireup="true" %>

<%@ Register Assembly="System.Web.Silverlight"
    Namespace="System.Web.UI.SilverlightControls" TagPrefix="asp" %>

<!DOCTYPE html PUBLIC "-//W3C//DTD XHTML 1.0 Transitional//EN"
  "http://www.w3.org/TR/xhtml1/DTD/xhtml1-transitional.dtd">

<html xmlns="http://www.w3.org/1999/xhtml" >
<head runat="server">
    <title>Test Page For SlidingBlocks</title>
</head>
<body style="height:100%;margin:0;">
    <form id="form1" runat="server" style="height:100%;">
    <div>
        <asp:ScriptManager ID="ScriptManager1" runat="server">
        </asp:ScriptManager>
        <asp:Silverlight ID="Xaml1" runat="server"
          Source="~/ClientBin/SlidingBlocks3.xap"
```

```
        MinimumVersion="3.0.40307.0" Width="100%" Height="100%" />
    </div>
    </form>
</body>
</html>
```

Note that this is an evolving technology, so your version number attributes and public key attributes might differ slightly. Don't worry—if your code was generated by the template, you should be in good shape.

Notice that there are two ASP.NET controls referenced on this page. The first is the *ScriptManager* control, which is an artifact of ASP.NET AJAX and is a terrific control that is used to manage the downloading and referencing of all necessary JavaScript libraries at the correct time and in the correct place.

The second is the *Silverlight* control. Notice that it takes the XAP that we discussed earlier as its parameter. This control will generate the correct HTML code to create the *<object>* that represents Silverlight to the browser.

When you run this page, you see that a lot of HTML and JavaScript is generated. Toward the bottom of the code, shown in bold type here, you'll see where Silverlight is created and pointed at the XAP file. Here's a snippet:

```
<script type="text/javascript">
//<![CDATA[
Sys.Application.initialize();
Sys.Application.add_init(function() {
    $create(Sys.UI.Silverlight.Control,
        {"source":"ClientBin/SlidingBlocks3.xap"},
         null, null, $get("Xaml1"));
        });
//]]>
</script>
```

This script is interpreted by the browser to instantiate the *Silverlight* control. Please note that this code relies on ASP.NET and the ASP.NET Silverlight controls to work properly. If you are instantiating from something other than ASP.NET, you can still use the SDK-based JavaScript tools to instantiate Silverlight. This is covered in depth in Chapter 6.

Building a Silverlight Game

Silverlight follows the model of separating the design from the development by having the design in XAML technology and the code for the development in code-behind technology, typically (though not exclusively) programmed with C#.

In this example, you use very little XAML—just enough to contain the *Canvas* in which the puzzle pieces will be kept and the image that shows the completed picture. If you refer back to Figure 3-3, you can see these on the left and right, respectively. Note that although the default page has a *Grid* as its main container, you use a *Canvas* in this game for simplicity.

Creating the UI in XAML

As you saw in Figure 3-3, the UI for this game is very simple, consisting of an area of the screen (contained in a *Canvas*) where the sliding blocks reside and another area that renders the finished image.

Here's an example of the XAML that provides the *Canvas* and the completed image:

```
<UserControl x:Class="SlidingBlocks.Page"
      xmlns="http://schemas.microsoft.com/client/2007"
      xmlns:x="http://schemas.microsoft.com/winfx/2006/xaml"
      Width="640"
      Height="480"
      >

    <Canvas x:Name="LayoutRoot" >
        <Canvas x:Name="GameContainer" />
        <Image Source="sl.JPG" Canvas.Left="500"
            Height="400" Width="400" Stretch="UniformToFill">
        </Image>
    </Canvas>
</UserControl>
```

As you can see, it is very straightforward. The *Canvas* that contains the pieces of the puzzle is called *GameContainer*, and the image that renders the completed puzzle image is static and thus does not need to be named. It is prefilled with the image sl.jpg that exists in the same Web project. That's everything you need for your design, so in the next section, you can start examining the code.

Writing the Game Code

The game code in this example is written using C#. You could easily translate it into VB.NET, IronPython, or any other supported language that you want to use, but in most cases, this book uses C#.

Initializing the Data Structures

The first step in writing the code for this game is initializing the data structures that will be used by the application. In this case, you break the image up into 16 tiles, 15 of which will be shuffled across the board. One tile is not used; instead, there is a blank space that is used by the player to slide the blocks around.

In Silverlight, you cannot create a subimage from an existing image, but you can clip an image according to a clipping path. Don't confuse clipping with cropping. In the former, you dictate which parts of the image to draw; in the latter, you remove all but the desired part of the image. Silverlight does not support cropping, so you have to clip an image.

The problem with clipping is that the rest of the image dimensions are still available and clickable. So, for example, if you have a 400 × 400 image and you clip a 100 × 100 square at position (100,100), you will still have a 400 × 400 object that will be blank (but still clickable) except for a 100 × 100 square at position (100,100). This doesn't suit your needs to create a sliding picture puzzle, so what can you do?

The answer is to contain the image in a *Canvas* that is the same dimensions as the clip, and then use a translate transform on it so that the clipped part of the image is at the upper-left corner of this *Canvas*, and thus the *Canvas* renders only the clipped region.

So, for a 4 × 4 puzzle made up of 16 blocks, you need 16 images and 16 *Canvas* objects. You also need something to represent the board so that you know which image is in which square. Here's the code to declare these:

```
Canvas[] cI = new Canvas[16];
Image[] i = new Image[16];
int[] board = new int[16];
```

Creating the Puzzle Pieces

To create the puzzle pieces, you have to load the sl.jpg image into each element in the array of images. You can do this by using a uniform resource identifier (URI) to point to the image and the *BitmapImage* class (from *System.Windows.Media.Imaging*) to read the data from that URI and point it at the image control:

```
i[nx].Source = new BitmapImage(uri);
```

From your constructor, you can call a function (*InitBoard*) that will be used to instantiate the pieces:

```
public MainPage()
{
    // Required to initialize variables
    InitializeComponent();
    InitBoard();
}
```

You can see this function here:

```
void InitBoard()
{
  Uri uri = new Uri("sl.jpg", UriKind.Relative);
  int nx = 0;
  for (int ix = 0; ix < 4; ix++)
    for (int iy = 0; iy < 4; iy++)
    {
      nx = (ix * 4) + iy;
      i[nx] = new Image();
      i[nx].Height = 400;
      i[nx].Width = 400;
```

```
            i[nx].Stretch = Stretch.UniformToFill;
            RectangleGeometry r = new RectangleGeometry();
            r.Rect = new Rect((ix * 100), (iy * 100), 100, 100);
            i[nx].Clip = r;
            i[nx].Source = new BitmapImage(uri);
            i[nx].SetValue(Canvas.TopProperty, Convert.ToDouble(iy * 100 * -1));
            i[nx].SetValue(Canvas.LeftProperty, Convert.ToDouble(ix * 100 * -1));

            cI[nx] = new Canvas();
            cI[nx].Width = 100;
            cI[nx].Height = 100;
            cI[nx].Children.Add(i[nx]);
            cI[nx].SetValue(Canvas.NameProperty, "C" + nx.ToString());
            cI[nx].MouseLeftButtonDown += new
              MouseButtonEventHandler(Page_MouseLeftButtonDown);
            if (nx < 15)
              GameContainer.Children.Add(cI[nx]);
        }

    // Mix up the pieces
    shuffle();

    // Draw the board
    drawBoard();

}
```

Be sure to add a reference to *System.Windows.Media.Imaging* at the top of your code page:

```
using System.Windows.Media.Imaging;
```

At first, this might look a little complex, but on closer inspection, it is actually quite
straightforward. A nested loop from 0–3 on the x- and y-axes is set up. This, as you might
have guessed, is used to manage the 4 × 4 array for the images themselves.

The *Image* and *Canvas* arrays used to store the blocks are one-dimensional arrays with 16
elements each (because less memory and code are used to store them this way). So, to figure
out how to map a two-dimensional *ix, iy* coordinate to a one-dimensional array, you need the
following calculation:

```
nx = (ix * 4) + iy;
```

You then set up each *Image* element with a 400 × 400 dimension with *UniformToFill* stretch.
You can find more about how to use images in Chapter 4, "Silverlight XAML Basics."

Next, calculate the clip region using a *RectangleGeometry*:

```
RectangleGeometry r = new RectangleGeometry();
r.Rect=new Rect((ix*100), (iy*100) ,100,100);
i[nx].Clip = r;
```

This defines a *Rectangle* at the appropriate coordinates (derived by multiplying *ix* and *iy* by 100) with the appropriate size (100 × 100), and then assigns it to be the clipping region for the current image (*i[nx]*).

Next, load the image by setting it to the value of the *BitmapImage*, which is initialized from the URI of the image, so that it is translated into position. An image that is clipped at position (100,100) has to be moved by (−100,−100) for the clipped area to appear in the upper-left corner. Thus, you have to set the *Top* and *Left* properties to −100 multiplied by the current *iy* and *ix* values, respectively.

```
i[nx].Source = new BitmapImage(uri);
i[nx].SetValue(Canvas.TopProperty, Convert.ToDouble(iy * 100 * -1));
i[nx].SetValue(Canvas.LeftProperty, Convert.ToDouble(ix * 100 * -1));
```

You have not yet added the images to a parent *Canvas*, so this is the next step. You need to initialize, size, and add the respective image to the *Canvas* as a child. Here's the code:

```
cI[nx] = new Canvas();
cI[nx].Width = 100;
cI[nx].Height = 100;
cI[nx].Children.Add(i[nx]);
```

Now that you have your *Canvas* and it contains the clipped image, you complete the initialization by naming the *Canvas* (so that you can track it later when you click it), defining an event handler to manage what happens when the user clicks it, and finally adding it to the parent *Canvas*. You don't need to position the block yet. That will happen after the board is shuffled. Note that you don't add the final image to the board because you want to have an empty space.

```
cI[nx].SetValue(Canvas.NameProperty, "C" + nx.ToString());
cI[nx].MouseLeftButtonDown += new
    MouseButtonEventHandler(Page_MouseLeftButtonDown);
if(nx<15)
    GameContainer.Children.Add(cI[nx]);
```

Finally, shuffle the pieces and draw the game board. You'll see the code for this in the next section.

Shuffling the Pieces

You can shuffle the puzzle pieces using a fairly simple shuffle algorithm that goes through the array 100 times, picking out two random elements on each occasion; if the two elements are different, it swaps their contents. At the end, it loads the value −1 into the last element to recognize that it is the empty square.

You can see the shuffle algorithm here:

```
void shuffle()
{
  // Initialize Board
  for (int n = 0; n < 15; n++)
  {
    board[n] = n;
  }
  Random rand = new Random(System.DateTime.Now.Second);
  for (int n = 0; n < 100; n++)
  {
    int n1 = rand.Next(15);
    int n2 = rand.Next(15);
    if (n1 != n2)
    {
      int tmp = board[n1];
      board[n1] = board[n2];
      board[n2] = tmp;
    }
  }
  board[15] = -1;

}
```

Now that the pieces are shuffled, the next step is to draw the board.

Drawing the Board

At this point, you have all of the blocks defined as *Image* elements within *Canvas* elements, and you have an array of integers, where the value at index *n* is the tile to display at that position. You've also shuffled this array of integers, so now it's time to draw the game board. You can achieve this simply by using this code:

```
void drawBoard()
{
  int nx = 0;
  int ny = 0;
  for (int n = 0; n < 15; n++)
  {
    nx = n / 4;
    ny = n % 4;
    if(board[n]>=0)
    {
      cI[board[n]].SetValue(Canvas.TopProperty, Convert.ToDouble(ny * 100));
      cI[board[n]].SetValue(Canvas.LeftProperty, Convert.ToDouble(nx * 100));

    }
  }
}
```

This code loops from 0 to 14 (there are 15 blocks in the puzzle) and calculates an *x,y* coordinate for each block in a 4 × 4 grid. The *x* value is simply the integer division of the loop index by 4, and the *y* value is simply the modulus of the loop index by 4. If you multiply these by 100, you then get the right position to draw the *Canvas* element.

At this point, you have fully initialized the game. The image is positioned on the right, and the shuffled board of image blocks is on the left.

Handling User Control

The next thing to do is to start handling the user interaction. In a game such as this, the expected behavior is that the user clicks an image block, and if this block is next to the empty space, the block that the user clicked will slide into the space, leaving a new empty space behind. So, you need to handle the clicking of the *Canvas* containing the *Image* block. If you remember all the way back to the initialization of the blocks, you saw this line:

```
cI[nx].MouseLeftButtonDown
        += new MouseButtonEventHandler(Page_MouseLeftButtonDown);
```

This defines that the *Page_MouseLeftButtonDown* event handler will fire when the *Canvas* is clicked. This event handler has been wired up for each of the *Canvas* blocks.

The code for this event handler has two sections. The first section identifies which *Canvas* raised the event and where that *Canvas* is in the board:

```
void Page_MouseLeftButtonDown(object sender, MouseButtonEventArgs e)
{
  Canvas c = sender as Canvas;
  int nCanvasID = -1;
  int nBoardLoc = -1;
  int nEmptyLoc = -1;
  for (int i = 0; i < 16; i++)
  {
    if (c == cI[i])
    {
      nCanvasID = i;
      break;
    }
  }
  for (int i = 0; i < 16; i++)
  {
    if (board[i] == nCanvasID)
    {
      nBoardLoc = i;
    }
    else if (board[i] == -1)
    {
      nEmptyLoc = i;
    }
  }
}
```

So, for example, the player might have clicked the block that represents the upper-left corner of the finished image (block 0), but it is currently in the lower-left corner of the board (position 12). When the click event is raised, you would look through the array of *Canvas* elements that represent the blocks until you find one that matches the *Canvas* that was actually clicked, and from here you could get its index in the array, loading it into the *nCanvasID* variable (which in the previous hypothetical case would be 0). You can then scan through the board to find where item 0 is and, when you find it, assign this value to the *nBoardLoc* variable (which in the hypothetical case is 12) and, while you are at it, find the location of the empty space on the board and load that into *nEmptyLoc*.

The second section of code then needs to check to see whether the player can move, and if so, it moves the block into the space and updates the board accordingly.

```
// Check if we can move
if ((nBoardLoc == nEmptyLoc + 1) ||
    (nBoardLoc == nEmptyLoc - 1) ||
    (nBoardLoc == nEmptyLoc + 4) ||
    (nBoardLoc == nEmptyLoc - 4))
{
    int nx = nEmptyLoc/4;
    int ny = nEmptyLoc%4;

    cI[nCanvasID].SetValue(Canvas.TopProperty, Convert.ToDouble(ny * 100));
    cI[nCanvasID].SetValue(Canvas.LeftProperty, Convert.ToDouble(nx * 100));

    board[nEmptyLoc] = nCanvasID;
    board[nBoardLoc] = -1;

    checkWinner();
}
else
{
    // do nothing
}


}
```

To do this, you first check the position of the empty location relative to the position of the location of the block that the player clicked. If it is immediately above, below, to the left, or to the right of the current block, you can move it. Because the board is a one-dimensional array representing a 4 × 4 board, this is easy to do. Items to the left and to the right of the current item are off by −1 and +1, respectively, and items above and below are off by −4 and +4, respectively, so if you seek the blocks at these indices for the empty block, you know that the player can move.

To move, you then need to get the *x* and *y* coordinates relative to the position of the empty block and assign them to the position of the clicked block. Then, assign the board location that previously contained the empty block to contain the value of the *Canvas* that the player just clicked, and the board location that previously contained the *Canvas* that the player just clicked to −1, indicating that it is now empty.

Finally, call the *checkWinner()* function to see whether the player has successfully unscrambled the board.

Checking Winning Condition

The *checkWinner* function checks to see whether the player has successfully unscrambled the board. This, again, is very straightforward. The board is unscrambled if every item at index *n* in the board array is equal to *n*—that is, *Canvas* 0 is at index 0, *Canvas* 1 is at index 1, and so on.

The most efficient way to do this is to assume that you have a winning board and scan through it until *board[n]* is not equal to *n*, at which point you have a losing board and you break the loop. If you make it all the way through the board, you have a winner.

```
void checkWinner()
    {
        bool bCompleted = true;
        for (int n = 0; n < 15; n++)
        {
            if (n != board[n])
            {
                bCompleted = false;
                break;
            }
        }
        if (bCompleted)
        {
            // The Player has won the game....do something nice for them.
        }
    }
```

At this point, you have all the elements for a basic image sliding picture puzzle game written in C# for Silverlight, and it is just over 100 lines of code. You can build on this sample as you progress through this book—adding animation to the sliding of the blocks, saving high scores, allowing images to be uploaded to the application, and so forth. The sky is the limit to the enhancements you can add!

Summary

In this chapter, you looked at Visual Studio 2008 and the various tools and templates that it offers you to develop Silverlight applications using .NET languages. You toured a project based on the default Silverlight templates, inspecting each of the files and how it is used to develop and deploy a Silverlight application. You then put the theory into practice by using XAML and C# to build a fully featured sliding picture puzzle game.

This gives you a taste of what you can do with Silverlight, but it barely scratches the surface of what is possible. In Part 2 of this book, "Programming Silverlight 3 with .NET," you start looking in more depth at some of the major areas of functionality that are available from the .NET Framework, including building your own controls, networking and communication, data and XML, dynamic languages, and the ASP.NET server controls.

Chapter 4
Silverlight XAML Basics

Extensible Application Markup Language (XAML) is at the core of your Microsoft Silverlight application. You use it to define your graphical assets, your interactions, your animations, and your timelines. It's based on Extensible Markup Language (XML), so everything is defined in text markup using attributes to declare properties, methods, and events.

This chapter explains the common XAML components used to define the visual elements of your application. First, you examine how to make a layout, including how elements can be drawn on the screen relative to their containers and each other. Next, you consider the various brushes that you can use to fill shapes and controls, as well as the strokes that you can use to draw their outlines. Then, you learn about paths and geometries and how they can help you generate complex shapes and groups of shapes as well as how you can use them to clip other objects or fills. Finally, you look at the controls that use these XAML components, including *Canvas*, which is at the heart of Silverlight layout, and examine how to render text using the *Glyphs* and *TextBlock* controls.

XAML Positioning Properties

Briefly, you use the *Canvas.Left* and *Canvas.Top* properties to position controls in XAML. These properties are referred to as *attached* properties, which simply means that they are available globally in your XAML code or that they modify a property that is really exhibited by their parent. In addition to this, you can use the *Canvas.ZIndex* attached property to determine the Z-order position of the item, which defines the topmost object to be rendered if two or more overlap. The default Z-order behavior in XAML is that the last item drawn (farthest down in the XAML document) is topmost, but you can override this default using *Canvas.ZIndex*.

So, consider the following XAML. It shows the code for a *Canvas* containing two rectangles. The rectangles use *Canvas.Left* and *Canvas.Top* to determine their upper-left corners relative to the canvas that contains them.

```
<Canvas>
    <Rectangle Fill="Red" Width="200" Height="128"
            Canvas.Left="8" Canvas.Top="8"/>
    <Rectangle Fill="Black" Width="280" Height="80"
            Canvas.Left="40" Canvas.Top="32"/>
</Canvas>
```

The black rectangle is drawn on top of the red one, as shown in Figure 4-1.

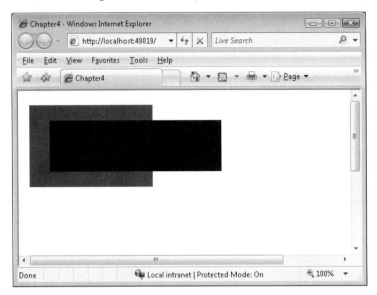

FIGURE 4-1 Rectangle layouts.

The red rectangle is positioned 8 pixels from the left and 8 pixels from the top of the parent canvas. The black one is positioned 40 pixels from the left and 32 pixels from the top. The black rectangle appears on top because it was the last one rendered.

You can use *ZIndex* to override this behavior. You can specify *ZIndex* to be a numeric value, and the highest numbered *ZIndex* will appear on top of lower numbered ones, as you see in the following code:

```
<Canvas>
    <Rectangle Canvas.ZIndex="2"
               Fill="Red" Width="200" Height="128"
               Canvas.Left="8" Canvas.Top="8"/>
    <Rectangle Canvas.ZIndex="1"
               Fill="Black" Width="280" Height="80"
               Canvas.Left="40" Canvas.Top="32"/>
</Canvas>
```

As shown in Figure 4-2, the red rectangle now appears on top of the black one, as you would expect, because the *ZIndex* value for the red rectangle is higher than the *ZIndex* value for the black rectangle.

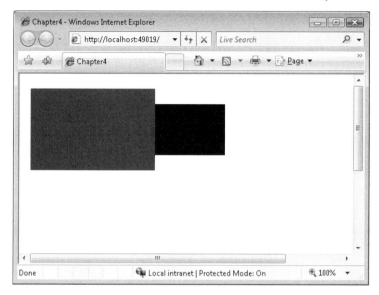

FIGURE 4-2 Changing the Z-order of elements.

XAML Brushes

You use *brushes* in XAML to determine how shapes are drawn and filled. In the earlier example, you saw that the two rectangles were filled using the known colors *Red* and *Black*. These are simple examples of using brushes. The next sections describe the more complex set of *Brush* types that XAML supports.

SolidColorBrush

The *SolidColorBrush* fills an area with a solid color. The color can be a named value, such as *Red* or *Black*, or it can be described in hexadecimal values indicating the alpha, red, green, and blue channel intensities. For example, the color white is described as *#FFFFFFFF* in hexadecimal notation, and the color red is *#FFFF0000*.

LinearGradientBrush

The *LinearGradientBrush* fills an area with a linear gradient defined in two-dimensional space. The default gradient is defined using a normalized rectangle—a rectangle with its upper-left corner at (0,0) and its lower-right corner at (1,1). This defines the gradient as extending from the upper-left corner to the lower-right corner. If you define a color at each of these points, Silverlight will draw the gradient between them.

As an example, consider the following rectangle definition:

```
<Canvas>
    <Rectangle Width="200" Height="128" Canvas.Left="8" Canvas.Top="8">
        <Rectangle.Fill>
            <LinearGradientBrush>
                <GradientStop Color="#FF000000" Offset="0"/>
                <GradientStop Color="#FFFFFFFF" Offset="1"/>
            </LinearGradientBrush>
        </Rectangle.Fill>
    </Rectangle>
</Canvas>
```

This XAML snippet defines a *LinearGradientBrush* that extends from the upper-left corner to the lower-right corner of the rectangle. The first gradient stop, at the beginning of the gradient, is black (#FF000000), and the second gradient stop, at the end of the gradient, is white (#FFFFFFFF). You can see this rectangle rendered in Figure 4-3.

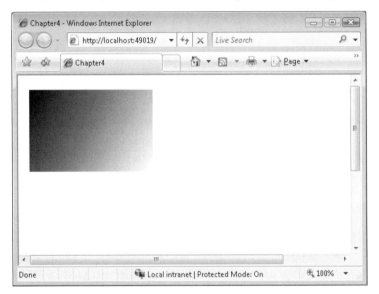

FIGURE 4-3 Using the *LinearGradientBrush*.

Changing the Gradient Direction

You can change the direction of the brush by setting the *StartPoint* and *EndPoint* properties of the *LinearGradientBrush*. To change the gradient fill direction to lower left to upper right, you can set these to (0,1) and (1,0), respectively, as shown:

```
<Rectangle Width="200" Height="128" Canvas.Left="8" Canvas.Top="8">
    <Rectangle.Fill>
        <LinearGradientBrush StartPoint="0,1" EndPoint="1,0">
            <GradientStop Color="#FF000000" Offset="0"/>
            <GradientStop Color="#FFFFFFFF" Offset="1"/>
```

```
        </LinearGradientBrush>
    </Rectangle.Fill>
</Rectangle>
```

Figure 4-4 shows how this rectangle is rendered.

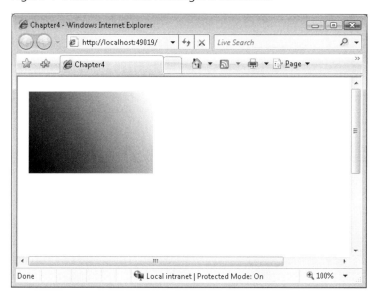

FIGURE 4-4 Changing the gradient direction.

Adding Gradient Stops

The previous examples show the minimum number of gradient stops, which is two. You can create other gradient stops containing colors and locations to control the gradient. For example, if you want your gradient to range from black to white to black again, you can define three stops like this:

```
<Rectangle Width="200" Height="128" Canvas.Left="8" Canvas.Top="8">
    <Rectangle.Fill>
        <LinearGradientBrush>
            <GradientStop Color="#FF000000" Offset="0"/>
            <GradientStop Color="#FFFFFFFF" Offset="0.5"/>
            <GradientStop Color="#FF000000" Offset="1"/>
        </LinearGradientBrush>
    </Rectangle.Fill>
</Rectangle>
```

The first stop, at position 0, is black; the second, half way along the gradient at position 0.5, is white; and the third stop, at the end of the gradient at position 1, is black again. If you render this, you will see something like the rectangle shown in Figure 4-5.

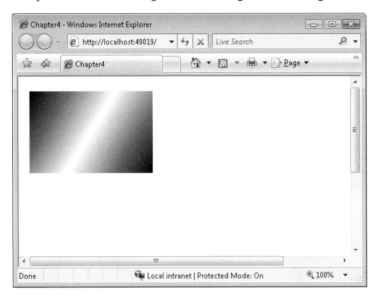

FIGURE 4-5 Using gradient stops.

The gradient stops are positioned using the *Offset* parameter; therefore, to move the white section of this gradient closer to the upper-left corner, you simply change its *Offset* so that it is closer to zero, as shown in this XAML snippet:

```
<Rectangle Width="200" Height="128" Canvas.Left="8" Canvas.Top="8">
    <Rectangle.Fill>
        <LinearGradientBrush>
            <GradientStop Color="#FF000000" Offset="0"/>
            <GradientStop Color="#FFFFFFFF" Offset="0.1"/>
            <GradientStop Color="#FF000000" Offset="1"/>
        </LinearGradientBrush>
    </Rectangle.Fill>
</Rectangle>
```

You can see how this changes the appearance of the rendered rectangle in Figure 4-6.

You can achieve some nice effects by experimenting with how you position and direct gradients. These properties can be used to fill shapes or to define strokes, as you will see later in this chapter.

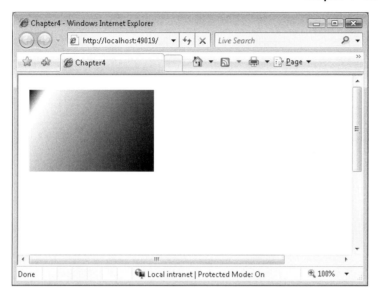

FIGURE 4-6 Positioning the gradient stop.

RadialGradientBrush

The *RadialGradientBrush* is similar to the *LinearGradientBrush* from a definition point of view, but it defines a circular gradient, with 0 marking the center of the circle of the gradient and 1 marking its outer edge. It's easier to show this by example, so consider this XAML:

```
<Rectangle Width="200" Height="128" Canvas.Left="8" Canvas.Top="8">
    <Rectangle.Fill>
        <RadialGradientBrush>
            <GradientStop Color="#FF000000" Offset="0"/>
            <GradientStop Color="#FFFFFFFF" Offset="1"/>
        </RadialGradientBrush>
    </Rectangle.Fill>
</Rectangle>
```

This fills the rectangle with a gradient brush with black at its center and white at its outer edge, as shown in Figure 4-7. Notice that because the outer edge of the rectangle is white, you see an ellipse. This is because the background color of the rectangle is the same as the outer gradient stop color for the brush.

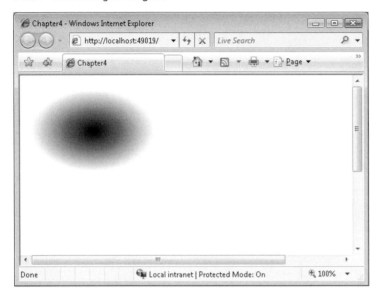

FIGURE 4-7 Filling a rectangle with the *RadialGradientBrush*.

Gradient stops for the *RadialGradientBrush* are defined using similar methods to those used for gradient stops for the *LinearGradientBrush*.

Setting the Focal Point

When you apply a fill with the *RadialGradientBrush*, you can set the focal point for the radial by using the *GradientOrigin* property. You use this to set the point from which the gradient emanates, usually at the center of the circle. Despite the circular nature of the *RadialGradientBrush*, the focal point is set in a rectangular normalized space. So, if you want the focal point to be at the upper-left corner, set the *GradientOrigin* to (0,0); if you want it at the lower-right corner, set the *GradientOrigin* to (1,1). The following example shows the gradient with the focal point set toward the lower right of the object, at (0.7,0.7):

```
<Rectangle Width="200" Height="128" Canvas.Left="8" Canvas.Top="8">
   <Rectangle.Fill>
      <RadialGradientBrush GradientOrigin="0.7, 0.7">
         <GradientStop Color="#FF000000" Offset="0"/>
         <GradientStop Color="#FFFFFFFF" Offset="1"/>
      </RadialGradientBrush>
   </Rectangle.Fill>
</Rectangle>
```

Figure 4-8 shows how it is rendered.

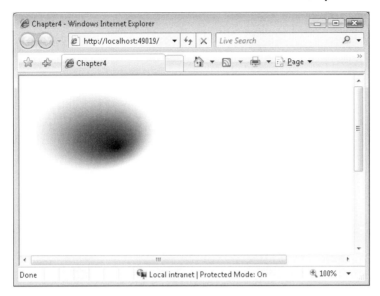

FIGURE 4-8 Setting the focal point of a *RadialGradientBrush*.

Changing the *SpreadMethod*

You can use the *SpreadMethod* property to determine how the gradient repeats. There are three possible values for *SpreadMethod*: *Pad*, *Reflect*, and *Repeat*. *Pad* fills the circle with the gradient as specified and is the default value. Figures 4-7 and 4-8 show a basic *RadialGradientBrush* with a spread set to *Pad*.

Following is the XAML for a rectangle filled with a gradient brush with its *SpreadMethod* set to *Reflect*. You can see the results in Figure 4-9.

```
<Rectangle Width="200" Height="128" Canvas.Left="8" Canvas.Top="8">
   <Rectangle.Fill>
      <RadialGradientBrush SpreadMethod="Reflect">
         <GradientStop Color="#FF000000" Offset="0"/>
         <GradientStop Color="#FFFFFFFF" Offset="1"/>
      </RadialGradientBrush>
   </Rectangle.Fill>
</Rectangle>
```

This XAML causes the gradient to reflect, as you can see in Figure 4-9. The gradient is defined to range from black to white, but then it starts phasing from white to black again as a reflection.

Similarly, you can use the *Repeat* method to repeat the gradient from black to white. Figure 4-10 shows the result of this. Where the gradient would usually stop, the gradient pattern is instead repeated, repeating the phasing from black to white to the outside edges of the rectangle.

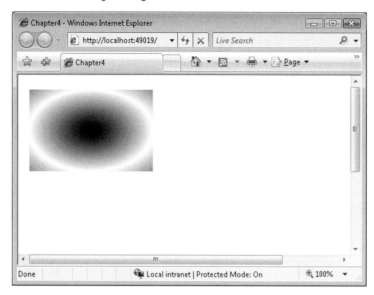

FIGURE 4-9 Using the *Reflect SpreadMethod*.

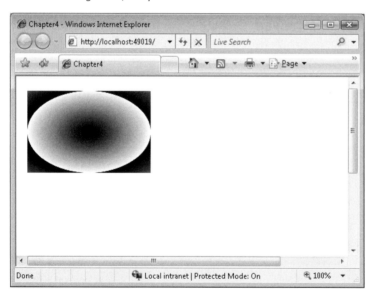

FIGURE 4-10 Using the *Repeat SpreadMethod*.

Setting the Radius of the *RadialGradientBrush*

You use the *RadiusX* and *RadiusY* properties to specify the desired radius for the gradient. The default value for each is 0.5. If you specify a value less than this, you will paint more than one circle with the *SpreadMethod* defining the rendering behavior. If you specify a value greater than 0.5, you effectively "zoom" the gradient.

For example, following is an XAML snippet that defines a *RadialGradientBrush* with *RadiusX* and *RadiusY* set to 0.1 and *SpreadMethod* not set (so that it defaults to *Pad*).

```
<Rectangle Width="200" Height="128" Canvas.Left="8" Canvas.Top="8">
   <Rectangle.Fill>
      <RadialGradientBrush RadiusX="0.1" RadiusY="0.1">
         <GradientStop Color="#FF000000" Offset="0"/>
         <GradientStop Color="#FFFFFFFF" Offset="1"/>
      </RadialGradientBrush>
   </Rectangle.Fill>
</Rectangle>
```

This XAML renders the rectangle with a *RadialGradientBrush* using a 0.1 radius, so it is effectively one-fifth the size of the objects you saw earlier. You can see this in Figure 4-11.

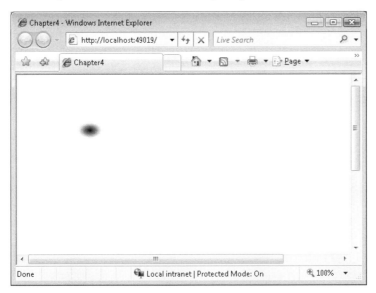

FIGURE 4-11 Setting the radius of the *RadialGradientBrush*.

When combined with the *SpreadMethod*, you can get some interesting effects. You can see an example with a *SpreadMethod* set to *Reflect* in Figure 4-12.

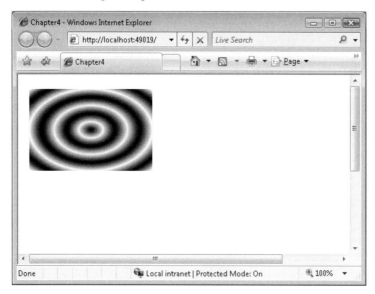

FIGURE 4-12 Combining a change in the radius setting and *SpreadMethod*.

Using *ImageBrush*

To fill a space with an image, you use the XAML *ImageBrush*. The default behavior will stretch the brush to fit the image to maintain the image's aspect ratio. The following XAML fills the contents of a rectangle with an *ImageBrush*:

```
<Rectangle Width="200" Height="128" Canvas.Left="8" Canvas.Top="8">
  <Rectangle.Fill>
    <ImageBrush ImageSource="smily.jpg" />
  </Rectangle.Fill>
</Rectangle>
```

You can see the results in Figure 4-13.

Stretching the Image

You can specify how the image fills the area that it is painting with the *Stretch* property. You can specify this using one of several different stretch modes: *None*, *Uniform*, *UniformToFill*, and *Fill*.

None renders the image untouched—no stretching takes place. *Uniform* scales the image to fit the rectangle dimensions but leaves the aspect ratio untouched. *UniformToFill* scales the image to fill the output area completely but preserves its aspect ratio (clipping the image as necessary). *Fill* scales the image to fit the output dimensions using independent scaling on the x-axis and y-axis. This distorts the image to fill the available space completely.

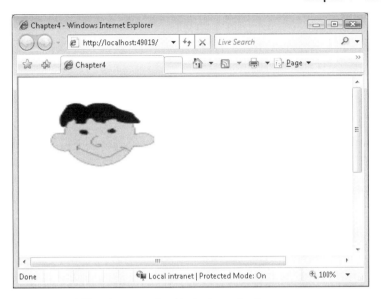

FIGURE 4-13 Filling the rectangle with the *ImageBrush*.

You can see these options in action in Figure 4-14, which shows four rectangles that have been filled with the same image but that use different stretch modes.

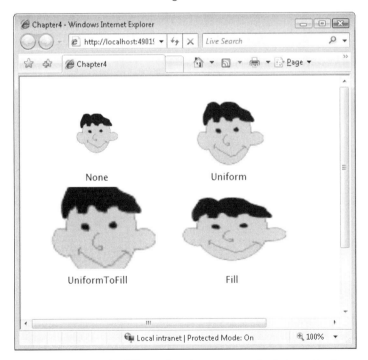

FIGURE 4-14 Using the different *Stretch* property modes in *ImageBrush*.

Aligning the Image

The alignment of the image along the x-axis and y-axis can be set with the *AlignmentX* and *AlignmentY* properties. You can align the image to the left, right, or center on the x-axis and to the top, center, or bottom on the y-axis. Note that if you are stretching the image to fill the surface, setting the alignment will have no effect—it will work only when *Stretch* is set to *None*. Following is an example of aligning the image to the right and bottom:

```
<Rectangle Stroke="Black" Width="200" Height="128" x:Name="r1">
   <Rectangle.Fill>
      <ImageBrush ImageSource="smily.jpg" Stretch="None"
                  AlignmentX="Right" AlignmentY="Bottom" />
   </Rectangle.Fill>
</Rectangle>
```

You can see how it appears in Figure 4-15.

FIGURE 4-15 Using image alignment.

VideoBrush

With the *VideoBrush*, you can fill an area with video. I discuss this brush in more detail in Chapter 10, "Media in Silverlight: Video," where I also describe the *MediaElement* control more completely.

XAML Visual Properties

Beyond brushes and location settings, XAML provides a number of other properties to help you to control the appearance of your object. By using these properties, you can set an object's dimensions, opacity, cursor behavior, and stroke.

Using XAML Dimension and Position Properties

XAML dimensions are set using the *Height* and *Width* properties, each of which takes a *double* value. To create a rectangle that is 100 pixels wide and 200 pixels high, for example, you would define the XAML as follows:

```
<Rectangle Fill="Black" Width="100" Height="200" />
```

In addition, keep in mind that the *Top* and *Left* properties attached to the parent canvas are used to specify the relative position of the object.

Consider the following XAML:

```
<Canvas>
  <Canvas Canvas.Top="40" Canvas.Left="40">
    <Rectangle Canvas.Top="40" Fill="Black" Width="100" Height="200" />
  </Canvas>
</Canvas>
```

Assume the outmost *Canvas* is the root canvas for the page. The *Rectangle* will be drawn 80 pixels down from the top of the page as a result. Its parent canvas is 40 pixels down, and the *Rectangle* is 40 pixels down from its parent, for a total of 80 pixels.

Using Opacity

You can set the opacity of an object in two ways. The first is to use the alpha channel in the brush that is used to fill the object. The following XAML creates a black rectangle on top of an image:

```
<Image Source="smily.jpg" />
<Rectangle Fill="#FF000000" Width="100" Height="200" />
```

The *Fill* is set to black (because the red, green, and blue channels are all set to zero), and the alpha is set to opaque (filled with #FF). You can make the rectangle semitransparent by changing the alpha channel value:

```
<Image Source="smily.jpg" />
<Rectangle Fill="#77000000" Width="100" Height="200" />
```

You'll see that the rectangle now appears gray, and the image is visible underneath it.

The second method is to use the *Opacity* property, which takes a value from 0 (totally transparent) through 1 (totally opaque). This property is used in conjunction with the alpha channel in the brush. If you use the brush color #77000000 to fill the shape, for example, and then set *Opacity* to 1, the rectangle will still be somewhat opaque. If you set it to 0, the rectangle will be totally transparent.

Using the *Opacity* property is useful when it comes to animating the opacity of an object. It makes it easy to fade an object in or out using a *DoubleAnimation*. You can learn more about animation in Chapter 5, "XAML Transformation and Animation."

Cursor Behavior

With most XAML elements, you can use the *Cursor* property to specify how the mouse will appear when it hovers over an item. This property is set to a value from the *MouseCursor* enumeration. Here are a number of the most commonly used enumerations:

- **Arrow**   Displays the typical default arrow cursor

- **Default**   No cursor preference; uses the parent's cursor if it is specified

- **Hand**   Displays a pointing hand cursor, usually used for a link

- **IBeam**   Specifies an I-beam cursor; typically used for text selection

- **None**   No cursor

- **Wait**   Specifies an icon that indicates a busy wait state

Controlling *Stroke*

The *Stroke* property determines how a shape's outline is painted on the screen. This is different from how the object is *filled* with a brush. In a rectangle, for example, the stroke determines how the outline of the rectangle is drawn.

Set the *Stroke* by using a brush. Following is an example of XAML that renders a rectangle using a simple stroke to specify a black outline:

```
<Rectangle Stroke="Black" Canvas.Left="40" Canvas.Top="40" Width="100" Height="200" />
```

In this case, the *Stroke* property is in fact using a *Black SolidColorBrush*. It is syntactically equivalent to the following XAML:

```
<Rectangle Canvas.Left="40" Canvas.Top="40" Width="100" Height="200">
   <Rectangle.Stroke>
      <SolidColorBrush Color="Black" />
```

```
      </Rectangle.Stroke>
</Rectangle>
```

By using this syntax (defining the brush as an attached *Stroke* property), you can specify different types of brushes to draw the shape's stroke. Following is an example of using a *LinearGradientBrush* to paint the rectangle's stroke:

```
<Rectangle StrokeThickness="10" Canvas.Left="40"
        Canvas.Top="40" Width="100" Height="200">
  <Rectangle.Stroke>
    <LinearGradientBrush >
       <GradientStop Color="#FF000000" Offset="0"/>
       <GradientStop Color="#FFFFFFFF" Offset="0.5"/>
       <GradientStop Color="#FF000000" Offset="1"/>
     </LinearGradientBrush>
  </Rectangle.Stroke>
</Rectangle>
```

You can see how this appears on the screen in Figure 4-16.

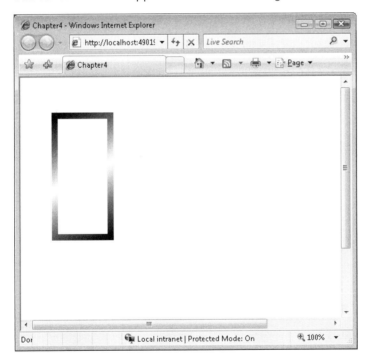

FIGURE 4-16 Using a *LinearGradientBrush* to define a shape's stroke.

Setting Stroke Width

You might have noticed in this example that the thickness of the stroke was set to 10. This was done to better demonstrate the gradient, which doesn't show up well using the default stroke thickness value of 1.

Set the stroke width using the *StrokeThickness* property. This specifies the stroke width in pixels:

```
<Rectangle StrokeThickness="10" Stroke="Black" Canvas.Left="40" Canvas.Top="40" Width="100"
Height="200" />
```

Setting Stroke Dash

The *StrokeDashArray* property is used to set the stroke dash pattern. You can combine this property with the *StrokeDashCap* and *StrokeDashOffset* properties to fine-tune stroke dash.

To set the stroke of the rectangle to be dashed with a repeating pattern of dashes, you define an array of *double* values that represents the length of the dashes as well as the space between them. To define a dash pattern using a dash 4 units long, followed by a space 1 unit long, followed by a dash 2 units long, followed by a space 1 unit long before repeating, you would set the *StrokeDashArray* property to (4,1,2,1). Here's an example:

```
<Rectangle StrokeThickness="10" Stroke="Black" Canvas.Left="40" Canvas.Top="40" Width="100"
Height="200" StrokeDashArray="4,1,2,1"/>
```

Figure 4-17 shows how this is drawn on the screen.

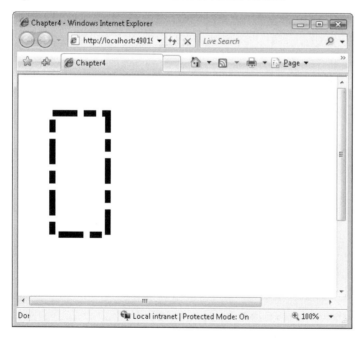

FIGURE 4-17 Setting the dash pattern for the stroke using *StrokeDashArray*.

You can see that these dashes are rectangular in shape, with squared dash edges. You can change this using the *StrokeDashCap* property. This property is set to a value from the *PenlineCap* enumeration. It can contain the following values:

- **Flat**   This is the default value, and it specifies that the cap doesn't extend beyond the end of the line—it is the same as not having a cap.

- **Round**   This specifies a semicircle with the same diameter as the line thickness.

- **Square**   This specifies a square end cap.

- **Triangle**   This specifies an isosceles triangle end cap, with the base length equal to the thickness of the stroke.

Following is an example of using the *StrokeDashCap* to set a rounded dash cap:

```
<Rectangle StrokeThickness="10" Stroke="Black" Canvas.Left="40" Canvas.Top="40" Width="100"
Height="200" StrokeDashArray="4,1,2,1" StrokeDashCap="Round"/>
```

Figure 4-18 shows how this will appear on the screen.

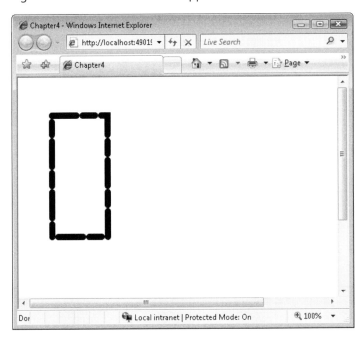

FIGURE 4-18 Using the *StrokeDashCap* property.

Controlling Line Joins

If you look at the previous examples, you will notice that the dash lines intersect at the corners and are drawn squared off. This is considered a line join, and with the *StrokeLineJoin* property you can control how the pen behaves at this line join. This property is set to the *PenLineJoin* enumeration, which can contain one of three values:

- **Bevel**   Shave off the edges of the join

- **Miter**   Keep the sharp edges

- **Round**   Round the edges of the join

This XAML creates a rectangle with the line join type set to *Bevel*:

```
<Rectangle StrokeThickness="10" Stroke="Black" Canvas.Left="40" Canvas.Top="40" Width="100"
Height="200" StrokeLineJoin="Bevel" />
```

You can see how this is drawn in Figure 4-19.

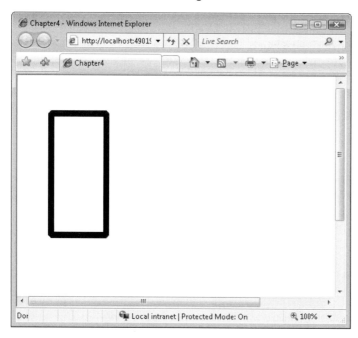

FIGURE 4-19 Using the *StrokeLineJoin* to specify a beveled corner.

Shapes in XAML

XAML supports a number of basic shapes that can be used to create more complex objects. These shapes are as follows:

- **Ellipse**   Draws an ellipse—a circle is an ellipse with equal radius distances for *X* and *Y*

- **Rectangle**   Draws a rectangle—a square is a rectangle with equal distances for *X* and *Y*

- **Line**   Draws a line

- **Path**   Draws a series of connected lines and curves according to a path language

- **Polygon**   Draws a closed shape made up of a connected series of lines

- **Polyline**   Draws a series of connected straight lines

The following subsections discuss how to create each of these shapes.

Using the *Ellipse* Object

Use the *Ellipse* shape to draw an ellipse or circle. You control the *Ellipse* by setting its height property to the desired vertical diameter (that is, twice the desired vertical radius) and its width property to the desired horizontal diameter. If these values are equal in value, the XAML will render a circle. The *Ellipse* outline is drawn using a *Stroke*, and the *Ellipse* is filled using a *Brush*.

Using the *Rectangle* Object

Use the *Rectangle* shape to draw a rectangle or square. You control the size of the shape using the *Width* and *Height* properties. If these properties are equal, you end up with a square. Like the *Ellipse*, the outline of the *Rectangle* is drawn using a *Stroke*, and it is filled using a *Brush*.

You can round the corners of a *Rectangle* shape using the *RadiusX* and *RadiusY* properties. You set these to a *double* specifying the radius of the desired circle. They default to 0.0, indicating no rounding. Because the *RadiusX* and *RadiusY* are set independently, you can obtain elliptical rounding effects by using different values.

Following is an example of a rectangle with rounded corners. *RadiusY* is set to 40, and *RadiusX* is set to 20, indicating that the corners will be smoother vertically than they are horizontally:

```
<Rectangle Fill="Black" Canvas.Left="40" Canvas.Top="40"
        Width="100" Height="200" RadiusX="20" RadiusY="40" />
```

You can see the results of these settings in action in Figure 4-20.

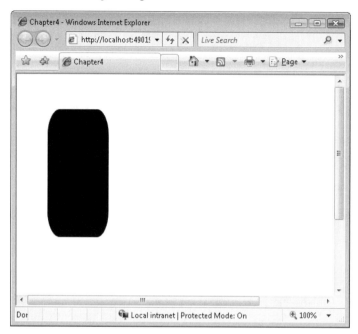

FIGURE 4-20 Rounding the corners of a rectangle.

Using the *Line* Object

You can draw a simple line in XAML using the *Line* object. You can specify the (X1,Y1) and (X2,Y2) coordinates with the line to be drawn between them. These coordinates are relative to the upper-left position of the line, specified using *Canvas.Top* and *Canvas.Left* in the usual manner. Note that you need to specify the line stroke using at least a stroke color before the stroke will be drawn.

Consider the following XAML:

```
<Line X1="40" Y1="40" X2="100" Y2="100" Stroke="Black" />
```

This draws a line from (40,40) to (100,100). However, if you add *Canvas.Top* and/or *Canvas.Left*, the line will be drawn relative to that. So, the following XAML draws the line from (40,140) to (100,200), assuming that there is no positioning on the parent canvas. If there is, Silverlight will draw the line relative to the parent positioning.

```
<Line Canvas.Top="100" X1="40" Y1="40" X2="100" Y2="100" Stroke="Black" />
```

Using Paths and Geometries

The *Path* object draws a connected series of lines and curves. These lines and curves can be defined using a geometry type. This section discusses the various geometry types.

The *EllipseGeometry* defines the path as a simple ellipse. Here's an example:

```
<Path Stroke="Black">
  <Path.Data>
    <EllipseGeometry RadiusX="100" RadiusY="100" />
  </Path.Data>
</Path>
```

The *EllipseGeometry* uses *RadiusX* and *RadiusY* to specify the dimensions of the ellipse that makes up the geometry. It also allows you to define the center point of the ellipse using the *Center* attribute. Following is an example:

```
<Path Stroke="Black">
  <Path.Data>
    <EllipseGeometry RadiusX="100" RadiusY="100" Center="50,50" />
  </Path.Data>
</Path>
```

The *LineGeometry* defines the path as a single line, starting at the *StartPoint* and ending at the *EndPoint*. These are set simply using string x- and y-coordinates, so the upper-left corner is specified as (0,0). Here's an example of a *LineGeometry*:

```
<Path Stroke="Black">
  <Path.Data>
    <LineGeometry StartPoint="10,10" EndPoint="100,100" />
  </Path.Data>
</Path>
```

The *RectangleGeometry* defines the path as a single rectangle, using the *Rect* property to define the dimensions of the rectangle. This is a string of four values, corresponding to the top, left, height, and width of the rectangle. So, to draw a rectangle that is 100 by 200 pixels with its upper-left corner at (0,0), you would use the following *Path*:

```
<Path Stroke="Black">
  <Path.Data>
    <RectangleGeometry Rect="0,0,100,200" />
  </Path.Data>
</Path>
```

Use the *PathGeometry* to put together a complex path of different segments, including arcs, Bezier curves, lines, poly-Bezier curves, polyquadratic Bezier curves, and quadratic Bezier curves. You can collect segments into a *PathFigure*, and one or more *PathFigure* objects make up a *PathGeometry*. The *PathGeometry* also sets the starting point of the path. If you have multiple segments, the starting point for each segment is the last point of the previous segment.

The *ArcSegment* Object

The *ArcSegment* object draws a simple elliptical arc between two points. You have a number of different properties to set to define the arc:

- **Point**   Sets the starting point for the arc

- **Size**   Sets the *x* and *y* radius of the arc

- **RotationAngle**   Sets the rotation angle—that is, how far the angle is rotated around the x-axis

- **IsLargeArc**   Sets the "largeness" of the arc, where an arc of more than 180 degrees is considered large

- **SweepDirection**   Sets the drawing direction of the arc (*Clockwise* or *CounterClockwise*)

Here's an example of a *Path* with a single arc segment, with these properties demonstrated:

```
<Path Stroke="Black">
    <Path.Data>
        <PathGeometry>
            <PathFigure>
                <ArcSegment Point="100,100" Size="200,200"
                    RotationAngle="10" IsLargeArc="False"
                    SweepDirection="ClockWise" />
            </PathFigure>
        </PathGeometry>
    </Path.Data>
</Path>
```

The *LineSegment* Object

You can add a line to a *PathSegment* using the *LineSegment* object. This simply draws a line from the current or starting point to the point defined using its *Point* property. So, to draw a line from (100,100) to (200,200) and then another back to (200,0), you create a *PathFigure* containing multiple line segments like this:

```
<Path Stroke="Black">
    <Path.Data>
        <PathGeometry>
            <PathFigure StartPoint="100,100">
                <LineSegment Point="200,200" />
                <LineSegment Point="200,0" />
            </PathFigure>
        </PathGeometry>
    </Path.Data>
</Path>
```

The *PolyLineSegment* Object

With the *PolyLineSegment*, you can draw a number of lines, as its name suggests, simply by providing the points. The first line is drawn from the start point to the first defined point, the second line from this point to the second defined point, and so forth.

Following is the XAML that demonstrates a *PolyLineSegment*:

```
<Path Stroke="Black">
   <Path.Data>
      <PathGeometry>
            <PathFigure StartPoint="100,100">
               <PolyLineSegment
                  Points="50,50,150,150,250,250,
                          100,200,200,100,300,300" />
            </PathFigure>
      </PathGeometry>
   </Path.Data>
</Path>
```

The *BezierSegment* Object

You can define a Bezier curve with the *BezierSegment* object. A Bezier curve is a curve between two points defined by one or two control points. The *BezierSegment* object takes as parameters three points, called *Point1*, *Point2*, and *Point3*. Depending on how many you use, you get different behavior. So, for example, if you set *Point1* and *Point2*, the curve will be rendered from the start point to *Point2*, using *Point1* as the control point. If you set *Point1*, *Point2*, and *Point3*, the curve will be rendered from the start point to *Point3*, using *Point1* and *Point2* as control points.

Following is an example of a *PathFigure* containing a *BezierSegment*:

```
<Path Stroke="Black">
   <Path.Data>
      <PathGeometry>
         <PathFigure StartPoint="100,100">
            <BezierSegment Point1="140,120" Point2="100,140" />
         </PathFigure>
      </PathGeometry>
   </Path.Data>
</Path>
```

The *PolyBezierSegment* Object

By using the *PolyBezierSegment* object, you can set a group of points that Silverlight will interpret into a set of control points for a group of Bezier curves. Consider the following XAML:

```
<Path Stroke="Black">
  <Path.Data>
    <PathGeometry>
      <PathFigure StartPoint="100,100">
        <PolyBezierSegment>
          <PolyBezierSegment.Points>
            <Point X="50" Y="50" />
            <Point X="150" Y="150" />
            <Point X="250" Y="250" />
            <Point X="100" Y="200" />
            <Point X="200" Y="100" />
            <Point X="300" Y="300" />
          </PolyBezierSegment.Points>
        </PolyBezierSegment>
      </PathFigure>
    </PathGeometry>
  </Path.Data>
</Path>
```

Alternatively, you can define the set of points using a points collection stored as comma-separated values in a string:

```
<Path Stroke="Black">
  <Path.Data>
    <PathGeometry>
      <PathFigure StartPoint="100,100">
        <PolyBezierSegment  Points="50,50,150,150,250,250,
                                    100,200,200,100,300,300" />
      </PathFigure>
    </PathGeometry>
  </Path.Data>
</Path>
```

The result of this XAML is shown in Figure 4-21. Here is an interpretation of this XAML: The starting point is defined as being at position (100,100), which is the upper-left side of the overall curve. The first Bezier then goes to the end point (250,250), using (50,50) and (150,150) as control points. Because these control points effectively cancel each other out (they are equidistant from the line from [100,100] to [250,250]), the first Bezier ends up being a straight line ending at (250,250). The second Bezier then starts at this point (250,250) and is drawn to the last point at (300,300), through control points at (100,200) and (200,100), which gives it the distinctive "loop back and then forward" look.

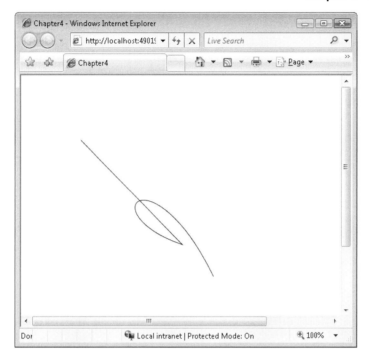

FIGURE 4-21 Using the *PolyBezierSegment*.

The *QuadraticBezierSegment* Object

A quadratic Bezier is a simple Bezier curve that is drawn as a regular quadratic curve using a single control point. It takes two point objects. If you use only one, that point becomes the end point of the curve with no control point and the curve is effectively a straight line from the start point to the point you defined. If you use two points, the second point is the end point of the curve, and the first is the quadratic control point. Here's an example:

```
<Path Stroke="Black">
    <Path.Data>
        <PathGeometry>
            <PathFigure StartPoint="100,100">
                <QuadraticBezierSegment Point1="200,0" Point2="300,100"  />
            </PathFigure>
        </PathGeometry>
    </Path.Data>
</Path>
```

You can see the curve rendered by this XAML in Figure 4-22.

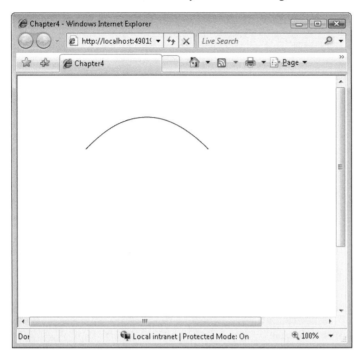

FIGURE 4-22 Simple quadratic Bezier curve.

The *PolyQuadraticBezierSegment* Object

As its name suggests, the *PolyQuadraticBezierSegment* object is a collection of connected quadratic Bezier curves defined and parsed from a list of control points in a similar manner to that described earlier in this chapter for the *PolyBezierSegment* object. Following is an example of a *PolyQuadraticBezierSegment* in action:

```
<Path Stroke="Black">
   <Path.Data>
      <PathGeometry>
         <PathFigure StartPoint="100,100">
            <PolyQuadraticBezierSegment Points="50,50,150,150,250,250,
                                        100,200,200,100,300,300" />
         </PathFigure>
      </PathGeometry>
   </Path.Data>
</Path>
```

The result of this XAML is shown in Figure 4-23.

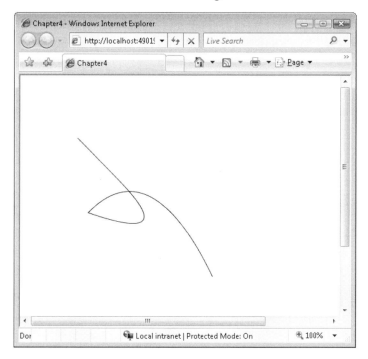

FIGURE 4-23 *PolyQuadraticBezierSegment* object in action.

The preceding code draws a number of quadratic Bezier curves. The first is from the starting point, (100,100), to (150,150), with a control point at (50,50), which yields a straight line ending at (150,150). The second is then a curve starting at (150,150) and ending at (100,200), with a control point at (250,250). This is shown as the curve sweeping toward the left. The third curve then starts at (100,200) and ends at (300,300), through a control point at (200,100), and this is rendered as the long smooth curve going from left to right in Figure 4-23.

Compound Path Segments

You can compound each segment type in a *PathFigure* segment in a collection. Additionally, you can collect *PathFigure* segments in a *PathGeometry* to create a complex set of segments.

Following is an example in which the *PathGeometry* contains two *PathFigure* objects. The first object has a *LineSegment*, a *PolyQuadraticBezierSegment*, and another *LineSegment*. The second object has a single *LineSegment*.

```
<Path Stroke="Black">
  <Path.Data>
    <PathGeometry>
      <PathFigure StartPoint="100,100">
```

```
            <LineSegment Point="200,200" />
            <PolyQuadraticBezierSegment Points="50,50,150,150,250,250,
                                        100,200,200,100,300,300" />
            <LineSegment Point="0,0" />
        </PathFigure>
        <PathFigure>
            <LineSegment Point="10,400" />
        </PathFigure>
    </PathGeometry>
  </Path.Data>
</Path>
```

Using the *GeometryGroup* Object

In the previous sections, you saw the various geometries that are available, from simple ones such as the *EllipseGeometry*, *LineGeometry*, and *RectangleGeometry*, to complex ones made up of many *PathSegments* in a *PathGeometry*. You can combine these together using a *GeometryGroup* object.

You simply define the geometries that you want as a collection in this object. Following is an example of a *GeometryGroup* containing an *EllipseGeometry*, a *RectangleGeometry*, and then the same complex *PathGeometry* that you used in the previous section:

```
<Path Stroke="Black">
  <Path.Data>
    <GeometryGroup>
      <EllipseGeometry RadiusX="100" RadiusY="100" Center="50,50" />
      <RectangleGeometry Rect="200,200,100,100" />
      <PathGeometry>
        <PathFigure StartPoint="100,100">
          <LineSegment Point="200,200" />
          <PolyQuadraticBezierSegment Points="50,50,150,150,250,250,
                                      100,200,200,100,300,300" />
          <LineSegment Point="0,0" />
        </PathFigure>
        <PathFigure>
          <LineSegment Point="10,400" />
        </PathFigure>
      </PathGeometry>
    </GeometryGroup>
  </Path.Data>
</Path>
```

Figure 4-24 shows how this will appear.

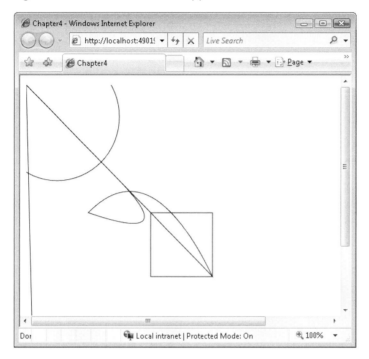

FIGURE 4-24 Using the *GeometryGroup* object to group many geometries together.

The *Path* Language

The *Path* object has a *Data* property that can use the *Path* language to define a complex path. This language uses the syntax of a command letter followed by a space, followed by a comma-separated list of numbers, followed by a space before the next command letter. Following is an example:

```
<Path Stroke="Black" Data="M 100,100 L 200,200" />
```

- In this instance, the path is drawn using the *M* command, for *Move*, to move to (100,100) and the *L* command, for *Line*, to draw a line between there and (200,200). These commands can either be uppercase letters (for example, *M*), which determines absolute coordinates, or lowercase letters (for example, *m*), which determines relative coordinates. The *M* command places the drawing pen at the specified point without drawing a line between the current point and the defined point; that is, it moves the starting point. It will draw the line from (100,100) to (200,200), assuming there is no positioning on the parent canvas. If there is, Silverlight will draw the line relative to the parent positioning.

- The *L* (for *Line*) command draws a line from the current point to the specified point.

- The *H* command takes a single number as a parameter and draws a horizontal line between the current point and the specified value on the x-axis.

- The *V* command takes a single number as a parameter and draws a vertical line between the current point and the specified value on the y-axis.

- The *C* command takes three points as parameters. It draws a cubic Bezier curve between the current point and the third of these points, using the first two points as control points.

- The *Q* command takes two points as parameters and draws a quadratic Bezier curve between the current point and the second one, using the first as a control point.

- The *S* command takes two points as parameters and draws a smooth cubic Bezier curve between the current point and the second of these. It uses two control points—the current point itself and the first of the two parameters—to generate a smoother curve.

- The *T* command works in the same way as the *S* command, except that it draws a smooth quadratic Bezier curve.

- The *A* command takes five parameters—for size, rotation angle, *isLargeArc*, *sweepDirection*, and end point. It uses these parameters to draw an elliptical arc.

- The *Z* command ends the current path and closes it to form a closed shape by drawing a line between the current point and the starting point of the path.

Clipping and Geometries in XAML

You can clip XAML elements according to a rule defined by a geometry type. As you saw in the previous section, these types can be simple (*EllipseGeometry*, *LineGeometry*, or *RectangleGeometry*), complex (using a geometry defined by *PathGeometry*), or a group of any of these contained within a *GeometryCollection*.

To define how an object is clipped, you simply set its attached *Clip* property to a geometry type. The following example is an image being clipped by an *EllipseGeometry*:

```
<Image Source="smily.jpg" Width="300" Height="300">
<Image.Clip>
   <EllipseGeometry Center="150,150" RadiusX="100" RadiusY="100" />
</Image.Clip>

</Image>
```

You can see how this looks in Figure 4-25.

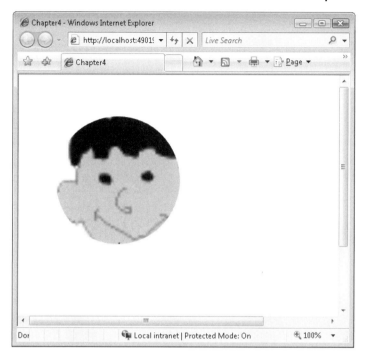

FIGURE 4-25 Clipping an image with a geometry.

Summary

With XAML, you can define your user interfaces. This chapter looks at some of the basic elements in XAML and how they work. It's a dip of your toe in the water, and in later chapters you'll see how XAML is used in more complex ways, including the XAML that you use to manage the layout of your controls as well as detailed configuration of the controls themselves.

In this chapter, you learned about many of the details involved in setting up visual elements using XAML. You were introduced to simple layout, positioning, filling, strokes, opacity, paths, geometries, and clipping, which give you control over what you see in the user interface.

In the next chapter, you'll examine how XAML is used to bring life to the user interface by adding transformations and animation.

Chapter 5
XAML Transformation and Animation

In Chapter 4, "Silverlight XAML Basics," you learned how you can use Extensible Application Markup Language (XAML) to render graphics on the screen, whether they are vector graphics, raster graphics (using the *Image* object), or video graphics. This chapter examines how to enhance these graphics using different types of transformations (to change how the object appears) and animations (to change attributes of the object over time). In addition, it introduces key frames and explains how they can be used to fine-tune animation behavior. Finally, it takes a quick look at Microsoft Expression Blend again to show how you can use it to design animations visually.

Transformations

In graphics, a transform defines how to map points from one coordinate space to another. This is typically described using a *transformation matrix*, a special mathematical construct that allows for simple mathematical conversion from one system to another. Microsoft Silverlight XAML abstracts this, and this book does not go into detail about the mathematics. Silverlight XAML supports four set transformations for rotation, scaling, skewing, and translation (movement), as well as a special transformation type that allows you to implement your own matrix, which is used to combine transformations.

Transformations are applied using transform properties. Several different types of transform properties are applied to different object types.

Thus, when using a *Brush* type, you define your transformation using either the *Brush.Transform* property when you want to affect the brush's content—if you want to rotate an image before using it in an *ImageBrush*, for example—or you might use the *Brush.RelativeTransform* property, which allows you to transform a brush using relative values—something you might do if you are painting different areas of different sizes using the same brush, for example.

When using a *Geometry* type, you apply a simple transform using the *Geometry.Transform* property. This type does not support relative transforms.

Finally, when using a user interface (UI) element, you specify the transformation to use with the *RenderTransform* property. If you are transforming an ellipse, for example, you use the *Ellipse.RenderTransform* to define the desired transform.

The following section looks at the different transformation types to see how these properties are used in their specific object types.

Rotating with the *RotateTransform* Property

With *RotateTransform*, you can rotate an element by a specified angle around a specified center point. You set the angle of rotation using the *Angle* property to set the number of degrees that you want to rotate the item. Consider the horizontal vector pointing to the right to be 0 degrees, and rotation takes place *clockwise*, so the vertical vector pointing down is the result of a 90-degree rotation.

You set the center of transformation using the *CenterX* and *CenterY* properties to specify the coordinates of the pivot. These default to 0.0, which makes the default rotation pivot the upper-left corner of the container.

Consider this example XAML, which rotates a *TextBlock* using a *RenderTransform* that contains a *RotateTransform* specifying a 45-degree rotation:

```
<TextBlock Width="320" Height="40"
         Text="This is the text to rotate" TextWrapping="Wrap">
   <TextBlock.RenderTransform>
      <RotateTransform Angle="45" />
   </TextBlock.RenderTransform>
</TextBlock>
```

You can see how this appears in Figure 5-1.

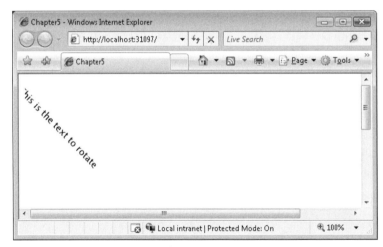

FIGURE 5-1 Using the *RotateTransform* property.

As you can see, this text is being rotated around a center point at (0,0) at the upper-left corner of the screen.

This XAML shows how to use *CenterX* and *CenterY* to rotate around a different point. In this next case, the rotation is done around the (100,200) point:

```
<TextBlock Width="320" Height="40"
          Text="This is the text to rotate" TextWrapping="Wrap" >
    <TextBlock.RenderTransform>
        <RotateTransform Angle="45" CenterX="100" CenterY="200" />
    </TextBlock.RenderTransform>
</TextBlock>
```

The results of this transformation are shown in Figure 5-2.

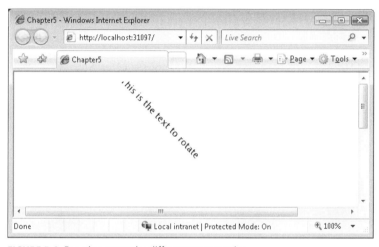

FIGURE 5-2 Rotating around a different center point.

Scaling with the *ScaleTransform* Property

You can use the *ScaleTransform* property to change the size of an object based on the horizontal axis, the vertical axis, or both axes.

When scaling an object, you need to specify at least one of the axes around which you want to scale and by how much you want to scale against that axis. You use the *ScaleX* property to scale the object on the horizontal axis, the x-axis, and *ScaleY* to scale it on the vertical axis, the y-axis. These are set to a *double* value, which represents the value by which you multiply the object's current size on the specified axis. Therefore, values greater than 1 will stretch the object by that multiple. For example, using a *ScaleX* value of 2 doubles the size of the object horizontally. Values less than 1, but greater than 0, shrink the object. By using a setting of 0.5, for instance, you can reduce the size of the object by half along the specific dimension.

So, for example, consider this XAML that creates a red rectangle 96 pixels wide by 88 pixels high:

```
<Rectangle Fill="#FFFF0404" Stroke="#FF000000" Width="96" Height="88"
Canvas.Left="112" Canvas.Top="72" />
```

Figure 5-3 shows what the rectangle looks like when it is rendered in Silverlight.

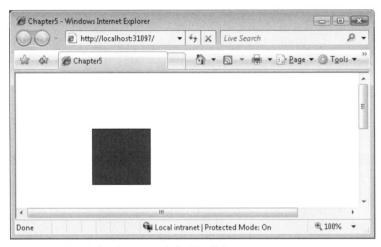

FIGURE 5-3 Rendering the rectangle in Silverlight.

To apply a *ScaleTransform* to this object, you use a *RenderTransform* and specify the transform to be a *ScaleTransform*. Here's the XAML:

```
<Rectangle Fill="#FFFF0404" Stroke="#FF000000"
        Width="96" Height="88" Canvas.Left="112" Canvas.Top="72">
   <Rectangle.RenderTransform>
      <ScaleTransform ScaleX="2" />
   </Rectangle.RenderTransform>
</Rectangle>
```

Figure 5-4 shows how this transform is rendered by Silverlight.

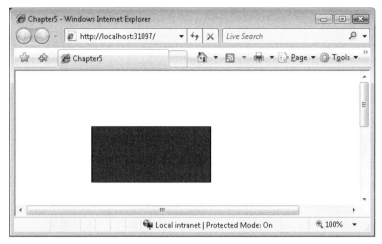

FIGURE 5-4 Scaling with the *ScaleTransform*.

Notice that the rectangle increased in size horizontally to the right using this *ScaleTransform* because the center of scaling was not specified. You can specify it with the *CenterX* property for horizontal scaling or the *CenterY* property for vertical scaling. These specify the coordinate of the center of scaling. This coordinate is relative to the upper-left corner of the rectangle. The coordinate default is 0, meaning that scaling takes place to the right on the horizontal axis and downward on the vertical axis.

If you set the *CenterX* property to a positive value (for example, 50), the scaling will be around the X point, 50 pixels to the right of the leftmost side of the rectangle. This will make it look like the rectangle has moved a number of pixels to the left of the rectangle where the *CenterX* hasn't been changed (the number depends on the size of the scaling factor). This is because the stretching is centered on that point, pushing the left side of the rectangle to the left as well as pushing the right side to the right. You'll get similar effects by setting the *ScaleY* and *CenterY* values in the same way. Following is an example:

```
<Rectangle Fill="#FFFF0404" Stroke="#FF000000"
    Width="96" Height="88" Canvas.Left="80" Canvas.Top="80">
  <Rectangle.RenderTransform>
    <ScaleTransform ScaleX="2" CenterX="50"/>
  </Rectangle.RenderTransform>
</Rectangle>
```

You can see how this affects the rectangle in Figure 5-5.

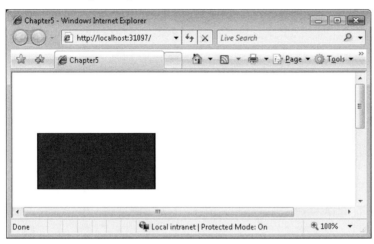

FIGURE 5-5 Scaling around a center point.

Moving an Object with the *TranslateTransform* Property

A *translation* is a transform that moves an object in a two-dimensional (2-D) plane from one position to another. It is defined by setting up vectors that define the object's motion along its x- and y-axes. These are set using the *X* and *Y* properties on the transform. To move an item two units horizontally (meaning it will move to the right), you set the *X* property to 2. To move it to the left, use a negative value, such as –2. Similarly, to move an object vertically, you would use the *Y* property. Positive values cause the object to move down the screen, and negative values move it up the screen.

Here's an example of a translate transform that moves the position of the red rectangle that you have been looking at by specifying *X* and *Y* values that move it up and to the left. These values effectively make up a *vector* that determines the transform.

```
<Rectangle Fill="#FFFF0404" Stroke="#FF000000"
        Width="96" Height="88" Canvas.Left="80" Canvas.Top="80">
  <Rectangle.RenderTransform>
    <TranslateTransform X="-50" Y="-50"/>
  </Rectangle.RenderTransform>
</Rectangle>
```

See the results of this transform in Figure 5-6. The rectangle has moved upward and to the left relative to its specified position compared with the position of the rectangle in Figure 5-3.

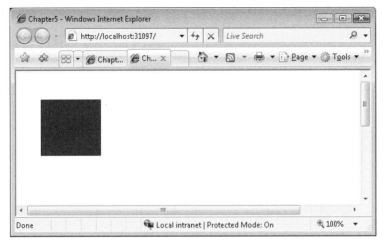

FIGURE 5-6 Using the *TranslateTransform* property.

Skewing an Object with the *SkewTransform* Property

Skewing an object involves changing it in a progressive, uniform manner along an axis. This has the effect of turning a square or rectangle into a parallelogram. This visual effect is very useful in creating the illusion of depth on a 2-D surface.

You can apply a skew at a certain angle on either the x- or y-axis and around a center point. These can, of course, be combined so that you can skew on both axes at the same time.

Following is the XAML that skews the rectangle on the x-axis by 45 degrees:

```
<Rectangle Fill="#FFFF0404" Stroke="#FF000000"
           Width="96" Height="88" Canvas.Left="80" Canvas.Top="80">
    <Rectangle.RenderTransform>
        <SkewTransform AngleX="45"/>
    </Rectangle.RenderTransform>
</Rectangle>
```

You can see the result of this skew in Figure 5-7.

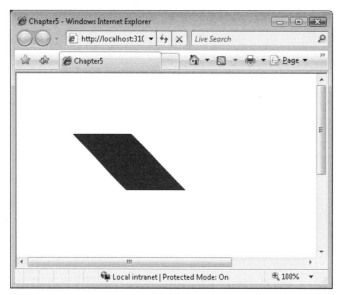

FIGURE 5-7 Skewing the rectangle using *SkewTransform*.

Simulating 3-D Perspective with *SkewTransform*

Skewing is useful for simulating three-dimensional (3-D) effects in graphics. Following is an example of some XAML that uses three rectangles, two skewed on the x-axis and one on the y-axis, that create an illusion of a 3-D perspective:

```
<Rectangle Fill="#FFFF0404" Stroke="#FF000000"
        Width="88" Height="88" Canvas.Left="80" Canvas.Top="80">
   <Rectangle.RenderTransform>
      <SkewTransform AngleX="45"/>
   </Rectangle.RenderTransform>
</Rectangle>
<Rectangle Fill="#FFFF0404" Stroke="#FF000000"
        Width="88" Height="88" Canvas.Left="80" Canvas.Top="168">
   <Rectangle.RenderTransform>
      <SkewTransform AngleX="45"/>
   </Rectangle.RenderTransform>
</Rectangle>
<Rectangle Fill="#FFFF0404" Stroke="#FF000000"
        Width="88" Height="88" Canvas.Left="80" Canvas.Top="80">
   <Rectangle.RenderTransform>
      <SkewTransform AngleY="45"/>
   </Rectangle.RenderTransform>
</Rectangle>
```

You can see the results of this in Figure 5-8.

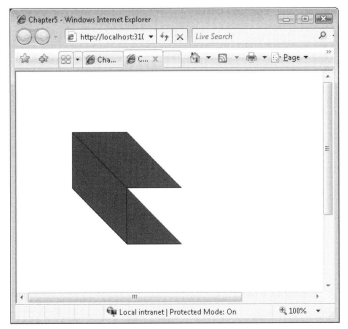

FIGURE 5-8 Simulating perspective with *SkewTransform*.

Defining Your Own Transforms with *MatrixTransform*

All transformations, at their heart, are performed by multiplying the coordinate space of the object by a transformation matrix. Each of the transforms that you've seen so far in this chapter is a well-known and well-defined transform.

Matrix mathematics and how transforms are implemented are beyond the scope of this book, but for the sake of syntactic completeness, this chapter discusses how you can define them in Silverlight XAML.

Note that the matrix used in the *MatrixTransform* is an *affine* matrix, which means that the bottom row of the matrix is always set to (0 0 1), and as such you set only the first two columns. You set these using the transform's *Matrix* property, which takes a string containing the first two rows of values separated by spaces. Following is an example:

```
<Rectangle Fill="#FFFF0404" Stroke="#FF000000"
        Width="96" Height="88" Canvas.Left="80" Canvas.Top="80">
  <Rectangle.RenderTransform>
    <MatrixTransform Matrix="1 0 1 2 0 1" />
  </Rectangle.RenderTransform>
</Rectangle>
```

Figure 5-9 shows the impact of the transform using this matrix, which renders a combined stretched and skewed rectangle.

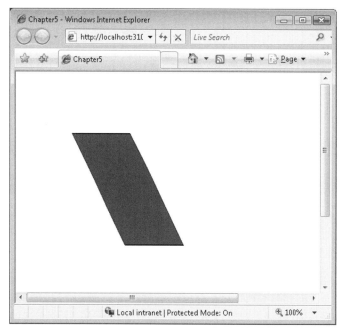

FIGURE 5-9 Using the *MatrixTransform*.

Combining Transformations

As you saw in the previous example, you can create a complex transformation by using a transformation affine matrix and specifying that using the *MatrixTransform* type. However, if you aren't an expert in matrix mathematics, another technique for using transforms is to combine them by means of the *TransformGroup* element. With *TransformGroup*, you can simply specify multiple transforms, and the combined effect of each is applied to the object. Here's an example:

```
<Rectangle Fill="#FFFF0404" Stroke="#FF000000"
        Width="96" Height="88" Canvas.Left="80" Canvas.Top="80">
  <Rectangle.RenderTransform>
```

```
        <TransformGroup>
            <ScaleTransform ScaleX="1.2" ScaleY="1.2" />
            <SkewTransform AngleX="30" />
            <RotateTransform Angle="45" />
        </TransformGroup>
    </Rectangle.RenderTransform>
</Rectangle>
```

This example combines a *ScaleTransform* that increases the size of the shape on both axes by 20 percent, with a 30-degree skew on the x-axis and a rotation of 45 degrees. You can see the results of this transformation in Figure 5-10.

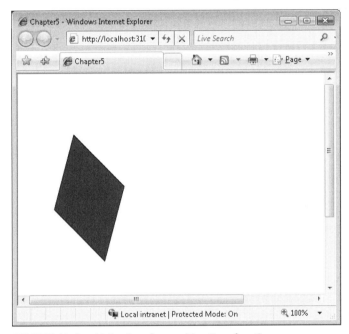

FIGURE 5-10 Combining transforms with a *TransformGroup*.

3-D Effects Using the Perspective Transform

One of the most exciting features in Silverlight 3 is the addition of perspective transforms. Perspective transforms, in a nutshell, are transforms that can be applied to XAML elements to simulate rotating them in a 3-D space. Note that it isn't *true* 3-D because it doesn't have 3-D mesh models, shading, hidden line removal, and so forth, but it is good for simulating 3-D effects with your XAML.

Take a look at how this works:

```
<Grid x:Name="LayoutRoot" Background="White">
    <Image Source="whack.jpg">
    </Image>
</Grid>
```

You can see XAML that defines the image of a kid "tearing the cover off" a baseball and hitting a huge home run! If you execute this in the browser with Silverlight, you see an image like the one shown in Figure 5-11.

FIGURE 5-11 Viewing the home run image without perspective.

Now, consider the screen to be a 3-D space with the x-axis going left to right, the y-axis going up and down, and the z-axis going in and out. If you want to rotate the image so that it appears to be in 3-D, with the perspective being that the left of the image is "inside" the screen and the right of the image is "outside" the screen, rotate the image *around* the y-axis. Similarly, if you want to rotate the image so that the top or bottom of the image is inside the screen and the rest is outside, rotate around the x-axis.

Think about this for a moment—at first you might think the image must rotate around the z-axis, but the z-axis is the in–out plane, so a rotation there in 3-D space would just change the angle at which the picture is viewed.

So, here's how to rotate the picture to give it perspective, with a 45-degree rotation on the y-axis:

```
<Grid x:Name="LayoutRoot" Background="White">
    <Image Source="bull.jpg">
        <Image.Projection>
            <PlaneProjection RotationY="45"></PlaneProjection>
        </Image.Projection>
    </Image>
</Grid>
```

You can see the results in Figure 5-12.

FIGURE 5-12 Rotating the image around the y-axis.

Similarly, you can rotate the image around the x-axis to produce a 3-D perspective effect where the top or bottom of the image is inside the screen and the other side is outside.

Here's an example:

```
<Grid x:Name="LayoutRoot" Background="White">
    <Image Source="bull.jpg" Width="640" Height="480" Canvas.Top="150"
Canvas.Left="0">
        <Image.Projection>
            <PlaneProjection RotationX="45"></PlaneProjection>
        </Image.Projection>
    </Image>
</Grid>
```

You can see the effect in Figure 5-13.

FIGURE 5-13 Rotation around the x-axis.

Do note that Silverlight treats the image as if it were *transparent* so that if you rotate the image in 3-D in a way that would make it appear that you have flipped the image and are now looking at its back, you would see the inverse of the image. If you change the rotation to 135 degrees from the previous example, you would see something like what is shown in Figure 5-14.

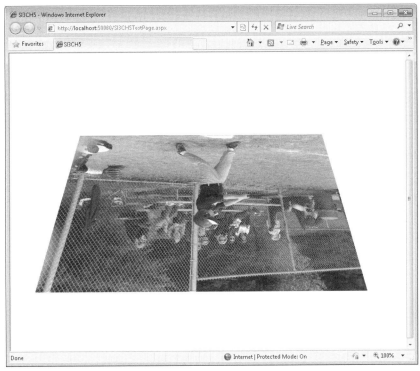

FIGURE 5-14 Viewing the back of the image with a perspective transform.

A neat trick that you can use is to animate the rotation property using a *Storyboard*. You see more on how to use the *Storyboard* element later in this chapter, so if this code looks a little odd, it will make more sense very soon!

```xml
<UserControl x:Class="sl3dtest.Page"
    xmlns="http://schemas.microsoft.com/winfx/2006/xaml/presentation"
    xmlns:x="http://schemas.microsoft.com/winfx/2006/xaml"
    Width="800" Height="600">
    <UserControl.Resources>
        <Storyboard x:Name="Storyboard1">
            <DoubleAnimationUsingKeyFrames BeginTime="00:00:00"
              Storyboard.TargetName="img"
              Storyboard.TargetProperty="(UIElement.Projection).(RotationX)"
              RepeatBehavior="Forever">
                <SplineDoubleKeyFrame KeyTime="00:00:00" Value="0"/>
                <SplineDoubleKeyFrame KeyTime="00:00:02" Value="360"/>
            </DoubleAnimationUsingKeyFrames>
        </Storyboard>
    </UserControl.Resources>
    <Grid x:Name="LayoutRoot" Background="White">
        <Image x:Name="img" Source="bull.jpg" Width="640" Height="480" Canvas.Top="150"
Canvas.Left="0">
            <Image.Projection>
                <PlaneProjection RotationX="0"></PlaneProjection>
```

```
            </Image.Projection>
        </Image>
    </Grid>
</UserControl>
```

This XAML simply creates a *Storyboard* that executes for two seconds, changing the *RotationX* from 0 to 360, and then repeating. This has the effect of rotating the image constantly through its x-axis in 3-D space.

Animation

The word *animation* literally means "imparting life onto something." So, with animation you can bring your creations to life by changing the attributes of the objects, such as their color, size, opacity, and other properties, over time or in response to user actions.

In XAML, you animate an item by changing one or more of its properties over time. Time is defined using a timeline. For example, to move an item across the screen in 5 seconds, you'd specify a 5-second timeline that animates the *Canvas.Left* property from 0 to the width of the screen. The following sections discuss each type of animation available, as well as the difference in animating these properties using key frames.

Before you look into the different animation types, you should know that there is a framework around animations that involves the *Trigger*, *EventTrigger*, and *Storyboard* objects. First, take a look at these concepts, and then examine the different animation types in more detail.

Using Triggers and Event Triggers

Animations in Silverlight take place in response to an event, which is defined using a trigger. At present, there is only one trigger type supported in Silverlight XAML, the *EventTrigger*. Each user interface (UI) property has a *Triggers* collection that is used to define one or more triggers (that is, one or more *EventTrigger* objects).

So, the first step in adding an animation to an element is to define its triggers collection; then, you need to add at least one event trigger to the collection you've created. For example, if you are animating a rectangle, the first step—specifying the triggers collection—looks like this:

```
<Rectangle x:Name="rect" Fill="Red" Canvas.Top="100"
        Canvas.Left="100" Width="100" Height="100">
    <Rectangle.Triggers>
    </Rectangle.Triggers>
</Rectangle>
```

Next, you need to define an *EventTrigger* to add to this collection. On this *EventTrigger*, you will use the *RoutedEvent* property to specify the event to run the animation in response. Chapter 6, "The Silverlight Browser Object," contains details on each event supported by each object in XAML, but note that *RoutedEvent* supports only the *Loaded* event.

To implement an animation that will begin when the rectangle is loaded, you can specify the *EventTrigger* as follows:

```
<EventTrigger RoutedEvent="Rectangle.Loaded">
</EventTrigger>
```

The XAML snippet to run this animation looks like this:

```
<Rectangle x:Name="rect" Fill="Red" Canvas.Top="100"
           Canvas.Left="100" Width="100" Height="100">
   <Rectangle.Triggers>
     <EventTrigger RoutedEvent="Rectangle.Loaded">
     </EventTrigger>
   </Rectangle.Triggers>
</Rectangle>
```

The next step is to define the animation that you want to use. Animations are contained in *Storyboard* objects, which are covered in the next section.

Using *BeginStoryboard* and *Storyboard*

BeginStoryboard is a trigger action that contains a *Storyboard* object. *Storyboard* objects contain the animation definitions. When you define an animation, you simply embed these objects in the *EventTrigger* definition. Here's how you can accomplish this using the rectangle from earlier:

```
<Rectangle x:Name="rect" Fill="Red" Canvas.Top="100"
           Canvas.Left="100" Width="100" Height="100">
   <Rectangle.Triggers>
     <EventTrigger RoutedEvent="Rectangle.Loaded">
         <BeginStoryboard>
            <Storyboard>
            </Storyboard>
         </BeginStoryboard>
     </EventTrigger>
   </Rectangle.Triggers>
</Rectangle>
```

Defining the Animation Parameters

Now that the framework for the animation is set up, you can specify the animation that you want to perform. At its most basic level, animation defines the changing of a property over time. You can animate three different property types:

- Double types are animated using the *DoubleAnimation* or *DoubleAnimationUsingKeyFrames*. This method is used to animate properties that contain a *double* value—for example, dimensions such as *Canvas.Left* or visual attributes such as *Opacity*.

- Point types are animated using a *PointAnimation* or *PointAnimationUsingKeyFrames* type. This method is used to animate properties that contain a *point* value, such as line segments or curves that are defined using points.

- Color types are animated using a *ColorAnimation* or *ColorAnimationUsingKeyFrames* type. This method is used to animate properties that contain a *color* value—the background or stroke of an element, for instance.

Each of these property types is animated from a value specified in the *From* attribute (or its current value if this is not set) either to a value specified in the *To* attribute or by a value specified in the *By* attribute.

Targeting the Animation

To define which object you want to apply the animation to, you use the *Storyboard.TargetName* property on these animation types. Set the value of the *Storyboard.TargetName* to the name of the object in question, which is set on the object using the *x:Name* property. Additionally, specify the property that will be animated by using the *Storyboard.TargetProperty*. Note that if you are specifying a complex or attached property (such as *Canvas.Left*), you place it in parentheses. So, for example, to specify a *Double* animation to target the *Canvas.Left* of a rectangle named *rect*, the resulting XAML will look like this:

```
<DoubleAnimation Storyboard.TargetName="rect"
Storyboard.TargetProperty="(Canvas.Left)" />
```

Setting the Duration

To define how long it will take to transition the properties in question from one value to another, you use the *Duration* property. It is defined in the HH:MM:SS format, wherein a five-second time duration for the animation is specified as 00:00:05, abbreviated to 0:0:5. Following is an example:

```
<DoubleAnimation Storyboard.TargetName="rect"
Storyboard.TargetProperty="(Canvas.Left)" Duration="0:0:5" />
```

Setting the Begin Time

If you do not want the animation to begin right away, you can insert a delay using the *BeginTime* property. It uses the same syntax as *Duration*.

```
<DoubleAnimation Storyboard.TargetName="rect"
Storyboard.TargetProperty="(Canvas.Left)" BeginTime="0:0:5" />
```

Using the *SpeedRatio* Property

You can also tweak the animation behavior by multiplying the duration by a speed ratio. This is achieved using the *SpeedRatio* property. For example, in the previous case, the duration was set to 5 seconds. You can change the speed ratio to make the animation last 10 seconds by setting *SpeedRatio* to 2, or, alternatively, you can speed the animation up to 1 second
by setting *SpeedRatio* to 0.2.

```
<DoubleAnimation Storyboard.TargetName="rect"
Storyboard.TargetProperty="(Canvas.Left)" SpeedRatio="2" Duration="0:0:5" />
```

Using the *AutoReverse* Property

Silverlight animation provides the facility to reverse the changes made as part of the animation. For example, if you are moving a *double* value from 0 to 500 over a specific time frame, an *AutoReverse* will cause the animation to move from 500 back to 0.

Note that if the animation is set to run for 5 seconds as previously stated, and the *AutoReverse* is set to *true*, the complete animation will take 10 seconds. Following is an example of XAML containing the *AutoReverse* property:

```
<DoubleAnimation Storyboard.TargetName="rect"
    Storyboard.TargetProperty="(Canvas.Left)" AutoReverse="True"
    Duration="0:0:5" />
```

Setting the *RepeatBehavior* Property

When the animation has finished running, you can apply a number of options to control how you want it to behave. You specify these using the *RepeatBehavior* property. This property can take three different types of values:

- A time defined in seconds   The timeline will wait for this period, and then start the animation again.

- A *Forever* value   You can set the animation for constant repetition by setting *Forever* as the repeat behavior.

- A discrete number of repetitions   By specifying a number followed by *x*, you can set the number of repetitions. For example, if you want the animation to run three times, you specify the value *3x*.

Following is the complete XAML for the animated rectangle to move it from 100 to 500 and back to 100 on the x-axis and then repeat that behavior three times:

```
<Rectangle x:Name="rect" Fill="Red"
    Canvas.Top="100" Canvas.Left="100" Width="100" Height="100">
  <Rectangle.Triggers>
    <EventTrigger RoutedEvent="Rectangle.Loaded">
```

```
        <BeginStoryboard>
          <Storyboard>
            <DoubleAnimation RepeatBehavior="3x"
                             Storyboard.TargetName="rect"
                             Storyboard.TargetProperty="(Canvas.Left)"
                             To="500" Duration="0:0:5"
                             AutoReverse="True" />
          </Storyboard>
        </BeginStoryboard>
      </EventTrigger>
    </Rectangle.Triggers>
</Rectangle>
```

The following sections look at each of these animation types in a little more detail, first, the attributes needed to animate each of the various types, and then where the associated key frame type of animation fits into the picture.

Animating a Value with *DoubleAnimation*

With the *DoubleAnimation* object, you can specify how a *double* value will change over a specified timeline. The animation is calculated as a linear interpolation between the property values over time.

When animating a *double*, you specify the value at the start of the animation using the *From* value, and then change it to either the *To* value, which is an absolute destination, or the *By* value, which is a relative destination.

For example, if you are moving the *Canvas.Left* property of an item from 100 (near the left of the screen) to 500, you can set *From* to 100 and *To* to 500 or *By* to 400. Note that if you set both, the *To* property takes precedence and the *By* property is ignored. Also, if the rectangle is already located at the desired *From* position, you do not need to specify the *From* property.

The previous XAML example displayed this behavior. The rectangle is located with a *Canvas.Left* value of 100, and the *DoubleAnimation* specifies the *To* value as 500. Hence, the animation moves the value from 100 to 500, which will cause the rectangle to move across the screen to the right.

Animating a Color with *ColorAnimation*

ColorAnimation operates in a manner that is very similar to *DoubleAnimation*. You use it to specify how the *color* value of an element will change over time. The animation is then calculated as a linear interpolation between the *color* values over the specified time.

When animating a color, you specify the value at the start of the animation using the *From* property. If you do not specify this value, the current color is used. You specify the desired end color using the *To* attribute. You can also specify a *By* attribute, which will provide the end color that is the result of adding the values of the *From* color (or the starting color) to the *By* color.

When you animate a color-based property, you do not animate the contents of the property directly because the contents of the property are usually a brush and not a color. So, if you want to animate the fill color of a rectangle, for example, you don't use the rectangle's *Fill* property as your target. Instead, you specify that you intend to animate the *Color* property of the *SolidBrush* that is used to perform the fill.

Following is an example of how to animate the color of a rectangle, changing it from black to white over a time duration of five seconds using a color animation:

```
<Rectangle x:Name="rect" Canvas.Top="100" Canvas.Left="100"
        Width="100" Height="100" Fill="Black">
   <Rectangle.Triggers>
      <EventTrigger RoutedEvent="Rectangle.Loaded">
         <BeginStoryboard>
            <Storyboard>
               <ColorAnimation Storyboard.TargetName="rect"
                            Storyboard.TargetProperty=
                               "(Shape.Fill).(SolidColorBrush.Color)"
                            To="#00000000" Duration="0:0:5" />
            </Storyboard>
         </BeginStoryboard>
      </EventTrigger>
   </Rectangle.Triggers>
</Rectangle>
```

As you can see, this XAML example specifies as its target property the *Color* property of the *SolidColorBrush* that is filling the shape. This is the typical XAML syntax used in addressing complex properties like this.

Animating a Point with *PointAnimation*

To change a value that is defined as a point over time, you use the *PointAnimation* type. The animation is then calculated as a linear interpolation between the values over the specified time.

In a manner similar to the *Color* and *Double* animations, you specify the start value using *From* and the destination either as a relative direction (using *By*) or an absolute point (using *To*). Following is an example of how you could animate the end point of a Bezier curve:

```
<Path Stroke="Black" >
   <Path.Data>
      <PathGeometry>
         <PathFigure StartPoint="100,100">
            <QuadraticBezierSegment x:Name="seg"
                        Point1="200,0" Point2="300,100"  />
         </PathFigure>
      </PathGeometry>
```

```
    </Path.Data>
    <Path.Triggers>
        <EventTrigger RoutedEvent="Path.Loaded">
            <BeginStoryboard>
                <Storyboard>
                    <PointAnimation Storyboard.TargetName="seg"
                                    Storyboard.TargetProperty="Point2"
                                    From="300,100" To="300,600" Duration="0:0:5" />
                </Storyboard>
            </BeginStoryboard>
        </EventTrigger>
    </Path.Triggers>
</Path>
```

In this case, the Bezier curve is defined with a start point at (100,100), an end point at (300,100), and a control point at (200,0). An animation is set up to trigger after the path loads, and it animates the end point of the curve (*Point2*) from (300,100) to (300,600) over a time duration of five seconds.

Using Key Frames

The three animation types that you've just learned about, *ColorAnimation*, *DoubleAnimation*, and *PointAnimation*, all work by changing a defined property over time using linear interpolation. For example, if you are moving a *double* value from 100 to 500 over 5 seconds, it will increment by 80 each second.

Each of these can have this transition defined through a set of milestones called *key frames*. To change the linear behavior of the animation from the starting property to the ending property, you insert one or more key frames. Then, you define the style of animation that you want between the various points.

Key frames are defined using *key times*. These are times that are specified relative to the start time of the animation, and they specify the end time of the key frame. So, imagine you need a nine-second animation with three evenly spaced key frames. Using key frames, you can specify the first key frame to end at 0:0:3, the second to end at 0:0:6, and the third to end at 0:0:9. You do not specify the *length* of the key time—instead, you specify the end time for each key frame.

As another example, consider a *Double* animation that you want to span half the range of 100 to 500. The animation should move very quickly in the first half and very slowly in the second half, requiring a six-second total transition. Because 350 is the midpoint between 100 and 500, you define a key frame to begin at point 350. You tell it to go for 1 second between the start point and the midpoint, using a key time of 0:0:1, and then set a time duration of 5 seconds between the midpoint and the end point by using a second key time of 0:0:6. The item will zip across the screen to the midpoint, and then will crawl the rest of the way.

In the previous example, both animated segments are linearly interpolated. To provide extra flexibility, two other types of key frames are provided: a discrete key frame that instantly "jumps" the value between the two values, and a spline key frame that moves the value between the first point and end point using a quadratic curve to define the interpolation. (In the following sections, you look at how to define an animation using key frames for the *Double* type. The same principles apply for *Point* and *Color* animation types.)

To specify key frames, you use the *UsingKeyFrames* postfix on your animation. That is, to define *Double* animations and use key frames, you use *DoubleAnimationUsingKeyFrames* on which you specify your target and property (in the same way that you use *DoubleAnimation*). *DoubleAnimationUsingKeyFrames* contains the key frame definitions. (And as mentioned earlier, the same applies to *PointAnimationUsingKeyFrames* or *ColorAnimationUsingKeyFrames*.)

Using Linear Key Frames

The default method for animation between two property values is linear interpolation in which the amount is divided evenly over time. You can also define linear steps between frames using the *LinearKeyFrame* type in which linear interpolation is still used, but it is used between key frames so that you can have an acceleration/deceleration effect.

Consider the following animation. Here, a *DoubleAnimationUsingKeyFrames* is used, and it defines two key frames. One defines a linear interpolation between 0 and 300 for *Canvas.Left* changes over 1 second, and the next defines a linear interpolation between 300 and 600 for *Canvas.Left* changes over 8 seconds. This has the effect of making the rectangle move quickly to the halfway point, and then slowly the rest of the way across. Similar principles apply for the *LinearPointKeyFrame* and *LinearColorKeyFrame*.

```
<Rectangle Fill="#FFFF0000" Stroke="#FF000000"
        Width="40" Height="40" Canvas.Top="40" x:Name="rect">
  <Rectangle.Triggers>
    <EventTrigger RoutedEvent="Rectangle.Loaded">
      <BeginStoryboard>
        <Storyboard>
          <DoubleAnimationUsingKeyFrames
              Storyboard.TargetName="rect"
              Storyboard.TargetProperty="(Canvas.Left)" >
            <LinearDoubleKeyFrame KeyTime="0:0:1" Value="300" />
            <LinearDoubleKeyFrame KeyTime="0:0:9" Value="600" />
          </DoubleAnimationUsingKeyFrames>
        </Storyboard>
      </BeginStoryboard>
    </EventTrigger>
  </Rectangle.Triggers>
</Rectangle>
```

Using Discrete Key Frames

If you want to change the property from one value to another and *not* use linear interpolation, you can use a discrete key frame. This causes the object to "jump" to the value at the specified key frame time. Following is the same example as the previous one except that it uses a discrete key frame. At 1 second into the animation, the rectangle jumps halfway across the screen. Then, at 9 seconds into the animation, it jumps to the right of the screen:

```
<Rectangle Fill="#FFFF0000" Stroke="#FF000000"
    Width="40" Height="40" Canvas.Top="40" x:Name="rect">
  <Rectangle.Triggers>
    <EventTrigger RoutedEvent="Rectangle.Loaded">
      <BeginStoryboard>
        <Storyboard>
          <DoubleAnimationUsingKeyFrames
              Storyboard.TargetName="rect"
              Storyboard.TargetProperty="(Canvas.Left)" >
            <DiscreteDoubleKeyFrame KeyTime="0:0:1" Value="300" />
            <DiscreteDoubleKeyFrame KeyTime="0:0:9" Value="600" />
          </DoubleAnimationUsingKeyFrames>
        </Storyboard>
      </BeginStoryboard>
    </EventTrigger>
  </Rectangle.Triggers>
</Rectangle>
```

Similar principles apply for the *DiscretePointKeyFrame* and *DiscreteColorKeyFrame*.

Using Spline Key Frames

To change the property from one value to another using a curved value that provides for acceleration and deceleration, you use a spline key frame. To do this, first you define a quadratic Bezier curve, and then the speed of the property as it moves from one value to another is determined by a parallel projection of that curve.

If this is hard to visualize, consider the following scenario: The sun is right overhead, and you hit a baseball into the outfield. You look at the shadow of the ball. As it is climbing into the air, the movement of the shadow appears to accelerate. As it reaches its apex, you see the shadow decelerate. As the ball falls, you see the speed of the shadow accelerate again until it is caught or hits the ground.

Imagine your animation in this case is the ball's shadow, and the spline is the curve of the baseball. You define the trajectory of the baseball, a spline, using a *KeySpline*. The *KeySpline* defines control points for a quadratic Bezier curve. It is normalized so that the first point of the curve is at 0 and the second is at 1. For a parabolic arc, which is the trajectory the baseball would follow, the *KeySpline* will contain two comma-separated normalized values.

To define a curve like the flight of a baseball, you can specify the spline using a *KeySpline*, such as 0.3,0 0.6,1. This defines the first point of the curve at (0.3,0) and the second at (0.6,1). This will have the effect of making the animation accelerate quickly until approximately one-third

of the movement of the baseball is complete, and then it will move at a uniform speed until approximately two-thirds of the ball's trajectory is reached, and then it will decelerate for the rest of the flight of the animated baseball as the animation simulates the ball's fall to earth.

Following is an example of using a *KeySpline* to define the spline for this simulation using *DoubleAnimationUsingKeyFrames*:

```
<Ellipse Fill="#FF444444" Stroke="#FF444444"
        Width="40" Height="40" Canvas.Top="40" x:Name="ball">
    <Ellipse.Triggers>
        <EventTrigger RoutedEvent="Ellipse.Loaded">
            <BeginStoryboard>
                <Storyboard>
                    <DoubleAnimationUsingKeyFrames
                        Storyboard.TargetName="ball"
                        Storyboard.TargetProperty="(Canvas.Left)" >
                        <SplineDoubleKeyFrame KeyTime="0:0:5"
                            KeySpline="0.3,0 0.6,1" Value="600" />
                    </DoubleAnimationUsingKeyFrames>
                </Storyboard>
            </BeginStoryboard>
        </EventTrigger>
    </Ellipse.Triggers>
</Ellipse>
```

This example animates the ellipse so that it moves across the screen in a manner similar to the shadow of a baseball, as if you were above the baseball looking down toward the ground as the ball flies through the air.

Animation and Expression Blend

You can define animation graphically in Microsoft Expression Blend. This generates the XAML for you to perform the animation, providing the different types of animation for you automatically.

When using Expression Blend, select Animation Workspace from the Window menu. This menu contains the tools you can use to design timelines graphically. When you edit the properties that you want changed using the visual editor, the XAML code for the animation is generated. You can see this in Figure 5-15.

In Figure 5-15, at the bottom of the screen, you can see the Objects And Timeline view. In this view, you can add a timeline, and then visually add key frames. To add a new timeline, click the plus sign (+) button in the Objects And Timeline view. See Figure 5-16.

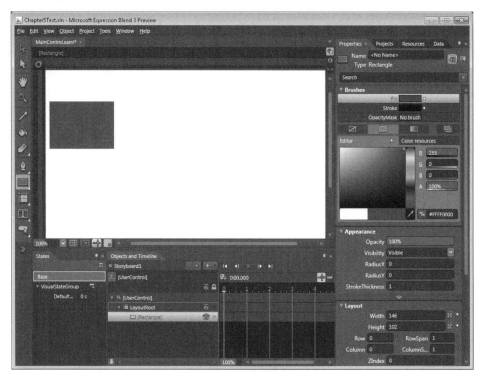

FIGURE 5-15 Expression Blend in Animation Workspace mode.

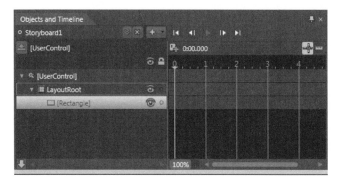

FIGURE 5-16 Adding a new timeline.

When you click the plus sign button, the Create Storyboard Resource dialog box appears and asks you for the name of the storyboard to create, as shown in Figure 5-17. In this case, I changed the default name from Storyboard1 to Timeline1.

FIGURE 5-17 Creating the storyboard.

When using Expression Blend, you can create an animation at the *Canvas* level or as a *Resource*. In the former case, animations then run in response to triggers on the canvas. Following is an example of the XAML created by Expression Blend from the Create Storyboard Resource dialog box, where the user specified to create the animation not as a *Resource*:

```
<Canvas.Triggers>
    <EventTrigger RoutedEvent="Canvas.Loaded">
        <BeginStoryboard>
            <Storyboard x:Name="Timeline1"/>
        </BeginStoryboard>
    </EventTrigger>
</Canvas.Triggers>
```

The Objects And Timeline view changes to show the timeline that you've just created. You can see this in Figure 5-18.

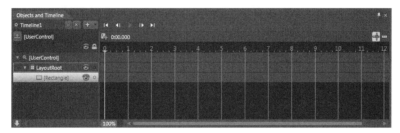

FIGURE 5-18 Objects And Timeline view showing a new timeline.

The vertical line at time zero that you see in Figure 5-18 denotes the current time. (In Expression Blend, this line is yellow.) To add a key frame, you simply drag this line to the time where you want a key frame, and click the Record Keyframe button. In Figure 5-18, this button is located just above the timeline to the left of 0:00:000.

Drag the line to the four-second mark, and add a key frame. You see the key frame added as a small oval on the timeline, as shown in Figure 5-19.

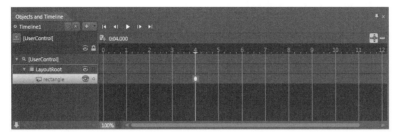

FIGURE 5-19 Adding a key frame.

Now that the timeline is on the four-second frame and you have added a key frame, you can edit the rectangle's color, location, opacity, or shape, and Expression Blend will calculate the correct transformations necessary to facilitate the animation. As an example, Figure 5-20 shows the same rectangle as shown in Figure 5-15, but now it has been moved, filled with a different color, and resized.

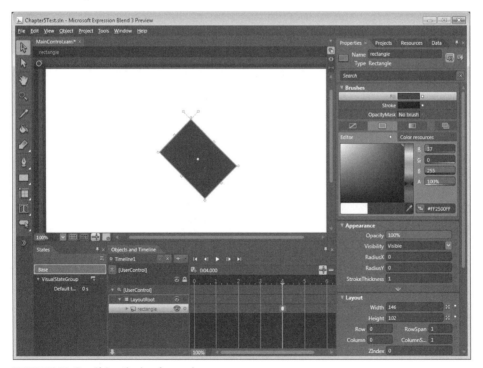

FIGURE 5-20 Specifying the key frame changes.

Finally, you might notice that if you drag the timeline indicator around, you can preview the animation and see how it appears at any particular time. Figure 5-21 shows how the rectangle appears at the two-second key time, achieved by dragging the yellow vertical line to the two-second point.

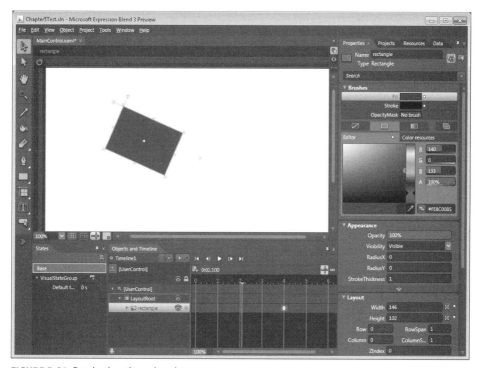

FIGURE 5-21 Previewing the animation.

Following is the complete XAML that Expression Blend generated when designing this animation:

```
<Canvas
  xmlns="http://schemas.microsoft.com/client/2007"
  xmlns:x="http://schemas.microsoft.com/winfx/2006/xaml"
  Width="640" Height="480"
  Background="White"
  x:Name="Page">
  <Canvas.Triggers>
    <EventTrigger RoutedEvent="Canvas.Loaded">
      <BeginStoryboard>
        <Storyboard x:Name="Timeline1">
          <DoubleAnimationUsingKeyFrames BeginTime="00:00:00"
            Storyboard.TargetName="rect"
            Storyboard.TargetProperty="(UIElement.RenderTransform).
                    (TransformGroup.Children)[3].(TranslateTransform.X)">
            <SplineDoubleKeyFrame KeyTime="00:00:04" Value="141"/>

          </DoubleAnimationUsingKeyFrames>
```

```
<DoubleAnimationUsingKeyFrames BeginTime="00:00:00"
        Storyboard.TargetName="rect"
        Storyboard.TargetProperty="(UIElement.RenderTransform).
            (TransformGroup.Children)[3].(TranslateTransform.Y)">
        <SplineDoubleKeyFrame KeyTime="00:00:04" Value="163"/>
    </DoubleAnimationUsingKeyFrames>

    <DoubleAnimationUsingKeyFrames BeginTime="00:00:00"
        Storyboard.TargetName="rect"
        Storyboard.TargetProperty="(UIElement.RenderTransform).
            (TransformGroup.Children)[2].(RotateTransform.Angle)">
        <SplineDoubleKeyFrame KeyTime="00:00:04" Value="35.107"/>
    </DoubleAnimationUsingKeyFrames>

    <ColorAnimationUsingKeyFrames BeginTime="00:00:00"
        Storyboard.TargetName="rect"
        Storyboard.TargetProperty="(Shape.Fill).(SolidColorBrush.Color)">
        <SplineColorKeyFrame KeyTime="00:00:04" Value="#FF9D0B0B"/>
    </ColorAnimationUsingKeyFrames>

    <DoubleAnimationUsingKeyFrames BeginTime="00:00:00" Storyboard.TargetName="rect"
        Storyboard.TargetProperty="(UIElement.RenderTransform).
            (TransformGroup.Children)[0].(ScaleTransform.ScaleX)">
        <SplineDoubleKeyFrame KeyTime="00:00:04" Value="1.7"/>
    </DoubleAnimationUsingKeyFrames>

    <DoubleAnimationUsingKeyFrames BeginTime="00:00:00"
        Storyboard.TargetName="rect"
        Storyboard.TargetProperty="(UIElement.RenderTransform).
            (TransformGroup.Children)[0].(ScaleTransform.ScaleY)">
        <SplineDoubleKeyFrame KeyTime="00:00:04" Value="1.549"/>
    </DoubleAnimationUsingKeyFrames>
    </Storyboard>
    </BeginStoryboard>
    </EventTrigger>
    </Canvas.Triggers>
    <Rectangle Width="87" Height="69" Fill="Red" Stroke="#FF000000"
            Canvas.Top="41" RenderTransformOrigin="0.5,0.5" x:Name="rect">
    <Rectangle.RenderTransform>
        <TransformGroup>
        <ScaleTransform ScaleX="1" ScaleY="1"/>
        <SkewTransform AngleX="0" AngleY="0"/>
        <RotateTransform Angle="0"/>
        <TranslateTransform X="0" Y="0"/>
        </TransformGroup>
    </Rectangle.RenderTransform>
    </Rectangle>
</Canvas>
```

Animation Easing

Easing functions are designed so that you can create and use a variety of specialized animation effects, including bouncing or "spring" effects. Silverlight 3 ships with a number of built-in easing functions in the *System.Windows.Media.Animation* namespace.

The use of animation easing functions makes it a lot easier for you to animate your objects with realistic behavior without having to figure out the physics of the movements yourself.

So, for example, if you want your animation to provide a realistic bounce, you can either do the physics calculations yourself and program it that way, or you can use the built-in bounce easing function, which is achieved using the new *EasingFunction* child of the animation tag.

Consider this scenario: With Silverlight, if you want to animate the movement of an ellipse, moving it from the top to the bottom of the screen, you would use a *<Storyboard>* object that contains a *<DoubleAnimation>* targeting the *Top* property of the ellipse. To add easing to this, you simply add the definition of the easing function as shown here:

```
<Canvas x:Name="LayoutRoot" Background="White">
  <Canvas.Resources>
    <Storyboard x:Name="bounce">
      <DoubleAnimation From="0" To="300" Duration="0:0:10"
        Storyboard.TargetName="myCircle"
        Storyboard.TargetProperty="(Canvas.Top)">
        <DoubleAnimation.EasingFunction>
          <BounceEase Bounces="10" EasingMode="EaseOut" Bounciness="2"></BounceEase>
        </DoubleAnimation.EasingFunction>
      </DoubleAnimation>
    </Storyboard>
  </Canvas.Resources>
  <Ellipse x:Name="myCircle" Width="40" Height="40" Fill="Red"
      Canvas.Top="0" Canvas.Left="50"></Ellipse>
</Canvas>
```

The *EasingFunction* definition (called *BounceEase*) contains the type of ease that you want to use, and each type has different parameters to define the ease. For example, to simulate a falling object bouncing, specify the starting and ending positions (*Top* from 0 to 300), and use the ease to define the bouncing behavior. In this case, it's set to bounce 10 times and to bounce at the *end* of the animation (the *EasingMode* is set to *EaseOut*).

Note that easing can take place in three modes: *EaseIn*, where the ease takes place at the *end* of the animation; *EaseOut*, where it takes place at the *beginning* of the animation; and *EaseInOut*, where both take place—you *EaseIn* to about half way, and then you *EaseOut*.

If you can imagine a bounce effect like the one demonstrated earlier, where a value is animated from 0 to 100 with a *Bounce* ease, the following will happen:

- *EaseIn* will start the value at 0 and move toward 100. Before it gets there, it will turn back and head toward 0 again. Before it reaches 0, it will turn and head toward 100, repeating this several times until it gets to 100.

- *EaseOut* will start the value at 0 and move past 100 before turning around and moving back to 100. It will go past 0 again, turning again and moving back toward 100. It repeats this overshooting and bouncing back a few times, based on your configuration, before it reaches 100.

- *EaseInOut* is a strange combination of the two, where the value bounces both at the beginning and at the end.

In the earlier example, you can see that the *EaseOut* function has the more natural effect of making the ball bounce beyond 100 when it hits the hard surface.

You can find the built-in easing functions in the *System.Windows.Media.Animation* namespace. In the following descriptions, the similes used to describe them are based on the *EaseIn* mode. You can deduce the *EaseOut* and *EaseInOut* effects from these descriptions. The differences between the ease modes can be subtle. It's best to experiment with them to get the best results!

These are the built-in easing modes:

- *BackEase*   This moves the animation *backward* a little before continuing. It's a little bit like starting a car on a hill: You roll back a little before you move forward.

- *BounceEase*   As you saw in the previous example, this creates a bouncing effect.

- *CircleEase*   This accelerates the animation based on a circular function, where the initial acceleration is slower and the latter acceleration is higher.

- *CubicEase*   This is similar to *CircleEase* but is based on the cubic formula of time, causing a slower acceleration in the beginning and a more rapid one toward the end of the animation.

- *ElasticEase*   This is similar to *BounceEase* in that it oscillates the value until it comes to a rest.

- *ExponentialEase*   This function is similar to *CircleEase* and *CubicEase* in that it is an exponential acceleration from one value to the next.

- *PowerEase* This is an exponential acceleration where the value of the ease is proportional to the power of the time.

- *QuadraticEase* This is very similar to *CubicEase* except that in this case the value is based on the square of the time.

- *QuarticEase* Similar to *QuadraticEase* and *CubicEase*. This time the value is based on the cube of the time.

- *QuinticEase* Again, similar to *QuadraticEase*, *CubicEase*, and *QuarticEase*. This time the value is based on the time to the power of five.

- *SineEase* This accelerates the value along a sine wave.

Note that these are classes, so each has its own relevant properties so that you can configure and fine-tune it. For example, if you look at the *BounceEase* from earlier, you can see that it has properties for the number of bounces that it provides and the "bounciness" of the animation (that is, the variation in value bounds as it changes direction). When using an easing function, check out the API documentation for it carefully to get it just right!

Summary

In this chapter, you learned how transformations and animations are defined in Silverlight XAML. You were introduced to different types of transformation used to rotate, scale, or skew an object, as well as to free-form transformations using an affine matrix as applied to a shape. You then learned about animations and saw how to define an animation to run based on an XAML trigger. You saw how animations change property values over time, and you looked at the XAML types that support animating *double*, *point*, and *color* values. You also learned how to use key frames for finer control over your animations. Finally, you took a look at the Expression Blend animation designer to see how easily you can generate animations visually by using it.

In Chapter 6, you look at how to use XAML controls for layout in your application to ensure that that your controls are drawn where you want them to be.

Chapter 6
The Silverlight Browser Object

In this chapter, you take an in-depth look at programming the Microsoft Silverlight plug-in, explore the properties and methods that are exposed to JavaScript programmers, discover how to use the *<object>* tag in HTML to instantiate Silverlight, and also learn how the object is used to execute Silverlight *out* of the browser.

When you build installers for applications, it is important for you to understand the Silverlight object and how to use its programming model to manage the user's installation experience. In this chapter, you look at this process and how the object behaves with different browsers and operating systems so that you can best manage the installation of Silverlight for users who don't already have it installed.

Hosting Silverlight in the Browser

You don't need any special software to be able to use and build Silverlight applications—in fact, you can use any software for building Web sites to build Silverlight sites, from Notepad to Eclipse to Microsoft Expression Web or Expression Blend. It's really up to you.

This section presents a basic primer that shows you what you need to do to begin to use Silverlight. So far in this book, you've been using an Expression Blend or Microsoft Visual Studio template to do the hard work for you, but now take a look at what it takes to get a simple Silverlight site up and running without any tools other than Windows Explorer and Notepad.

First, you create an HTML file that will host Silverlight. You do this using an *<object>* tag for Silverlight. Here's an example:

```
<!DOCTYPE html PUBLIC "-//W3C//DTD XHTML 1.0 Transitional//EN"
"http://www.w3.org/TR/xhtml1/DTD/xhtml1-transitional.dtd">
<html xmlns="http://www.w3.org/1999/xhtml" >
<head>
    <title>App1</title>
</head>

<body>
  <div id='errorLocation' style="font-size: small;color: Gray;"></div>
  <div id="silverlightControlHost">
    <object type="application/x-silverlight"
      width="100%" height="100%" id="slPlugin">
        <param name="source" value="ClientBin/App1.xap"/>
        <param name="onerror" value="onSilverlightError" />
        <param name="background" value="white" />
        <param name="minRuntimeVersion" value="3.0.40211.0" />
```

```
            <param name="autoUpgrade" value="true" />
            <p>Silverlight isn't installed</p>
            </object>
            <iframe style='visibility:hidden;height:0;width:0;border:0px'></iframe>
        </div>
    </body>
</html>
```

You use the *<object>* tag to instantiate Silverlight. This is a standard HTML tag, and as such supports the standard parameters. Explaining the full list of parameters is beyond the scope of this book, but following are the ones used in the preceding listing:

- The *Type* attribute specifies the type of object to load. In this case, you specify it using *application/x-silverlight*, which instructs the browser to load the Silverlight plug-in to access this content.

- The *Width* attribute specifies the control width by percentage or in pixels.

- The *Height* attribute specifies the control height by percentage or in pixels.

- The *ID* attribute specifies the control name to be used in JavaScript programming.

Because not every *<object>* supports the same set of configurable parameters, with the HTML *<object>* tag you can specify nonstandard parameters using list *<Param>* elements. You use these elements to specify a name/value pair. Table 6-1 lists the optional values.

TABLE 6-1 Parameters Supported by the Silverlight Object

Parameter Name	Description
source	Specifies either the XAP containing the application to load and run or an XAML document to render.
width	Sets the width of the control in pixels or by percentage.
height	Sets the height of the control in pixels or by percentage.
background	Determines the background color of the control. See the section titled "*SolidColorBrush*" in Chapter 4, "Silverlight XAML Basics," for more details on how to set colors. You can use an ARGB value, such as #FFAA7700, or a named color, such as *Black*.
framerate	Sets the maximum frame rate to allow for animation. It defaults to 24.
isWindowless	This parameter is set to *true* or *false* and defaults to *false*. When it is set to *true*, the Silverlight content is rendered behind the HTML content so that HTML content can be written on top of it.
enableHtmlAccess	Determines whether the content that is hosted in the Silverlight control is accessible from the browser DOM. It defaults to *true*.

Parameter Name	Description
minRuntimeVersion	Determines the minimum version of Silverlight to support.
onLoad	Specifies the function to run when the control is loaded.
onError	Specifies the function to run when the control hits an error.
onFullScreenChange	Fires when the *FullScreen* property of the Silverlight control changes.
onResize	Fires when the *ActualWidth* or *ActualHeight* property of the Silverlight control changes.

One nice feature of the *<object>* tag is that it is stackable in the sense that, if the initial *<object>* instantiation fails, the browser will render the next piece of HTML in its place, provided that the HTML is located before the closing *</object>* tag. This makes it easy to make a simple banner to put on the screen if Silverlight is not installed.

Here's an example:

```
<object data="data:application/x-silverlight,"
  type="application/x-silverlight-2-b1"
  width="100%" height="100%">
  <param name="source" value="Page.xaml"/>
  <param name="onerror" value="onSilverlightError" />
  <param name="background" value="white" />

  <a href="…" style="text-decoration: none;">
    <img src="…" alt="Get Microsoft Silverlight"
        style="border-style: none"/>
  </a>
</object>
```

In this situation, a hyperlink (*<a>* tag) is embedded in the object, so if Silverlight is not present in the system, this tag provides a clickable installation for it.

Responding to Page Load Events

You can respond to the page that contains Silverlight loading in a number of ways.

The first is to specify a JavaScript function to execute in response to the *Onload* event of the *<Body>* tag in HTML. This method is recommended if you are checking to see whether *Silverlight* can load—and not necessarily your application. The Silverlight application will load after your page does, so a positive on the page load does not mean a positive on the Silverlight application loading.

The second method is to specify a JavaScript event handler to manage page load events using the *onLoad* parameter introduced in Table 6-1. This parameter fires after the Extensible Application Markup Language (XAML) content or XAP file in the Silverlight control has completely loaded. Note that if you have defined a loaded event on any XAML UI element, those events will fire before the Silverlight control's *onLoad* event does. In addition, the control has a read-only *IsLoaded* property that is set immediately before the *onLoad* event fires.

When you use an *onLoad* event handler, the JavaScript function should take three parameters: The first is a reference to the control, the second is the user context, and the third is a reference to the root element of the XAML. Following is an example:

```
function handleLoad(control, userContext, rootElement)
{
    ...
}
```

The third method of responding to the page loading is to use the code-behind in Silverlight to specify what to do in response to either the application loading or any of the XAML elements in your application loading (such as the default Page).

For the *Application*, the default Silverlight application template defines *Application_Startup* as the event handler in the App.xaml.cs code-behind file.

For individual pages, you can specify the event handler in the *Loaded* parameter in XAML like this:

```
<UserControl x:Class="SLTestApp1.Page"
    xmlns="http://schemas.microsoft.com/winfx/2006/xaml/presentation"
    xmlns:x="http://schemas.microsoft.com/winfx/2006/xaml"
    Width="400" Height="300"
    Loaded="UserControl_Loaded">
    <Grid x:Name="LayoutRoot" Background="White">

    </Grid>
</UserControl>
```

You then need a function with this footprint in your code-behind for the page, or Silverlight will throw an error:

```
        private void UserControl_Loaded(object sender, RoutedEventArgs e)
        {

        }
```

Alternatively, you can execute code in the constructor for the page so that if your page is called Page.xaml, you'll see a constructor function called *Page()*.

Responding to Page Error Events

Silverlight provides several methods for error handling, depending on the type of error. Errors are raised when the XAML parser encounters a problem, the XAP code throws an error, loading isn't completed properly, run-time errors are encountered, and event handlers defined in the XAML document do not have a JavaScript or code-behind function associated with them.

When initializing a control using the *onError* event handler, you specify a JavaScript function that will be called when an error occurs. However, if you do not specify a function (or if you specify it as *null*), the default JavaScript event handler will fire.

The Default Event Handler

The JavaScript default event handler displays an error message alert box that contains basic details about the Silverlight error, including the error code and type as well as a message defining the specific problem and the method name that was called.

Following is an example of a badly formed XAML document in which the closing tag of the *TextBlock* element is misnamed *</TextBlok>*:

```
<Canvas xmlns="http://schemas.microsoft.com/client/2007"
        xmlns:x="http://schemas.microsoft.com/winfx/2006/xaml">
  <TextBlock>Hello, World!</TextBlok>
</Canvas>
```

If the error handler is set to *null*, the default error handler will fire and display the default Silverlight error message, as shown in Figure 6-1.

FIGURE 6-1 Default error message.

Using Your Own Error Handler

You can use your own error handler by setting the *onError* property of the Silverlight control to a custom event handler function. Your error handler function will need to take two parameters: the sender object and the event arguments that define the specifics of the error that occurred.

There are three types of event argument that you can receive. The first is the basic *ErrorEventArgs* object that contains the error message type and code. The *errorType* property defines the type of error as a string containing *RuntimeError* or *ParserError*. Based on this information, you can use one of the two associated derived error types.

When processing a parsing error in XAML, the *ParserErrorEventArgs* is available. This contains a number of properties:

- The *charposition* property contains the character position where the error occurred.

- The *linenumber* property contains the line where the error occurred.

- The *xamlFile* identifies the file in which the error occurred.

- The *xmlAttribute* identifies the XML attribute in which the error occurred.

- The *xmlElement* defines the element in which the error occurred.

Run-time errors are defined in the *RuntimeErrorEventArgs* object. This object also contains a number of properties:

- The *charPosition* property identifies the character position where the error occurred.

- The *lineNumber* property identifies the line in which the error occurred.

- The *methodName* identifies the method associated with the error.

In the previous section, you saw a parsing error as trapped by the default error handler. Here's how you could capture the same error with your own error handler. First, you create the *<object>* tag that specifies the error handler:

```
<div id="silverlightControlHost">
  <object data="data:application/x-silverlight-2,"
      type="application/x-silverlight-2" width="100%" height="100%">
    <param name="source" value="doError.xaml"/>
    <param name="onerror" value="onSilverlightError" />
    <param name="background" value="white" />
```

```
    <param name="minRuntimeVersion" value="3.0.40211.0" />
    <param name="autoUpgrade" value="true" />
    </object>
    <iframe style='visibility:hidden;height:0;width:0;border:0px'></iframe>
</div>
```

This defines the JavaScript function *onSilverlightError* as the function to call whenever you hit an error.

Here's an example function that handles and reports on an error:

```
<script type="text/javascript">
    function onSilverlightError(sender, args) {

        var appSource = "";
        if (sender != null && sender != 0) {
            appSource = sender.getHost().Source;
        }
        var errorType = args.ErrorType;
        var iErrorCode = args.ErrorCode;

        var errMsg = "Unhandled Error in Silverlight Application " +  appSource + "\n" ;

        errMsg += "Code: "+ iErrorCode + "     \n";
        errMsg += "Category: " + errorType + "        \n";
        errMsg += "Message: " + args.ErrorMessage + "       \n";

        if (errorType == "ParserError")
        {
            errMsg += "File: " + args.xamlFile + "       \n";
            errMsg += "Line: " + args.lineNumber + "      \n";
            errMsg += "Position: " + args.charPosition + "      \n";
        }
        else if (errorType == "RuntimeError")
        {
            if (args.lineNumber != 0)
            {
                errMsg += "Line: " + args.lineNumber + "      \n";
                errMsg += "Position: " +  args.charPosition + "       \n";
            }
            errMsg += "MethodName: " + args.methodName + "       \n";
        }

        alert(errMsg);
    }
</script>
```

When this code is executed and the error is tripped, the alert box will display the contents of the error. Figure 6-2 shows an example of a customized alert box.

FIGURE 6-2 Using your own event handler.

Silverlight Control Properties

The Silverlight control has a number of properties, some of which were discussed earlier in the section titled "Hosting Silverlight in the Browser." In addition to being able to set them when you initialize the control, you can also set the control's properties using script.

The control splits properties into three types: direct, content, and settings properties. *Direct* properties are properties of the control itself that are accessible using the *control.propertyname* syntax. *Content* properties and *settings* properties are accessed using the *control.content.propertyname* and *control.settings.propertyname* syntax, respectively.

Direct Properties

Following are the direct properties that are supported:

- ***initParams***   The initialization parameters that are passed to the control are stored in this property. It can be set only as part of the control initialization.

- ***isLoaded***   The *isLoaded* property is *true* after the control is loaded; otherwise, it is *false*. It is read-only.

- ***source***   The *source* property is the XAML content that you want to render. It can be a reference to a file, a URI to a service that generates XAML, or, when prefixed with a number sign (#), a DIV containing XAML code in a script block.

Content Properties

To access content properties, you can use the *control.content.propertyname* syntax. For example, if you want to access the *actualHeight* property, you use the *control.content.actualHeight* syntax. The following content properties are available:

- ***actualHeight***   The *actualHeight* property returns the height of the rendering area of the Silverlight control in pixels. The value returned depends on a number of different criteria. First, it depends on how the height of the control was initially set. Recall that it can be a percentage or an absolute pixel value. In the case of the former, the *actualHeight* property is the current height of the control, but if the user changes the browser dimensions, the *actualHeight* property will change. If the height was set using an absolute pixel value, that value will be returned. When the control is used in full screen mode, the *actualHeight* property will return the current vertical resolution of the display.

- ***actualWidth***   The *actualWidth* property returns the width of the display. The value returned depends on a number of criteria and is similar to the *actualHeight* parameter.

- ***fullScreen***   The *fullScreen* property switches the Silverlight control display between embedded and full screen mode. It defaults to *false*, which is the embedded mode. When set to *true*, Silverlight will render to the full screen.

Settings Properties

The control also contains a number of properties that are defined as settings properties, where they are accessed using the *control.settings.propertyname* syntax:

- ***background***   The *background* property sets the background color of the Silverlight control. It can take several different formats, including a named color (such as *Black*), 8-bit *Red/Green/Blue* (*RGB*) values with or without alpha, and 16-bit *RGB* values with or without alpha.

- ***enableFrameRateCounter***   When set to *true*, Silverlight will render the current frame rate (in frames per second) in the browser's status bar. The *enableFrameRateCounter* property defaults to *false*.

- ***enableHtmlAccess***   When set to *true*, the *enableHtmlAccess* property will allow the XAML content to be accessible from the browser Document Object Model (DOM). The default value is *true*.

- *enableRedrawRegions*   When set to *true*, the *enableRedrawRegions* property shows the areas of the plug-in that are being redrawn upon each frame. It's a useful tool to help you optimize your application. The default value is *false*.

- *maxFrameRate*   The *maxFrameRate* property specifies the maximum frame rate to render Silverlight content. It defaults to 24 and has an absolute maximum of 64.

- *version*   The version property reports the version of the Silverlight control that is presently being used. It is a string containing up to four integers, separated by dots, that contains the major, minor, build, and revision numbers, although only the first two values (major and minor version numbers) are required.

- *windowless*   The *windowless* property determines whether the control is displayed as a windowless or windowed control. When set to *true*, it is windowless, meaning the Silverlight content is effectively rendered "behind" the HTML content on the page.

Silverlight Control Methods

The Silverlight control has a number of methods that you can use to control its behavior and function. Similar to Silverlight property groups, the Silverlight methods are grouped into "families" of methods. At present, one direct and three content methods are supported. You see which is which in the following sections, including samples showing their syntax and how to access them.

The *createFromXaml* Method

The *createFromXaml* method is a Silverlight content method with which you can define XAML content to add dynamically to your Silverlight control. It takes two parameters. The first is a string containing the XAML that you want to use, and the other is the *namescope* parameter that, when set to *true* (it defaults to *false*), creates unique *x:Name* references in the provided XAML that do not conflict with any existing XAML element names.

You can add a constraint around the XAML using *createFromXaml*. The XAML you add has to have a single root node. So, if you have a number of elements to add, make sure that they are all contained within a single node containing the *Canvas* element.

Additionally, *createFromXaml* does not add the XAML to the Silverlight control until it has been added to the children of one of the *Canvas* elements within the control. So, when you call *createFromXaml*, you get a reference to the node returned, and this reference is then used to add the node to the render tree. Following is an example:

```
function handleLoad(control, userContext, sender)
{
   var xamlFragment = '<TextBlock Canvas.Top="60" Text="A new TextBlock" />';
   var textBlock = control.content.createFromXaml(xamlFragment);
   sender.children.add(textBlock);
}
```

Here the XAML code for a *TextBlock* control is created that contains the text "A new TextBlock". This is then used to create an XAML node in the control content; after it is complete, Silverlight will return a reference to the *TextBlock*. This reference is then added to the Silverlight control's render tree and is used to render the context of the *TextBlock*.

The *createFromXamlDownloader* Method

The *createFromXamlDownloader* method is a content method used in conjunction with a *Downloader* object, which you will learn about later in this chapter. It takes two parameters. The first parameter is a reference to the *Downloader* object that downloads the XAML code or a package containing the XAML code. The second parameter is the name of the specific part of the download content package to use. If this is a .zip file, you specify the name of the file within the .zip file that contains the XAML code you want to use. When the downloaded content is not in a .zip package, you should set this parameter to an empty string.

The *createObject* Method

The *createObject* method is a direct method designed so that you can create a disposable object for a specific function. In Silverlight, the only object that is supported is the *Downloader* object. The *Downloader* object is covered in greater detail later in this chapter.

The *findName* Method

With the *findName* content method, you can search for a node in the XAML code based on its *x:Name* attribute. If *findName* finds a node with the provided name, it returns a reference to it; otherwise, it returns *null*.

The *Downloader* Object

With the *Downloader* object in the Silverlight control, you can download additional elements using asynchronous downloading functionality. By using this functionality, you can download individual assets or assets that are packaged in a .zip file.

Downloader Object Properties

The *Downloader* object supports the following properties:

- **downloadProgress**   The *downloadProgress* property provides a normalized value (between 0 and 1) representing the percentage of progress of the content downloaded, where 1 is equal to 100 percent complete.

- **status**   The *status* property gets the HTTP status code for the current status of the downloading process. It returns a standard HTTP status code, such as "404" for "Not Found" or "200" for "OK."

- **statusText**   The *statusText* property gets the HTTP status text for the current status of the downloading process. This corresponds to the status code for the *status* property. For a successful request, the *status* will be "200," and the *statusText* will be "OK." For more information about HTTP status codes, check out the standard HTTP codes provided by W3C (*http://www.w3.org/Protocols/rfc2616/rfc2616-sec10.html*).

- **uri**   The *uri* property contains the URI of the object that the downloader is presently accessing.

Downloader Object Methods

The *Downloader* object supports the following methods:

- **abort**   The *abort* method cancels the current download and resets all properties to their default state.

- **getResponseText**   The *getResponseText* method returns a string representation of the downloaded data. It takes an optional parameter that is used to name the contents of the file name in a downloaded package.

- **open**   The *open* method initializes the download session. It takes two parameters. The first is the verb for the action. The set of HTTP verbs is documented by the W3C; however, only the *GET* verb is supported in Silverlight. The second parameter is the URI for the resource that is to be downloaded.

- **send**   The *send* method executes the download request that was initialized with the *Open* command.

Downloader Object Events

The *Downloader* object supports the following events:

- **completed**   The *completed* event fires when the download is complete. It takes two parameters. The first is the object that raised the event (in this case, the downloader control itself), and the second is a set of event arguments (*eventArgs*).

- **downloadProgressChanged**   The *downloadProgressChanged* event fires while content is being downloaded. It fires every time the progress (which is a value between 0 and 1) changes by 0.05 (5 percent) or more, as well as when it reaches 1.0 (100 percent). When it reaches 1.0, the *completed* event also fires.

Using the *Downloader* Object

With the *Downloader* object, you can access network resources from JavaScript. Please note that this object works only if you are running the Silverlight application from a Web server, and it will throw an error if you are simply loading the page from the file system.

You create a *Downloader* object using the *createObject* method provided by the Silverlight control. Here's an example:

```
<script type="text/javascript">
    function handleLoad(control, userContext, sender)
    {
       var downloader = control.createObject("downloader");
    }
</script>
```

The next step is to initialize the download session by using the *open* method of the *Downloader* object to declare the URI of the file and then to call the *send* method to kick off the download. Following is an example that downloads a movie file called *movie.wmv*:

```
function handleLoad(control, userContext, sender)
{
   var downloader = control.createObject("downloader");
   downloader.open("GET","movie.wmv";
   downloader.send();
}
```

To trap the download progress and completion, you need to wire the appropriate event handlers. Following is the same function updated accordingly:

```
function handleLoad(control, userContext, sender)
{
   var downloader = control.createObject("downloader");
   downloader.addEventListener("downloadProgressChanged","handleDLProgress");
   downloader.addEventListener("completed","handleDLComplete");
   downloader.open("GET","movie.wmv";
   downloader.send();
}
```

Now you can implement these event handlers. In this example, the *DownloadProgressChanged* event is wired to a JavaScript function called *handleDLProgress*, and the *Completed* event is wired to the *handleDLComplete* JavaScript function. You can see these functions here:

```
function handleDLProgress(sender, args)
{
   var ctrl = sender.getHost();
   var t1 = ctrl.content.findName("txt1");
   var v = sender.downloadProgress * 100;
   t1.Text = v + "%";
}

function handleDLComplete(sender, args)
{
    alert("Download complete");
}
```

> **Note** You can use the *Downloader* object only on applications that are hosted on a Web server. If you try to use it from a page that is loaded from the file system, you'll get an error.

Do also note that the *Downloader* object is how you can download resources using JavaScript. If you are building Silverlight applications that use the Microsoft .NET Framework, a plethora of options to access network resources is available. These are covered in much more detail in Chapter 12, "Networking and Interoperability in Silverlight."

Using the Object Model to Build an Install Experience

The Silverlight object model exposes events that you can use to build a very friendly user experience for installing Silverlight.

When it comes to using a Web site that requires a plug-in to render content, the user is generally faced with a choice: Is it worth spending the time and effort to install the plug-in to get to the content that I want? Is it clear to me what I am installing? Do I *want* to install it?

Through research on popular Web sites such as the NBC Olympics and the Democratic National Conference sites and also a myriad of Microsoft-owned sites, Microsoft has found a number of key factors that make this decision easier for the user, help manage users through the process of installation, and make it more likely, ultimately, for more people to choose the plug-in to interact with your content.

This section outlines the possible scenarios that users might encounter when they are installing Silverlight and the code that you can write to overcome any issues that might arise in these scenarios. There are more issues than you might expect. Sometimes the user will not have Silverlight to begin with; other times the user has an older version installed; sometimes users will be in a state where they need to restart the browser, and yet others need only to refresh.

Programming the Install User Experience

Silverlight projects that are built using Silverlight Tools for Visual Studio offer a default installation experience (called the Silverlight badge) for users who do not have the Silverlight runtime already installed. It's a very simple experience that is designed to be a lowest common denominator approach.

It's important to note that this experience is generic in nature, and as such is not tailored to any particular application. Thus, when users see the install badge, they might become confused.

Consider a scenario in which a user visits a site that provides casual games. The user selects to play a game, but instead of the game appearing, the user sees a blank screen with the Silverlight badge in the top left corner. Is it a banner ad? Did the user click the wrong button? With this confusion, there's a high probability that the user will not click the badge, will not download Silverlight, and will not play the game.

Additionally, if the user does click the badge, then what happens? Clicking the badge doesn't install the application but triggers the download of an executable that has to be acted upon by the user to install. After installation, there's no guarantee that the content will work right away. Sometimes performing a refresh is enough. Sometimes a browser restart is necessary. To give the best possible experience to the user, you must manage all of these scenarios effectively and coherently.

To do this, you need to understand two main artifacts. The first is the *technology* and the code that can be used to provide the best install user experience (UX). The second is the *solicitation* and the correct language and prompts to use to ensure that the user fully understands and is properly guided through the installation experience.

Before getting your hands dirty with the code, it's a good idea to understand all the installation cases that you are likely to face.

After the installation experience has been designed, a Web author should generate several variants of that experience to account for special states that a user might be in when visiting the Silverlight-enabled application. These variations are different only in text, but will greatly improve the user's confidence in the application and the platform.

Users can view the Silverlight installation experience on a Web site in one of six states. The message users are presented with, if any, should be a variant of the installation experience that is semantically equivalent to the recommendations given in Table 6-2.

TABLE 6-2 Silverlight Install States

State	Message Type
Silverlight is installed and loaded.	Don't give a message, just show the content.
The correct version of Silverlight is installed but not loaded.	Thank the user, and ask the user to restart the browser before coming back to this page.
An older version of Silverlight is installed.	Tell users that they need to upgrade to the latest version of Silverlight, and direct them to where they can get it.
The upgrade has started.	Inform users that the upgrade is under way, and that once it is finished, they'll have to restart the browser.
Silverlight is not installed.	Prompt users that to get the content they need to install the Silverlight plug-in. Emphasize the content, not Silverlight.
The installation has started.	Thank users for installing Silverlight, and let them know that they might need to refresh their browser when the installation is finished.
This is an unsupported configuration.	Prompt and show users an HTML view that is delivered for people who cannot install Silverlight in their environment. This can be a note that discusses the compatibility issue or an alternative HTML experience.

These states are represented visually in Figure 6-3.

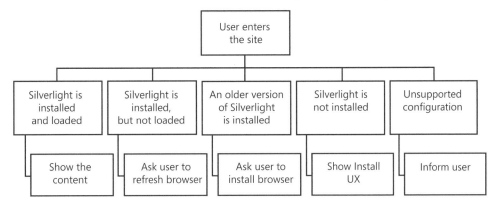

FIGURE 6-3 Different install states.

These states and user expectations can be managed by following these steps in your code.

Task 1. Integrate Silverlight.js and use the *<object>* Tag

Step 1. Integrate Silverlight.js

Silverlight.js must be included using a *<script>* tag in the page's *<head>* element. This JavaScript file defines the required APIs and includes the code required to check whether Silverlight is installed to begin with.

```
<head>
    <script src="Silverlight.js" type="text/javascript" ></script>
</head>
```

Step 2. Use an *<object>* tag for Silverlight

As you saw earlier, the Web page embeds Silverlight on the page using an HTML *<object>* tag. This tag must include the *data* and *type* attributes. Notice that the default state for Silverlight projects is to use *"application/x-silverlight-2"* as the MIME type for these attributes.

Note that to detect the installation state for Silverlight 1.0 users, you should use the Silverlight 1.0 MIME type for both the *data* and *type* attributes. By doing this, you force the user to upgrade the control with minimal impact on the Web site author.

Thus, these attributes should be defined like this:

```
type="application/x-silverlight"
```

and

```
data="data:application/x-silverlight,"
```

Step 3. Use the *minRuntimeVersion* parameter

The *minRuntimeVersion* parameter is part of the *<object>* tag that is used to ensure that the user has the proper version of Silverlight installed. If not, the control will not download the XAP and will instead ask the user to upgrade the control. Additionally, this state will trigger the *OnError* event with the *args.ErrorCode* set to 8001 "Upgrade Required" or 8002 "Restart Required."

Do note that because Silverlight 1.0 did not support the *minRuntimeVersion* parameter, checking the error state is not enough to see whether an action is required on the part of the user. You can determine whether the user must take action only by following the steps in this chapter and by using Silverlight.js.

The correct value for the *minRuntimeVersion* parameter is "2.0.31005" for the RTM version of Silverlight 2. The RTM of Silverlight 3 is not available at the time of this writing but this information will be updated after the book is published. Check the author's blog at *http://blogs.msdn.com/webnext* for more details.

Step 4. Use the *autoUpgrade* parameter

When *autoUpgrade* is *true*, the default Silverlight experience for upgrading will take place. If you want to control this with your own UX, you should set this parameter to *false*.

Note that you can test the UX by creating a Silverlight object on a page with *data*, *type*, *minRuntime*, and *autoUpgrade* properties set like this:

```
<object data="data:application/x-silverlight,"
    type="application/x-silverlight">
    <param name="minRuntimeVersion" value="9.9.99999" />
    <param name="autoUpgrade" value="true" />
</object>
```

Step 5. Turn on error handling

The *<object>* tag must use the *onError* parameter and its definition function must call *Silverlight.IsVersionAvailableOnerror(sender,args)*.

If this function returns *true*, the right version of Silverlight is already installed *and* loaded, so normal error handling code should be executed.

If the parameter on the *<object>* tag looks like this:

```
<param name="onError" value="onSilverlightError" />
```

you have a handler that looks like this:

```
function onSilverlightError(sender, args)
{
    if (Silverlight.IsVersionAvailableOnError(sender, args)) {
        //run error handling code
    }
}
```

Step 6. Capture the *onLoad* event

The *onLoad* parameter of the *<object>* tag must define a handler function, and this function must call *Silverlight.IsVersionAvailableOnLoad(sender)*. By calling this function, you can identify earlier versions of Silverlight (beta builds, for example) and trigger an upgrade or restart to handle them.

So, if the parameter on the *<object>* tag looks like this:

```
<param name="onLoad" value="onSilverlightLoad" />
```

you have a handler that looks like this:

```
function onSilverlightLoad(sender)
{
    Silverlight.IsVersionAvailableOnLoad(sender);
}
```

Step 7. Address incompatible configuration

Although the Silverlight control is available for installation by a majority of the Internet's users, some platforms are not currently supported. When users on unsupported platforms click the Silverlight installation URL they are redirected to a Web page at *http://www.microsoft.com/silverlight* that informs them that their platform is not supported. This experience is fine for most pages, but some Web sites want to be able to identify these users without redirecting to *http://www.microsoft.com*. You can accomplish this goal in several different ways:

o   Identify the user as being unsupported server-side based on the HTTP request

o   Identify the user as being unsupported client-side based on *navigator.userAgent*

A default implementation of client-side-supported user detection is available in Silverlight.supportedUserAgent.js (*http://code.msdn.microsoft.com/SLsupportedUA*).

One way that user detection could be used is as follows:

First, add a reference to the script file to your page.

```
<script type="text/javascript" src="Silverlight.supportedUserAgent.js"></script>
```

Then, create an HTML prompt for the not supported scenario and load it into a JavaScript *var*:

```
var PromptNotSupported = "<div><p>This browser doesn't support Silverlight,
sorry!</p></div>";
```

Finally, create a JavaScript function that uses the *supportedUserAgent* API to determine whether the current browser is supported. Note that for this to work, the Silverlight object must be contained in a *<div>* called *silverlightControlHost*.

```
<script type="text/javascript">
function CheckSupported() {
  var tst = Silverlight.supportedUserAgent();
  if (tst) {
    // Do nothing
  }
  else{
    document.getElementById("silverlightControlHost").innerHTML =
        PromptNotSupported;
  }
}
</script>
```

To use this, you have to call this script when the page loads.

```
<body onload="CheckSupported()">
```

It is very important to note that as Web browsers and Silverlight evolve, the supported user agent detection code will also change. Therefore, Web developers should be sure to check the Silverlight.supportedUserAgent Web page often to ensure that they have the latest version.

Task 2. Render the UI Prompts at the Appropriate Time

In Figure 6-4 you can see the potential install states and from it you can derive that there are five main prompts that you need to give to the user.

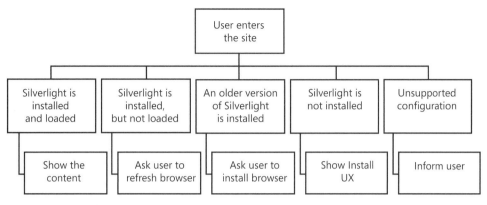

FIGURE 6-4 The different install states.

Reading from left to right, the first path is the simple state—the correct version of Silverlight is installed and present, so just show the content.

The next state is when the user *does not* have Silverlight installed. In this case, the user is first prompted with a Click to Install button, and when installation is complete the user is requested to refresh the browser.

The next state is when the user *has* Silverlight, but it is an older version. In this case, the user is prompted with a Click to Upgrade button, and when installation is complete the user is requested to restart the browser.

The next state is when the correct version of Silverlight is detected, but it hasn't been loaded. In this case, the user is asked to restart the browser.

The last state is when an incompatible configuration is detected.

Note that the substates on the paths where Silverlight needs to be installed or updated are not automatically detected. You have to generate these prompts in response to the users clicking the Click to Install or Click to Upgrade options. You will see how to do this later.

To summarize, following are the six ways in which the user needs to be prompted that correlate to the six states:

- Silverlight is not installed; click to install.

- You are now installing Silverlight; refresh when done.

- An older version of Silverlight is installed; click to upgrade.

- You are not upgrading Silverlight; restart when done.

- Please restart your browser.

- Your browser is incompatible with this experience.

The following steps will show you what to follow to be able to build a full install UX for Silverlight.

Step 1. Define the HTML to prompt user to install Silverlight

In the *<object>* tag definition, you can render HTML that shows when the object cannot be created. This fires if Silverlight is not installed. This step is very straightforward—just add a *<div>* after the parameter installs that renders the HTML.

Note that somewhere in this HTML you should capture a click and use it to run a JavaScript function. This JavaScript is necessary to render the installing message.

Here's an example of a fully formed *<object>* tag containing this HTML:

```
<object data="data:application/x-silverlight," type="application/x-silverlight"
                    width="100%" height="100%">
  <param name="source" value="bin/debug/Memory.xap"/>
  <param name="background" value="white" />
  <param name="minRuntimeVersion" value="2.0.31005.0" />
  <param name="autoUpgrade" value="false" />
  <param name="onerror" value="onSilverlightError" />
  <param name="onload" value="onSilverlightLoad" />
  <div id="SLInstallFallback" class="silverlightInstall" >
    <img src="images/install.PNG" onclick='InstallClicked();'
        class="silverlightInstallImage"
        alt='Click to Install' style='cursor:pointer;'/>
  </div>
</object>
```

This code defines an image (images/install.PNG) to show when Silverlight isn't installed. You can replace this HTML with your own, depending on your situation. Do be sure to have an *onclick* handler though. You explore handlers in step 3 of this procedure.

Step 2. Define the UI for other prompt states

The other five prompt states can be defined as JavaScript variables.

Here are the variables that are used for the states in this example:

- ***var PromptFinishInstall***   Used for "You are now installing Silverlight, refresh when done."

- ***var PromptUpgrade***   Used for "An older version of Silverlight is installed, click to upgrade."

- ***var PromptFinishUpgrade***   Used for "You are now upgrading Silverlight, restart when done."

- *var PromptRestart*   Used for "Please restart your browser."

- *Var PromptIncompatible*   Used for "Your browser is incompatible with this experience."

These should simply be HTML *<div>* objects that are used to replace the *innerHTML* of a portion of your page when you need to issue a prompt to the user.

Do note that the *PromptUpgrade* (similar to the prompt in step 1) should have a call to a JavaScript function when an area within it is clicked. This JavaScript function will change the on-screen prompt to the "You are now upgrading Silverlight, restart when done" state. You see this in step 3.

Here's an example of what this call to the JavaScript function should look like. Note the definition of the *onclick* event handler:

```
var PromptUpgrade =
  "<div id='SLInstallFallback' class='silverlightInstall' >" +
  "   <img src='images/upgrade.PNG' onclick='UpgradeClicked();'
        class='silverlightInstallImage'" +
  "       alt='Click to Upgrade' style='cursor:pointer;'/>" +
  "</div>";
```

Step 3. Write JavaScript functions to handle user actions for install and upgrade

In step 1, you defined the prompt to solicit users to click an area on your page to install Silverlight. The response to this action should trigger the download of the installer and update the screen to inform users that they are not in the installation state.

The JavaScript to achieve this is as follows:

```
function InstallClicked()
{
 window.location = "http://go2.microsoft.com/fwlink/?linkid=124807";
 document.getElementById("silverlightControlHost").innerHTML =
    PromptFinishInstall;
}
```

Note that it changes the *innerHTML* of the *<object>* tag to the value of *PromptFinishInstall* as defined in step 2.

In step 2, when defining the upgrade prompt you specified an *onClick* event handler called *UpgradeClicked*. This is similar to the *InstallClicked* event handler in that it downloads the software and changes the prompt, this time to the one to finish the upgrade.

```
function UpgradeClicked()
{
  window.location = "http://go2.microsoft.com/fwlink/?linkid=124807";
  document.getElementById("silverlightControlHost").innerHTML =
    PromptFinishUpgrade;
}
```

Task 3. Capture the Callbacks from Silverlight.js

Silverlight.js has some helper functions that trap the different states so that you can update the UI accordingly.

These functions are as follows:

- *Silverlight.onRequiredVersionAvailable*   The correct version of Silverlight is installed and available. You can use this function to let users know that they are ready to go, or you can just ignore it and render the content.

- *Silverlight.onRestartRequired*   The user needs to restart the browser. In this case, you change the prompt area HTML to the contents of your *PromptRestart* var.

- *Silverlight.onUpgradeRequired*   The user needs to upgrade from an older version of Silverlight. In this case, you change the prompt area HTML to the contents of your *PromptUpgrade var.*

- *Silverlight.onInstallrequired*   Silverlight isn't installed but needs to be. You don't need to take any action here because you are capturing this state in the *<object>* tag.

Here's the code:

```
function onSilverlightLoad(sender)
{
  Silverlight.IsVersionAvailableOnLoad(sender);
}

Silverlight.onRequiredVersionAvailable = function()
{
};

Silverlight.onRestartRequired = function()
{
  document.getElementById("silverlightControlHost").innerHTML =
    PromptRestart;
};
```

```
Silverlight.onUpgradeRequired = function()
{
  document.getElementById("silverlightControlHost").innerHTML =
    PromptUpgrade;
};

Silverlight.onInstallRequired = function()
{
};
```

Task 4. Work Around Known Issues

A known issue affects Firefox users that are upgrading from Silverlight 1.0 or a beta of Silverlight 2 to the release of Silverlight 2. It has been fixed for future versions of Silverlight but needs to be worked around for Silverlight 2.

Firefox users will see the *<object>* tag's fallback experience after an upgrade to Silverlight 2 unless they restart their browser.

This is fixed by using the following script *after* the *<object>* definition.

```
<script type="text/javascript">
  try
  {
    if (navigator.plugins["Silverlight Plug-In"].description)
    {
      document.getElementById("SLInstallFallback").innerHTML = PromptRestart;
    }
  }
  catch (e)
  {
  }
</script>
```

Another issue is that Mac Firefox users are misidentified as being in the upgrade required state when they are actually in the restart required state. There is no known workaround at this time, but the scenarios that lead to this are complex, and in most cases you will not encounter this state.

Exploring the Finished Page with Install UX

Microsoft Visual Studio creates a default HTML page to host your Silverlight content. It is pretty easy to follow the preceding steps to upgrade this page from the default UX to one that manages the installation states as demonstrated.

Listing 6-1 is the complete code for the page, with the new sections shown in bold type.

LISTING 6-1 Finished Page

```
<!DOCTYPE html PUBLIC "-//W3C//DTD XHTML 1.0 Transitional//EN"
"http://www.w3.org/TR/xhtml1/DTD/xhtml1-transitional.dtd">
<html xmlns="http://www.w3.org/1999/xhtml" >
<!-- saved from url=(0014)about:internet -->
<head>
    <title>SilverlightApplication1</title>

    <style type="text/css">
    html, body {
        height: 100%;
        overflow: auto;
    }
    body {
        padding: 0;
        margin: 0;
    }
    #silverlightControlHost {
        height: 100%;
    }
    </style>
    <script type="text/javascript" src="Silverlight.js"></script>
    <script type="text/javascript" src="Silverlight.supportedUserAgent.js"></script>
    <script type="text/javascript">
        var PromptFinishInstall = "<div><p>You are now installing Silverlight,
refresh your browser when done.</p></div>";
        var PromptUpgrade = "<div><p onclick='UpgradeClicked()'>This application
needs you to upgrade the Silverlight plug-in that runs it. An older version is
installed. Click here to upgrade it.</p></div>";
        var PromptFinishUpgrade = "<div><p>You are now upgrading Silverlight. When
this is done, please restart your browser.</p></div>";
        var PromptRestart = "<div><p>Please restart your browser.</p></div>";
        var PromptNotSupported = "<div><p>This browser doesn't support Silverlight,
sorry!</p></div>";
        function onSilverlightError(sender, args) {

            if (Silverlight.IsVersionAvailableOnerror(sender, args)) {
                var appSource = "";
                if (sender != null && sender != 0) {
                    appSource = sender.getHost().Source;
                }
                var errorType = args.ErrorType;
                var iErrorCode = args.ErrorCode;

                var errMsg = "Unhandled Error in Silverlight 2 Application " +
appSource + "\n";

                errMsg += "Code: " + iErrorCode + "    \n";
                errMsg += "Category: " + errorType + "        \n";
                errMsg += "Message: " + args.ErrorMessage + "      \n";
```

```
            if (errorType == "ParserError") {
                errMsg += "File: " + args.xamlFile + "     \n";
                errMsg += "Line: " + args.lineNumber + "     \n";
                errMsg += "Position: " + args.charPosition + "      \n";
            }
            else if (errorType == "RuntimeError") {
                if (args.lineNumber != 0) {
                    errMsg += "Line: " + args.lineNumber + "     \n";
                    errMsg += "Position: " + args.charPosition + "      \n";
                }
                errMsg += "MethodName: " + args.methodName + "      \n";
            }

            throw new Error(errMsg);
        }
    }

    function onSilverlightLoad(sender) {
        Silverlight.IsVersionAvailableOnLoad(sender);

    }

    Silverlight.onRequiredVersionAvailable = function() {
};

    Silverlight.onRestartRequired = function() {
        document.getElementById("silverlightControlHost").innerHTML =
PromptRestart;
    };

    Silverlight.onUpgradeRequired = function() {
        document.getElementById("silverlightControlHost").innerHTML =
PromptUpgrade;
    };
    Silverlight.onInstallRequired = function() {
    };
    function UpgradeClicked() {
        window.location = "http://go2.microsoft.com/fwlink/?linkid=124807";
        document.getElementById("silverlightControlHost").innerHTML =
PromptFinishUpgrade;
    }
    function InstallClicked() {
        window.location = "http://go2.microsoft.com/fwlink/?linkid=124807";
        document.getElementById("silverlightControlHost").innerHTML =
PromptFinishInstall;
    }
        function CheckSupported() {
        var tst = Silverlight.supportedUserAgent();
        if (tst) {
            // Do nothing
            }
        else{
            document.getElementById("silverlightControlHost").innerHTML =
```

```
PromptNotSupported;
                }
        }


    </script>
</head>

<body onload="CheckSupported()">
    <!--Run-time errors from Silverlight will be displayed here.
    This will contain debugging information and should be removed or hidden when
debugging is completed -->
    <div id='errorLocation' style="font-size: small;color: Gray;"></div>

    <div id="silverlightControlHost" style="height:100%;">
            <object data="data:application/x-silverlight," type="application/x-
silverlight" width="100%" height="100%">
                    <param name="source"
value="ClientBin/SilverlightApplication1.xap"/>

                    <param name="background" value="white" />
                    <param name="minRuntimeVersion" value="2.0.31005.0" />
                    <param name="autoUpgrade" value="false" />
                    <param name="onerror" value="onSilverlightError" />
                    <param name="onload" value="onSilverlightLoad" />
                    <div id="SLInstallFallback"><div><p
onclick='UpgradeClicked()'>This application needs you to use the Silverlight plug-in
to use it. Click here to install it.</p></div></div>
            </object>
            <iframe style='visibility:hidden;height:0;width:0;border:0px'></iframe>
    </div>
    <div id="silverlightExperienceHost" style="visibility:hidden;">
    </div>
    <script type="text/javascript">
        try {
            if (navigator.plugins["Silverlight Plug-In"].description) {
                document.getElementById("SLInstallFallback").innerHTML =
PromptRestart;
            }
        }
        catch (e) {
        }
    </script>
</body>
</html>
```

In this scenario, you've built the code, but not the installation solicitation. It's recommended that you build the solicitation carefully for your application and focus on your application content, not Silverlight. So, for example, if you are building a site to show off a widget, you should have big friendly text with the value proposition of the widget with a short and smaller indication that to access the widget, users must install a plug-in, which is a quick, easy, and secure procedure. Look at some existing sites to see what works and what doesn't. You can find a good example of an install solicitation at *http://movies.msn.com/pretty-in-ink/*. You can see the solicitation in Figure 6-5.

FIGURE 6-5 Well-designed install solicitation.

By creating a well-designed install solicitation along with a well-managed set of install states, you should expect less drop-off of users and more access to your new, rich Silverlight content.

Running Silverlight Applications Out of the Browser

In Silverlight 3, you can write out-of-browser applications so that you can create an application that encapsulates its own window and that can be added to the Start menu or the desktop. Creating an out-of-browser application is very straightforward, as you'll see in a moment. You simply add some configuration to the application manifest to inform it that you want it to run offline also.

Create a new Silverlight application called SLOOB. Add something simple, like a Hello World *TextBlock* to the default page, and then execute it. You can see it running in the browser as usual. However, if you right-click the Silverlight content, the new Install Onto This Computer menu item appears but is unavailable. Figure 6-6 shows the Install Onto This Computer option. The name of the application is used in the menu—you'll see how to configure this n a moment!

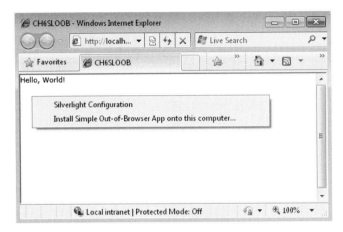

FIGURE 6-6 Out-of-browser capabilities are disabled.

To enable this functionality, you have to make some changes to the application manifest. You can find AppManifest.xml in the Properties folder, and it looks like this:

```
<Deployment xmlns="http://schemas.microsoft.com/client/2007/deployment"
        xmlns:x="http://schemas.microsoft.com/winfx/2006/xaml">
    <Deployment.Parts>
    </Deployment.Parts>
</Deployment>
```

The first thing you need to add is the *EntryPointAssembly* and *EntryPointType* settings. For the SLOOB application, these should be *SLOOB* and *SLOOB.App*, respectively.

So now, your manifest should look like this:

```
<Deployment xmlns="http://schemas.microsoft.com/client/2007/deployment"
        xmlns:x="http://schemas.microsoft.com/winfx/2006/xaml"
            EntryPointAssembly="SLOOB"
            EntryPointType="SLOOB.App">

    <Deployment.Parts>
    </Deployment.Parts>
</Deployment>
```

Next, you need to add an *Application Identity* section to the manifest. This section contains the short name, title, and blurb settings for your application.

The *Title* is displayed in the title bar of the stand-alone window that runs the application.

The *Short name* is displayed on the desktop and/or Start menu shortcuts.

The *Blurb* is used in the Comments section of the file. You can view this section in the properties of the application in Windows Explorer.

You can see these elements in the manifest here:

```
<Deployment xmlns="http://schemas.microsoft.com/client/2007/deployment"
       xmlns:x="http://schemas.microsoft.com/winfx/2006/xaml"
            EntryPointAssembly="SLOOB"
            EntryPointType="SLOOB.App">

   <Deployment.Parts>
   </Deployment.Parts>
  <Deployment.ApplicationIdentity>

    <ApplicationIdentity ShortName="Simple Out-of-Browser App"
                        Title="My Cool App's Title">

      <ApplicationIdentity.Blurb>
        Do really cool stuff at home or on the go.
      </ApplicationIdentity.Blurb>

    </ApplicationIdentity>

  </Deployment.ApplicationIdentity>
</Deployment>
```

Now, when you run the application and right-click it you see that the Save for Offline Use option is available.

When you click Save for Offline Use, the Microsoft Silverlight – Saving for Offline Use dialog box opens, as shown in Figure 6-7.

FIGURE 6-7 Saving for offline use.

Note that this is a very early version of the dialog box, and its appearance might change before the final release of Silverlight.

The Microsoft Silverlight – Saving for Offline Use dialog box contains options to save your application for offline use on the Start menu or desktop. In Figure 6-7, you can see that the option to save a shortcut on the Start menu is selected. Click OK to allow the application to be saved, or click Cancel to disallow it.

When you click OK, shortcut icons are saved to your desktop and/or Start menu (depending on what you selected) and the application will open in its own window, as shown in Figure 6-8.

FIGURE 6-8 Application running in its own window.

Note that when you right-click this application the Remove This Application option is available. The Remove This Application option removes the application from wherever you installed it.

These examples show the application with the default icons that Silverlight provides. You can override these by using PNG files that represent four different sizes of icon. So, you need to provide a 16 × 16, a 32 × 32, a 64 × 64, and a 128 × 128 PNG file that represents the desired icons.

You need to add a definition to the application manifest that defines these sizes and file locations and sets the *Icons Build Action* in Visual Studio to *Content*.

Here's the application manifest:

```
<Deployment xmlns="http://schemas.microsoft.com/client/2007/deployment"
        xmlns:x="http://schemas.microsoft.com/winfx/2006/xaml"
            EntryPointAssembly="SLOOB"
            EntryPointType="SLOOB.App">

    <Deployment.Parts>
    </Deployment.Parts>
  <Deployment.ApplicationIdentity>
```

```
    <ApplicationIdentity ShortName="My Cool App's Short Name"
                         Title="My Cool App's Title">

      <ApplicationIdentity.Blurb>
        Do really cool stuff at home or on the go.
      </ApplicationIdentity.Blurb>
      <ApplicationIdentity.Icons>
        <Icon Size="16x16">sl16.png</Icon>
        <Icon Size="32x32">sl32.png</Icon>
        <Icon Size="64x64">sl64.png</Icon>
        <Icon Size="128x128">sl128.png</Icon>
      </ApplicationIdentity.Icons>
    </ApplicationIdentity>

  </Deployment.ApplicationIdentity>
</Deployment>
```

So now, when you run the application and save it for offline use, it will use your icon!

Summary

This chapter tours what can be done with the Silverlight object. You started by looking at the plumbing of the object itself, how to host it on a page, and how to use the various parameters that it exposes. Then, you saw how, using JavaScript, you can build a nice customized install UX through the fallbacks to the browser offered by the *<object>* tag. Finally, you saw how the Silverlight object can be executed outside of the browser to provide desktop applications. In the next chapter, you'll see the browser bridge functionality that complements what you've learned in this chapter and how Silverlight is a first-class browser citizen.

Part II

Programming Silverlight 3 with .NET

Chapter 7
The Silverlight Browser Bridge

We stand at a crossroads in Web development. A wide chasm is open before us, with different camps evangelizing different philosophies about how you should develop for the Web. On one side, a camp says that the unenhanced browser is enough. You can do everything you want to do with clever JavaScript, Dynamic HTML, cascading style sheets, and AJAX. The other side preaches the fact that the browser was designed to render *documents* and not *applications*; to build applications that meet increasingly sophisticated user experience requirements, to rely on the browser alone is to build a house of cards.

But there's a happy medium between the two when you use Microsoft Silverlight. Silverlight provides a bridge across this chasm so that you can choose which philosophy to use. You might have already invested significant time and effort in building JavaScript-based APIs and don't want to throw them away to start again, but perhaps you are tempted by the performance improvements and richness that Silverlight offers. Well, fear not! Silverlight includes a "browser bridge" that makes it a first-class browser citizen. When using the browser bridge, the following are possible:

- Any code that is compiled into a Microsoft .NET Framework assembly can be exposed to the browser and called from JavaScript.

- Any JavaScript code in the browser can be accessed from within the .NET assembly and called from in your Silverlight application.

- Your Extensible Application Markup Language (XAML) render tree is exposed to the browser. From JavaScript, you can create XAML elements and add them to the render tree, delete existing items in the render tree, or edit existing items in the render tree.

This chapter looks at how you can work in each of these scenarios. You'll look at the Microsoft Virtual Earth API, which is JavaScript-based, and see just how easy it is to interact with the JavaScript functions in Virtual Earth.

Creating the Base Application

Before you begin, you need a simple application that exposes its functionality to and from the browser using the bridge.

In this section, you build a simple Silverlight application, and then explore the hooks that allow it to be used from JavaScript.

First, build the framework for the .NET application. It will render data for three different cities for each of three different European countries.

Use Microsoft Visual Studio to create a new Silverlight solution and call it Sample1. Make sure that you select the option to add a Web project to the solution.

Creating the Data Class

Start with a class that represents this data. Add a new class called *CityData* to your Silverlight project.

You can see the code for this class here:

```
public class CityData

{

    public string CityName { get; set; }
    public double Latitude{get;set;}
    public double Longitude{get;set;}

    public CityData(string strCityName, double nLatitude, double nLongitude)
    {
        CityName = strCityName;
        Latitude = nLatitude;
        Longitude = nLongitude;
    }
}
```

As you can see, *CityData* is a very straightforward class that contains a string and two doubles for the city name, latitude, and longitude, respectively.

Creating the Data in Silverlight

This Silverlight application uses the *CityData* class to store data for three cities. In a real scenario, this data would be stored in the cloud, but for the sake of simplicity you can store the data directly in the application.

Here is a function that returns city data for the country that is passed into it:

```
private List<CityData> getCities(string strCountry)
    {
        List<CityData> ret = new List<CityData>();

        switch (strCountry)
        {
            case "france":
                {
                    ret.Add(new CityData("Paris", 48.87, 2.33));
                    ret.Add(new CityData("Lourdes", 43.1, 0.05));
```

```
                        ret.Add(new CityData("Toulouse", 43.6, 1.38));
                        break;
                    }
                case "uk":
                    {
                        ret.Add(new CityData("London", 51.5, 0));
                        ret.Add(new CityData("Stratford-Upon-Avon", 52.3, -1.71));
                        ret.Add(new CityData("Edinburgh", 55.95, -3.16));
                        break;
                    }
                case "germany":
                    {
                        ret.Add(new CityData("Berlin", 52.52, 13.42));
                        ret.Add(new CityData("Munich", 48.13, 11.57));
                        ret.Add(new CityData("Hamburg", 53.58, 9.98));
                        break;
                    }
            }
            return ret;
    }
```

The function is quite straightforward, returning a *List<CityData>* that is built in the function. This *List<>* is built by creating new instances of the aforementioned *CityData* class, with the name, latitude, and longitude passed in as the constructor.

Rendering the Data with an *ItemsControl*

Now, look at how you can use this data. Because you are using a *List<>* to represent the data, you can take advantage of the data binding functionality in Silverlight. With the *ItemsControl* control, you can specify in XAML how you want the data to appear and have Silverlight automatically populate the *ItemsControl* with the correct number of items. Item contents are generated from the data according to a specified template.

```xml
<UserControl x:Class="Sample1.Page"
    xmlns="http://schemas.microsoft.com/winfx/2006/xaml/presentation"
    xmlns:x="http://schemas.microsoft.com/winfx/2006/xaml"
    Width="400" Height="300">
    <Grid x:Name="LayoutRoot" Background="White">
        <ItemsControl x:Name="itmCities">
            <ItemsControl.ItemTemplate>
                <DataTemplate>
                        <TextBlock FontSize="14" Height="30"
                            Text="{Binding CityName}" ></TextBlock>
                </DataTemplate>
            </ItemsControl.ItemTemplate>
        </ItemsControl>
    </Grid>
</UserControl>
```

If you're not familiar with the syntax, you'll see more on data binding in Chapter 13, "Data Binding in Silverlight," but for now think of it this way: The *ItemsControl* is a dumb control that just draws data the way that you want it to. You define the items using the *ItemTemplate*, and because you are binding to data, this *ItemTemplate* is a *DataTemplate*.

The *DataTemplate* in Silverlight is very powerful. It defines *what* the data you want is and *how* you want to present it.

The preceding code example specifies that you want to render the data using a *TextBlock* with *FontSize="14"*. The *{Binding CityName}* in the *Text* field denotes that you want to bind to the data and extract the *CityName* field from it to populate this *TextBlock*.

Putting It All Together

The next step is to get the data. You wrote the preceding function that generates the data, and here you can see how to ask Silverlight to render it.

Following is a function that creates the data for a country, loads it into a *List<CityData>*, and binds it to the *ItemsControl*:

```
private void upDateCities(string strCountry)
{
    List<CityData> myCities = getCities(strCountry);
    itmCities.ItemsSource = myCities;
}
```

Now all we have to do is call this. Let's add code to call it and pass it the country 'uk' in the Page() constructor.

```
public Page()
{
    InitializeComponent();
    upDateCities("uk");
}
```

Now the application is ready to go. Execute it and see what results. You should see something like the result shown in Figure 7-1.

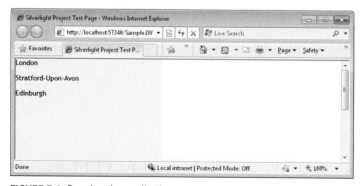

FIGURE 7-1 Running the application.

Even though it doesn't look like much, fear not! This is the basis for what you are going to build. Remember the *upDateCities* function? It was called from the page constructor and was passed the value *uk* to get these cities in the United Kingdom. In the next section, you open this function to JavaScript so that the JavaScript code can change the state of the Silverlight page.

Controlling the Application with JavaScript

This section builds on the example that you created in the previous section. You add some HTML and JavaScript to the application and add the hooks to the Silverlight application that allow the JavaScript code to manipulate it.

Editing the Hosting Page

When you created the Silverlight application, you added a Web application to the solution. This solution contains a test ASP.NET page (called Sample1TestPage.aspx if you followed the naming suggestion) and a test HTML page (similarly, called Sample1TestPage.html).

Right-click the Sample1TestPage.html page in Solution Explorer, and click Set As Start Page on the shortcut menu. This ensures that when you run the application, this page will be the default page that renders.

Next, open the page for editing. At the bottom of the page, you can see a *<div>* called *silverlightControlHost*. This contains the *<object>* tag that defines the Silverlight content. Right now, the Silverlight object doesn't have an ID, so add an *id="slControl"* attribute to the object tag, and name it *slControl*.

Toward the bottom of the page you can see an *<iframe>* before the closing *</div>*.

Add the following code to create HTML buttons on the page:

```
<div style="position: absolute; width: 400px; height: 76px;  left: 0px; top: 200px"
id="JSLayer">
  <input id="bUK" type="button" value="uk"
         onclick="doCities('uk');" />
  <input id="bGermany" type="button" value="germany"
         onclick="doCities('germany');"/>
  <input id="bFrance" type="button" value="france"
         onclick="doCities('france');" />
</div>
```

Before you run the page, you need to make one more change. The cascading style sheets code at the top of the page specifies that the Silverlight content should take up 100 percent of the screen. You must change the content size to be smaller so that you can see the HTML content; otherwise, Silverlight will overwrite all of it.

Change the cascading style sheets code that specifies the height of the Silverlight control to look like this:

```
#silverlightControlHost {
        height: 100px;
}
```

Now, when you execute the application and the HTML page loads, you'll see something like the result shown in Figure 7-2.

FIGURE 7-2 Adding HTML to the application.

Writing the JavaScript

Perhaps you tried clicking one of the buttons. If so, this triggered a JavaScript error because when you added the buttons you specified that the JavaScript function *doCities* should execute. The *doCities* function hasn't been written yet, so you can add it now:

```
function doCities(country)
{
  var slPlugin = document.getElementById("slControl");
  slPlugin.content.MySilverlightObject.upDateCities(country);
}
```

The *doCities* function uses the HTML Document Object Model (DOM) to get a reference to the Silverlight plug-in. It then calls the *upDateCities* function that you created in .NET in Silverlight to change the state of the Silverlight application and render the new cities.

But wait—it doesn't work. Not yet, anyway, because you must still specify to Silverlight which functions to expose and how to expose them. So, switch back to the Silverlight application.

You must do two things to get the application to work with the browser bridge.

Making Silverlight Scriptable

First, register the Silverlight object with the page as a scriptable object. This gives the browser bridge permission to access functions in Silverlight. Usually, you do this when the Silverlight application first loads. Add a *Page_Loaded* event handler like this:

```
void Page_Loaded(object sender, RoutedEventArgs e)
{
    HtmlPage.RegisterScriptableObject("MySilverlightObject", this);
}
```

This isn't an event handler until you wire it up. In the *Page()* constructor, add the wire-up. Here's the full constructor:

```
public Page()
{
    InitializeComponent();
    this.Loaded += new RoutedEventHandler(Page_Loaded);
    upDateCities("uk");
}
```

Make sure that you include a reference to *System.Windows.Browser* at the top of your code page like this:

```
using System.Windows.Browser;
```

Now when the page is loaded, it registers itself with the browser bridge.

There's one more change to make to open the .NET code to JavaScript: You must attribute the functions that you want to allow access to by using the *[ScriptableMember]* attribute. This protects your code from unwanted JavaScript probing.

You want to expose the *upDateCities* function, so attribute it like this:

```
[ScriptableMember]
public void upDateCities(string strCountry)
{
    myCities = getCities(strCountry);
    _cities.ItemsSource = myCities;
}
```

Note that any functions that are attributed as scriptable like this should be *public* functions. Now your app is fully ready to be called from JavaScript. The JavaScript function that calls this is

```
slPlugin.content.MySilverlightObject.upDateCities(country);
```

The Silverlight control exposes its content through the *<control>.content collection*. You registered the scriptable object using the name *MySilverlightObject*, so that is why it is present and its exposed methods are available to call on it. You can simply call it from here.

Putting It All Together

Now when you execute the application, clicking the buttons sends the name of the country to Silverlight. This is then used to build the *List<CityData>* to which the user interface is bound. This binding then draws the new cities on the Silverlight surface.

You can see this in action in Figure 7-3, where Germany has been selected.

Not too difficult, right? You've just opened up your Silverlight application to be manipulated from within the browser. As such, you can see that you can enhance your existing sites and JavaScript code with the rich rendering layer that Silverlight provides.

Not only is your *code* accessible to Silverlight, but the XAML that Silverlight renders (using its render tree) can be directly modified from outside your Silverlight application. You examine this in the next section.

FIGURE 7-3 Changing the Silverlight content using JavaScript.

Manipulating the Silverlight Render Tree

In the previous section, you saw how you could expose your .NET code so that your functions could be called from JavaScript residing on the hosting page. In addition to this, you can use JavaScript to edit the Silverlight render tree by adding, removing, or editing the XAML.

This section discusses what is involved in manipulating the render tree. In this section, you also add the following functionality: When the user clicks a country button and the country label does not exist, your Silverlight application will create a new country label.

When the country label is created, the user interface (UI) needs to change to allow it. In this case, the data needs to move downward to make room for the new label.

If the country label already exists when the user clicks one of the buttons, you can edit the label using the contents of the country. You can see how this would appear in Figure 7-4.

FIGURE 7-4 Manipulating the XAML tree.

The code that handles the button click is the *doCities* function, shown again here for your convenience:

```
function doCities(country)
{
  var slPlugin = document.getElementById("slControl");
  slPlugin.content.MySilverlightObject.upDateCities(country);
}
```

As you can see, the first line gets a reference to the Silverlight control and loads it into the *slPlugin* var.

In Figure 7-4, you can see that there's a large headline at the top of the screen. This label is rendered by an XAML element called *titleText*, so the first thing you need to do is see whether this label exists. If it does, simply edit it using the name of the country in question.

You can do this with the *findName* method of the Silverlight control. Here's the code:

```
var titleExists = slPlugin.content.findName("titleText");
if (titleExists) {
    slPlugin.content.findName("titleText").Text = country;
}
```

Now, of course, the *titleText* might not actually exist yet (it won't when you first run the application). Look back at the XAML that defines the user interface, and you'll see there is no *TextBlock* with the name *titleText*. You have to add an *else* clause to the preceding *if* and use it to create the *TextBlock*.

Let's look, line by line, at how this is done.

The steps to creating an XAML element are simple. First, you create a JavaScript *var* containing a string that defines the XAML. Then, you create an XAML element from this on the Silverlight control. Finally, you add or insert the XAML element into the render tree.

Here is step 1, creating the XAML:

```
var xamlFragment = '<TextBlock FontSize="20" Foreground="Blue">' + country + '</TextBlock>';
```

This XAML isn't named, and you want to call it *titleText*, so there's a little more you need to add. As you might remember, naming an element in XAML uses the *x:Name* syntax, which uses a namespace. So, not only do you have to add the tag, you also need to add the namespace declaration, like this:

```
var xamlFragment = '<TextBlock
    xmlns:x="http://schemas.microsoft.com/winfx/2006/xaml"
    x:Name="titleText" FontSize="20" Foreground="Blue">' + country + '</TextBlock>';
```

Step 2 involves creating an XAML element from this string in the Silverlight control. You can do this by using the *createFromXaml* method. Here's how:

```
var tb = slPlugin.content.createFromXaml(xamlFragment, false);
```

This does not *render* the XAML, it just creates the objects and allows Silverlight to render them. For them to be rendered, you must add or insert them into the render tree, which is step 3.

To add or insert an object into the render tree, you need to be aware of a few things. First, know *where* you want to add the content. You have to add it as a child of a current element, so first you need to know which element you want to make the object a child of. If you use the *Add* method, the content will be added as the last child of the element. If you use the *Insert* method, the content will be added at a specified position.

The XAML for this application has a *<Grid>* with *LayoutRoot* as its root element. Place the new content in the root element. You can make it the first child so that it can be written above the existing content.

Here's the code:

```
slPlugin.content.findName("LayoutRoot").children.insert(0, tb);
```

Now put it all together to see how it looks:

```
<script type="text/javascript">
    function doCities(country) {
        var slPlugin = document.getElementById("slControl");
        var titleExists = slPlugin.content.findName("titleText");
        if (titleExists) {
            slPlugin.content.findName("titleText").Text = country;
        }
        else {
            var xamlFragment = '<TextBlock
              xmlns:x="http://schemas.microsoft.com/winfx/2006/xaml"
              x:Name="titleText" FontSize="20"
              Foreground="Blue">' + country + '</TextBlock>';
            var tb = slPlugin.content.createFromXaml(xamlFragment, false);
            slPlugin.content.findName("LayoutRoot").children.insert(0, tb);

        }

        slPlugin.content.MySilverlightObject.upDateCities(country);
    }
</script>
```

When you run the application, you might expect to see something like what was shown previously in Figure 7-4. Well, give it a try. You can see the actual results in Figure 7-5.

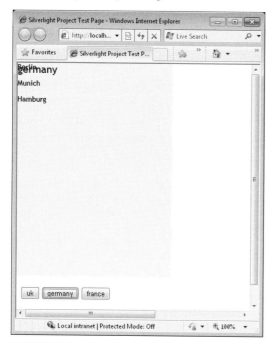

FIGURE 7-5 Running the new application.

As you can see in Figure 7-5, the new title block has been written over the text despite the fact that you placed it above the content by inserting it at position 0. Why is it written like this? The reason is that the content wasn't positioned automatically because it is rendered in a *<Grid>*. If the container was one that provided automatic layout, for example, a *<StackPanel>*, the title block would render properly. But the container does not provide layout.

The content is presented using an *<ItemsControl>* called *itmCities*. This is a child of the *Grid*, and you can position content in the grid by using the *Margin* property.

Following is the JavaScript code to set the *Margin* property and push the content down the screen by a few pixels:

```
slPlugin.content.findName("itmCities").SetValue("Margin", "0,22,0,0");
```

Put this code at the bottom of the *else* clause in the JavaScript so that it is executed only once—when you create the title.

Now when you run the application, you see what is shown in Figure 7-6, which is the desired effect.

FIGURE 7-6 Running the application.

Although this might seem to be a lot of work to do something simple, think about the implications of what you've just done: You radically altered the functionality and display of the running Silverlight application without recompiling the code. You did this by using external JavaScript code and the browser bridge!

In the next section, you see what it takes to allow your JavaScript code and HTML content to be manipulated from within your .NET code in Silverlight.

Accessing JavaScript Functions from .NET

This section closes the loop on what you've been looking at thus far. You can see how you can use .NET code to interact with JavaScript functions on your page. This is particularly useful because there are many JavaScript APIs out there, and you don't need to rewrite them in Silverlight to use them.

For example, the Microsoft Virtual Earth platform can be used for building mapping applications. In this section, you will interact with this API.

For this example, continue editing the HTML page. To use Virtual Earth, do the following to your page.

First, add a *<div>* to the page that will contain the map.

Look for the *<div>* called *errorLocation* on your page, and place the new *<div>* immediately beneath it (and above the *<div>* containing the *<object>* tag):

```
<div id='mapDIV' style="position: absolute; width: 443px; height: 417px; z-index: 2; left:
301px; top: 0px"></div>
```

Next, add a reference to the JavaScript libraries for Virtual Earth. You can add these anywhere in the *<head>* section of the page:

```
<script type="text/javascript"
src="http://dev.virtualearth.net/mapcontrol/mapcontrol.ashx?v=6.2"></script>
```

Then, write a JavaScript function that loads the *Map* control into the *div* you created. Here's the code:

```
var map = null;

function GetMap()
{
    map = new VEMap('mapDIV');
    map.LoadMap();
}
```

This code defines a *map var* that will be shared across this and another JavaScript function (which you'll see in a moment). The *GetMap()* then creates a new *VEMap* object (representing a Virtual Earth map) in the *div* that you created earlier and loads it.

Finally, call the *GetMap* when the page loads. Amend the *<Body>* tag to call *GetMap* by specifying its *OnLoad* behavior:

```
<body onload="GetMap();">
```

When you execute this page, you see the default map loaded in place, as shown in Figure 7-7.

For the .NET code to be able to manipulate this map, you next need to add a JavaScript function that finds the required location and moves the map to that location. This function can be called from other JavaScript or .NET.

Here's the function:

```
function MoveMap(where) {
    try {
        map.Find(null, where);
    }
    catch (e) {
        alert(e.message);
    }

}
```

FIGURE 7-7 Integrating the Virtual Earth map.

The *map* var was created earlier when the Virtual Earth map was loaded. This function simply uses its *Find* API and passes it a string called *where*. As you can see, *where* is a parameter to this function, so if you were to call it like this:

```
MoveMap("London,England");
```

the map would move to the specified location.

In the final step, look at the .NET code that implements the functionality of moving the map to the specified location when the user clicks one of the locations.

The first step is to make the data points clickable. Remember that when you defined the XAML earlier you used an *<ItemsControl>* to host the data. The control has a *<DataTemplate>* template that defines how the data will appear, and this template contains a simple *<TextBlock>* for each control. All you have to do to make *each* item clickable is to make the *<TextBlock>* in the *<DataTemplate>* clickable. You can do this by wiring up its *MouseLeftButtonUp* event:

```
<ItemsControl x:Name="itmCities">
    <ItemsControl.ItemTemplate>
        <DataTemplate>
            <TextBlock FontSize="14" Height="30"
                Text="{Binding CityName}"
                MouseLeftButtonUp="TextBlock_MouseLeftButtonUp" >
            </TextBlock>
        </DataTemplate>
```

```
            </ItemsControl.ItemTemplate>
        </ItemsControl>
```

Now, whenever the user clicks *any TextBlock*, the function *TextBlock_MouseLeftButtonUp* fires.

This function must derive the city and country, build a string containing them, and use the browser bridge to call the JavaScript *MoveMap* function to update the map location.

First, create two strings to contain the city and country:

```
        String strCity = "";
        String strCountry = "";
```

Event handlers in Silverlight have an object that raises the event as their first parameter. To get the city, simply cast this to a *TextBlock* and take its text parameter:

```
        TextBlock clickedText = sender as TextBlock;
        strCity = clickedText.Text;
```

The country is a little more tricky because the *TextBlock* containing it is added to the render tree at run time. (See the previous section for more details.) To find the country in the render tree, use this code:

```
TextBlock title = this.FindName("titleText") as TextBlock;
```

There's no guarantee that the country exists in the render tree because it is added only when a user first clicks a country button. You must check to see whether the title text is *null* before you derive the country from it, or else you might generate a run-time error.

```
        if (title != null)
        {
            strCountry = title.Text;
        }
```

When you have the city and country, build a string from them:

```
string toFind = strCity + "," + strCountry;
```

Here is where the magic takes place. You must pass the string out through the browser bridge to the JavaScript function and invoke the function.

With the *HtmlPage* collection in .NET, you can find the JavaScript function as a property of the page. Because it is script, you need to cast this into a script object. Here's the code:

```
ScriptObject sMoveMap = (ScriptObject)HtmlPage.Window.GetProperty("MoveMap");
```

Now, all that you have to do is run the script and pass it the string *toFind*. You can do this by using the *InvokeSelf* method of the *ScriptObject*:

```
sMoveMap.InvokeSelf(toFind);
```

Here is a look at the full event handler:

```
private void TextBlock_MouseLeftButtonUp(object sender, MouseButtonEventArgs e)
{
  String strCity = "";
  String strCountry = "";
  TextBlock clickedText = sender as TextBlock;
  strCity = clickedText.Text;

  TextBlock title = this.FindName("titleText") as TextBlock;
  if (title != null)
  {
    strCountry = title.Text;
  }

  string toFind = strCity + "," + strCountry;

ScriptObject sMoveMap = (ScriptObject)HtmlPage.Window.GetProperty("MoveMap");
  sMoveMap.InvokeSelf(toFind);
}
```

That's all you need to call your JavaScript functions from within .NET.

In Figure 7-8, you can see the results of clicking Hamburg, Germany, and in Figure 7-9, clicking Paris, France.

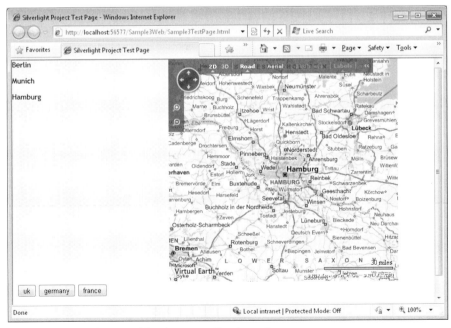

FIGURE 7-8 Using the UI to drive the map to Hamburg, Germany.

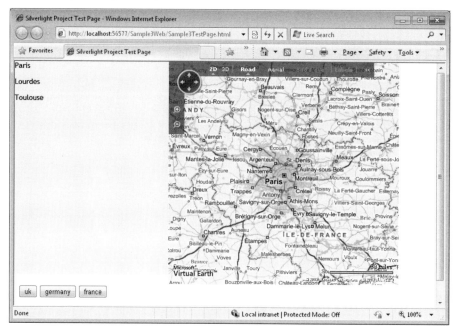

FIGURE 7-9 Using the UI to drive the map to Paris, France.

This is just a brief look at the power of the browser bridge. The browser bridge exemplifies the flexibility and power of Silverlight and how Silverlight is a first-class browser citizen!

Summary

The Silverlight browser bridge is a great piece of technology that you can use to integrate Silverlight into your existing Web applications. It has a variety of functions. You can use it to call .NET code and use .NET code from JavaScript, amend your visual rendering in Silverlight from within an HTML page, and call existing functionality in JavaScript from .NET code.

In this chapter, you built, step by step, an example application that follows the scenario of someone who has already invested in JavaScript APIs, namely the Microsoft Virtual Earth APIs. This example shows how you could add Silverlight content to an application that uses these APIs. In the next chapter, you switch gears and look at some of the core XAML controls available in Silverlight.

Chapter 8
Silverlight Core Controls

The *System.Windows* namespace contains a number of core controls that are at the heart of every Microsoft Silverlight application. This chapter introduces the following core controls, and you will learn how you can use them in Silverlight:

- *Button*
- *CheckBox*
- *ComboBox*
- *HyperlinkButton*
- *Image*
- *ListBox*
- *RadioButton*
- *TextBlock*
- *TextBox* and *PasswordBox*

This chapter looks at the specific properties, methods, and events that each control exposes, as well as the general ones that are shared across all controls. The information in this chapter is not intended to be an exclusive reference for everything associated with each control, but it should contain more than enough basics to get you started and make it easier for you to experiment with these controls on your own.

The *Button* Control

In Silverlight, you implement a push button using the *Button* control. A button reacts to user input from input devices such as the mouse, keyboard, or stylus, raising a *Click* event when it does so. A button raises the *Click* event in several configurable ways. You set these using the *ClickMode* property, which can contain the values of *Hover*, *Press*, and *Release*. These values determine when the *Click* event is raised. In the first case, *Hover*, the *Click* event is raised when the mouse pointer hovers over the button. In the second, *Press*, the *Click* event is raised when the mouse button is held down while the pointer is over the button. In the third, *Release*, the *Click* event is raised when the user presses *and* releases the mouse button while the pointer is over the button.

```
<Canvas x:Name="LayoutRoot" Background="White">
  <Button x:Name="b1" ClickMode="Hover"
      Content="Button1" Click="Button_Click"></Button>
  <Button x:Name="b2" Canvas.Top="40" ClickMode="Press"
      Content="Button2" Click="Button_Click"></Button>
  <Button x:Name="b3" Canvas.Top="80" ClickMode="Release"
      Content="Button3" Click="Button_Click"></Button>
</Canvas>
```

You can see that the *Click* event handler has been defined on these buttons and that the same function, *Button_Click*, is defined for each.

Here is the code that handles the event:

```
private void Button_Click(object sender, RoutedEventArgs e)
{
  Button b = (Button)sender;
  string strTest = b.Name;
}
```

This code follows a typical event handler pattern. It receives an object sender that contains a reference to the control on which the event was raised, in this case one of the buttons, and a set of arguments associated with the event (*RoutedEventArgs*) that contains metadata about the event.

Notice that only one event handler is declared in this instance. This is particularly useful in keeping your code tidy. You will, of course, want to figure out which item raised the event, and that's where the sender comes in.

The sender is of type *Object*, so to figure out some of the button-specific properties, you simply cast it to a *Button*. In this case, you can see that it is cast to a *Button*, and from there the name can be derived. If you run the application now, you'll see three buttons, and you'll see how the *ClickMode* property associated with each button causes it to behave differently!

An additional, useful property is *IsEnabled*. When *IsEnabled* is set to *false*, the button is still rendered, but it appears unavailable on the screen and does not raise any events.

You set the label on a button using the *Content* property, which you can set to some simple text to create a caption for the button. However, *Button* is also a container control, so you can customize the content of your button using Extensible Application Markup Language (XAML).

Here's an example of a (very ugly) button that contains XAML as its content:

```
<Button x:Name="b1" Click="Button_Click" Width="100" Height="100">
  <Canvas>
    <Ellipse Fill="Green" Width="50" Height="50"></Ellipse>
    <TextBlock Text="Hello"></TextBlock>
  </Canvas>
</Button>
```

As you can see, the *Button* control gives you great flexibility in how your button is presented, so you can easily put together rich buttons—similar to those on the Microsoft Office 2007 ribbon—in your Web applications.

The *CheckBox* Control

The *CheckBox* control presents the user a selectable option that typically takes the form of a box that the user can select or clear. You use a *CheckBox* control when you want to present a set of options to the user and allow the user to select more than one option simultaneously.

A *CheckBox* raises the *Checked* event when it is selected, the *Unchecked* event when it is cleared, and the *Click* event whenever it is clicked. Similar to the *Button* control, *CheckBox* has a *ClickMode* property that you can set to *Hover, Press,* or *Release,* which configures it to raise the event in different circumstances.

The *CheckBox* can also be a three-state check box with an indeterminate state between selected and cleared. You turn this on or off using the *IsThreeState* property. When you are in this mode, if the user puts the check box into the indeterminate state, the *IsChecked* property will be *null.*

You can get the value of the *CheckBox* using the *IsChecked* property. Be careful when using *IsChecked* if you are using the *CheckBox* in the three-state mode because the *IsChecked* property value will be *null* when the *CheckBox* is in the indeterminate state.

Similar to the *Button* control, the *CheckBox* is a *Content* container, so you can use the *Content* property to hold a simple text string as the caption for a check box in your application, or you can use XAML in the *<Content>* child tag to get something richer.

Following is an example that shows each type of text:

```
<StackPanel>
  <CheckBox Checked="CheckBox_Checked"
      Unchecked="CheckBox_Unchecked"
      IsThreeState="True" Content="Test1">
  </CheckBox>
  <CheckBox Checked="CheckBox_Checked"
      Unchecked="CheckBox_Unchecked"
      IsThreeState="True">
    <CheckBox.Content>
      <StackPanel Orientation="Horizontal">
        <TextBlock Text="The Caption"></TextBlock>
        <Image Source="..."/>

      </StackPanel>
    </CheckBox.Content>
  </CheckBox>
</StackPanel>
```

When handling the *Clicked, Checked*, and *Unchecked* events, the *sender* will be an object that you should cast to the *CheckBox* type to access the properties.

Here's an example:

```
private void CheckBox_Checked(object sender, RoutedEventArgs e)
{
  CheckBox c = (CheckBox)sender;
  bool b = (bool)c.IsChecked;
}

private void CheckBox_Unchecked(object sender, RoutedEventArgs e)
{
  CheckBox c = (CheckBox)sender;
  bool b = (bool)c.IsChecked;
}
```

The *ComboBox* Control

You can use the *ComboBox* control to present a list of selectable items where only one item at a time is visible and a drop-down menu allows the user to open the list of selectable items, select an item, and continue.

The list is made up of *ComboBoxItem* objects, as in this example:

```
<ComboBox>
  <ComboBoxItem>
    <TextBlock Text="Item1"></TextBlock>
  </ComboBoxItem>
  <ComboBoxItem>
    <TextBlock Text="Item2"></TextBlock>
  </ComboBoxItem>
  <ComboBoxItem>
    <TextBlock Text="Item3"></TextBlock>
  </ComboBoxItem>
 </ComboBox>
```

You can manage the user's selection of the items that make up the *ComboBox* using the *SelectionChanged* event and the *SelectedItem* property.

These events are declared on the *<ComboBox>* and not its items, so you use *SelectionChanged* like this:

```
<ComboBox SelectionChanged="ComboBox_SelectionChanged">
  ...
</ComboBox>
```

This declares an event handler for the change of selection called *ListBox_SelectionChanged*. You handle this event by casting the *SelectedItem* to the appropriate type and then reading its properties. In the preceding case, the items in the *ComboBox* contained *TextBlock* controls, so you can derive their contents like this:

```
private void ComboBox_SelectionChanged(object sender, SelectionChangedEventArgs e)
{
  ComboBox theBox = sender as ComboBox;
  ComboBoxItem theItem = theBox.SelectedItem as ComboBoxItem;
  TextBlock theTextBlock = theItem.Content as TextBlock;
}
```

Note that the *SelectedItem* from the *ComboBox* returns an *object* and not a *ComboBoxItem* because the *ComboBox* can host many different types of content in the *ComboBoxItem*. In this case, you cast the *SelectedItem* to a *ComboBoxItem* to use it.

You can see a demonstration of how the *ComboBox* can contain different types of items. Following is an example in which the *ComboBox* contains compound items made up of *StackPanel* components each containing a *Rectangle*, an *Image*, and a *TextBlock*:

```
<ComboBox x:Name="theList" SelectionChanged="theList_SelectionChanged">
  <ComboBoxItem>
    <StackPanel Orientation="Horizontal">
      <Rectangle Fill="Black" Height="100" Width="100"></Rectangle>
      <Image Height="100" Width="100" Source="sl.jpg"/>
      <TextBlock Text="Item 1"></TextBlock>
    </StackPanel>
  </ComboBoxItem>
  <ComboBoxItem>
    <StackPanel Orientation="Horizontal">
      <Rectangle Fill="Black" Height="100" Width="100"></Rectangle>
      <Image Height="100" Width="100" Source="sl.jpg"/>
      <TextBlock Text="Item 2"></TextBlock>
    </StackPanel>
  </ComboBoxItem>
</ComboBox>
```

This code renders the items on the *ComboBox* as richer content (a rectangle, an image, and a text block), and you can capture the content you want in the event handler by casting the appropriate child to the appropriate value. Here's an example:

```
ComboBoxItem item = theList.SelectedItem as ComboBoxItem;
StackPanel s = item.Content as StackPanel;
TextBlock t = s.Children[2] as TextBlock;
string strValue = t.Text;
```

Note that in this example, the *ComboBox* is named *theList*, so you don't need to cast from the *sender* parameter.

You see another example similar to this one that also shows how Silverlight content controls can render flexible content in the section titled "The *ListBox* Control" later in this chapter.

The *HyperlinkButton* Control

The *HyperlinkButton* provides a clickable element on the page that navigates to a URI specified in the *NavigateUri* property.

Here's an example:

```
<HyperlinkButton Content="Microsoft"
    NavigateUri="http://www.microsoft.com" />
```

The *HyperlinkButton* is a content control, meaning that it can have a simple *Content* property containing text to render for the hyperlink, or it can contain much richer—and more exciting—content.

For example, if you want a hyperlink button that appears as an image, it's very easy to do using the *<Hyperlink.Content>* child, which can contain an image. Here's an example:

```
<HyperlinkButton NavigateUri="http://www.silverlight.net" >
  <HyperlinkButton.Content>
    <Image Source="sl.jpg"/>
  </HyperlinkButton.Content>
</HyperlinkButton>
```

Now when you run the application, you get a clickable image that navigates to the specified URL.

You use the *TargetName* property to specify where the content at the URL will be rendered. The options that you can use to display the URL content include the following:

- **_blank**   Opens a new browser window with no name.

- **_self**   Replaces the current HTML page with the new content. If it is in a frame, it only replaces that frame.

- **_top**   Replaces the current HTML page with the new content. If it is in a frame, the entire browser still has the new content.

- **_parent**   Replaces the entire HTML page.

If you are in a frameset, you can also specify the name of the frame to use.

Here's an example that specifies that a new browser window should open when the user selects the control:

```
<Grid x:Name="LayoutRoot" Background="White">
  <HyperlinkButton NavigateUri="http://www.silverlight.net"
      TargetName="_blank" >
```

```
    <HyperlinkButton.Content>
      <Image Source="sl.jpg"/>
    </HyperlinkButton.Content>
  </HyperlinkButton>
</Grid>
```

Note that the *Click* event for the *HyperlinkButton* fires before the navigation takes place. This can be very useful so that any preprocessing is completed prior to the new content loading.

Here's an example with the *Click* event configured. Notice that the *NavigateUri* is set to *http://www.microsoft.com*, but the page actually navigates to *http://www.silverlight.net* because the *Click* runs before the navigation, and then changes the *NavigateUri*.

First, here is the XAML:

```
<HyperlinkButton NavigateUri="http://www.microsoft.com"
    TargetName="_blank" Click="HyperlinkButton_Click">
  <HyperlinkButton.Content>
    <Image Source="sl.jpg"/>
  </HyperlinkButton.Content>
</HyperlinkButton>
```

And now here is the C# code-behind that handles the *HyperlinkButton_Click* event:

```
private void HyperlinkButton_Click(object sender, RoutedEventArgs e)
{
  HyperlinkButton h = (HyperlinkButton)sender;
  string strTest = h.NavigateUri.AbsoluteUri;
  if (strTest == "http://www.microsoft.com/")
  {
    h.NavigateUri = new Uri("http://www.silverlight.net");
  }
}
```

When you run this code, you see that despite the fact that the *HyperlinkButton* is configured for one URL, this is changed to another URL as part of the *Click* event handler, and the new URL is opened instead.

The *Image* Control

You can use the *Image* control to render an image. It can handle .bmp, .jpg, and .png file formats. You specify the path to the image using the *Source* property. Here's an example:

```
<Image Source="sl.jpg"/>
```

> **Note**　If the code references an invalid format or if the *Source* is improperly set, an *ImageFailed* event is raised.

When the actual image has different dimensions from those that you specify for an *Image* control (that is, if you have a 100 × 100 *Image* element that loads a 2000 × 2000-pixel .jpg), you can control the rendering behavior using the *Stretch* property. *Stretch* takes the following values:

- **Fill**   Scales the image to fit the output dimensions using independent scaling on the x- and y-axes

- **Uniform**   Scales the underlying image to fit the dimensions of the Image control, but leaves the aspect ratio untouched

- **UniformToFill**   Scales the image to completely fill the output area, clipping it where necessary

- **None**   Renders the image completely untouched, causing clipping if the underlying image is larger than the Image element

Many times you won't want to set the image at design time, hard coding a URI into the XAML, but will want to set it at run time, perhaps as the result of a database call or something similar. In these instances, you can use the *BitmapImage* class (from the *System.Windows. Media.Imaging* namespace) as the source for the *Image* control. Following is an example of how this works.

First the XAML:

```
<Image x:Name="theImage"/>
```

And here is the code that loads the image from a URL when the page loads:

```
public Page(){
  InitializeComponent();
  this.Loaded += new RoutedEventHandler(Page_Loaded);
}

void Page_Loaded(object sender, RoutedEventArgs e)
{
  Uri uri = new Uri("sl.jpg",UriKind.Relative);
  theImage.Source = new BitmapImage(uri);
}
```

In this case, a new *Uri* object is constructed using the path of the image. The second parameter in the constructor is the option for how the path to the *Uri* should be calculated. The URI referenced here can be relative (in which case the specified resource will be sought in the same directory as the one in which the component resides), absolute (in which case the specified resource will be sought directly, so you should specify the location using syntax such as *http://server/resource*), or a combination of the two.

After the *Uri* is constructed, it can be used to construct a new *BitmapImage*, which is set to the source of the *Image* control.

The *ListBox* Control

You can use the *ListBox* control to present content as an ordered list. The *ListBox* is flexible enough so that you can create list items from any type of content, but the typical list is made up of *ListBoxItem* elements, as shown in the following example:

```
<ListBox x:Name="theList" SelectionChanged="ListBox_SelectionChanged">
  <ListBoxItem Content="1"/>
  <ListBoxItem Content="2"/>
  <ListBoxItem Content="3"/>
  <ListBoxItem Content="4"/>
  <ListBoxItem Content="5"/>
</ListBox>
```

You can manage the user's selection of the items that make up the *ListBox* using the *SelectionChanged* event and the *SelectedItem* property. In the previous XAML, you can see that the *SelectionChanged* event is handled by a method handler called *ListBox_SelectionChanged*. Here's the code:

```
private void ListBox_SelectionChanged(
    object sender, SelectionChangedEventArgs e)
{
  ListBoxItem x = theList.SelectedItem as ListBoxItem;
  string strTest = x.Content.ToString();
}
```

Note that the *SelectedItem* from the *ListBox* returns an *object* and not a *ListBoxItem* because (as mentioned earlier) the *ListBox* can host many different types of content. In this case, you cast the *SelectedItem* to a *ListBoxItem* to use it.

Remember that a *ListBox* can contain different types of items. Following is an example in which the *ListBox* contains compound items made up of *StackPanel* components each containing a *Rectangle*, an *Image*, and a *TextBlock*:

```
<ListBox x:Name="theList" SelectionChanged="ListBox_SelectionChanged">
    <StackPanel Orientation="Horizontal">
        <Rectangle Fill="Black" Height="100" Width="100"></Rectangle>
        <Image Height="100" Width="100" Source="sl.jpg"/>
        <TextBlock Text="Item 1"></TextBlock>
    </StackPanel>
    <StackPanel Orientation="Horizontal">
        <Rectangle Fill="Black" Height="100" Width="100"></Rectangle>
        <Image Height="100" Width="100" Source="sl.jpg"/>
        <TextBlock Text="Item 2"></TextBlock>
    </StackPanel>
</ListBox>
```

You can see how this *ListBox* is rendered in Figure 8-1.

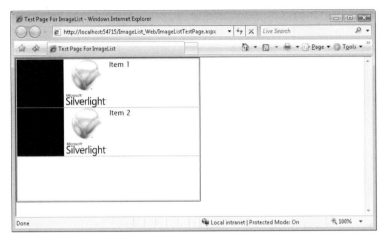

FIGURE 8-1 *ListBox* with complex items.

When you have a complex item like this, you can easily pull the content out by using the *SelectedItem* to get the container (in this case a *StackPanel*), and then derive the content that you want from it. Here's an example:

```
StackPanel s = theList.SelectedItem as StackPanel;
TextBlock t = s.Children[2] as TextBlock;
string strTest = t.Text;
```

The *RadioButton* Control

The *RadioButton* control is similar to the *CheckBox* in that you use it for catching user selections. However, it is different from the *CheckBox* in that you typically use it for situations in which the user makes a *single* selection from a range of options.

One way you can control the range of options that allow a single selection is by setting up the *RadioButton* controls for the options as siblings in a container. Consider this example:

```
<StackPanel Orientation="Vertical" Background="Yellow">
  <RadioButton Content="Option 1" IsChecked="true" ></RadioButton>
  <RadioButton Content="Option 2"></RadioButton>
  <RadioButton Content="Option 3"></RadioButton>
  <RadioButton Content="Option 4"></RadioButton>
  <StackPanel Orientation="Vertical" Background="White">
    <RadioButton Content="Option 5" IsChecked="true"></RadioButton>
    <RadioButton Content="Option 6"></RadioButton>
    <RadioButton Content="Option 7"></RadioButton>
    <RadioButton Content="Option 8"></RadioButton>
  </StackPanel>
</StackPanel>
```

This XAML contains two *StackPanel* containers, one within the other. The first contains options 1, 2, 3, and 4, and the second contains options 5, 6, 7, and 8. As a result, the user can select only one from options 1 through 4 and only one from options 5 through 8. You can see how this works in Figure 8-2.

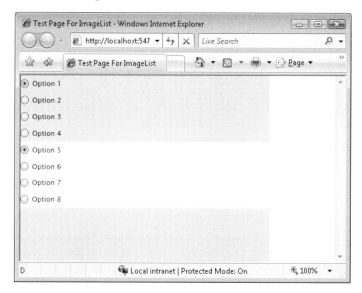

FIGURE 8-2 Using the *RadioButton* control.

Additionally, you can assign a *GroupName* to each *RadioButton* to subdivide the options into logical groups. In the previous example, you had options 1 through 4 in a *StackPanel*, and Silverlight allowed the user of the application to select only one of those four options.

If you wanted to subdivide this set of options into two groups so that the user could select one from options 1 and 2 and one from options 3 and 4, instead of using a container, you can use *RadioButton* groups.

```
<StackPanel Orientation="Vertical" Background="Yellow">
  <RadioButton Content="Option 1" IsChecked="true"
     GroupName="G1" ></RadioButton>
  <RadioButton Content="Option 2" GroupName="G1" />
  <RadioButton Content="Option 3" GroupName="G2" />
  <RadioButton Content="Option 4" GroupName="G2" />
  <RadioButton Content="Option 5" GroupName="G3"
     IsChecked="true" />
  <RadioButton Content="Option 6" GroupName="G3" />
  <RadioButton Content="Option 7" GroupName="G3" />
  <RadioButton Content="Option 8" GroupName="G3" />
</StackPanel>
```

You can see this in action in Figure 8-3.

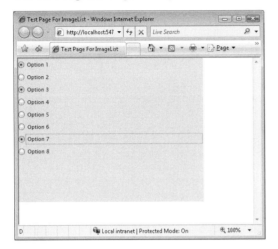

FIGURE 8-3 Using the *RadioButton* control with groups.

Similar to the *Button* and *CheckBox* controls, a *RadioButton* has a *ClickMode* property that determines what type of user interaction causes the *Click* event to be raised. This can be *Hover,* so that just moving the mouse pointer over the selection generates the event; *Press,* which raises the event when the mouse button is pressed down; and *Release,* in which the mouse button must be pressed and then released while the pointer is over the option button to generate the event. Also similar to the *CheckBox* control, you can evaluate the *IsChecked* property for a particular *RadioButton* option to see whether it is set.

The *TextBlock* Control

You can use the *TextBlock* control to render text in Silverlight applications. In its simplest case, you use the *TextBlock* along with its *Text* property to render the text. Here's an example:

```
<TextBlock Text="1234"></TextBlock>
```

You change the size of the rendered text using the *FontSize* property in pixels. You change the font that you are going to use with the *FontFamily* property; for example, if you want to use the Arial Black font at size 20, the XAML would look like this:

```
<TextBlock Text="1234" FontFamily="Arial Black" FontSize="20" />
```

You use the *FontStyle* property to set the text to be either italicized or normal. To use italics, set the property to *Italic* like this:

```
<TextBlock Text="1234" FontFamily="Arial Black"
    FontSize="20" FontStyle="Italic"></TextBlock>
```

To use normal text, you can set it to *Normal* or just leave the *FontStyle* property unset.

You can control line breaking and mixed text using the *<LineBreak>* and *<Run>* subelements of the *TextBlock*. As its name suggests, the *<LineBreak>* creates a break in the text; the text that follows this element sets on a new line.

However, the *TextBlock* is not a content presenter control as are some of the controls that you saw earlier in this chapter, so if you want to continue text beyond the bounds of the original contents of the *Text* property, you must use the *Run* control:

```
<TextBlock Width="400" Text="My first text">
  <LineBreak/>
  <Run>My Second Text</Run>
  <LineBreak/>
  <Run>My Third Text</Run>
  <LineBreak/>
  <Run>My Fourth Text</Run>
</TextBlock>
```

The nice thing about the *Run* control is that it supports the same properties as the *TextBlock* for font, size, color, and so forth, so you have the same level of control over its content as you have with the *TextBlock*, which means there is no disparity between the *TextBlock* text and the text that is displayed using the *Run* control.

Silverlight uses a set of system font fallback rules, so if the font exists on the system, the text is rendered in that font; if the font is not available on the system, a fallback font, defined by the operating system, is used to render the text.

Look at this example of some XAML created to display a *TextBlock* containing Webdings as well as some Chinese and Hebrew text:

```
<StackPanel Orientation="Vertical" Background="Yellow">
    <TextBlock Width="400" Text="My first text">
      <LineBreak/>
      <Run FontFamily="Webdings">My Second Text</Run>
      <LineBreak/>
      <Run>微软助力基础教育</Run>
      <LineBreak/>
      <Run>דיון וקבוצות בישראלקהילות פיתוחזה מרכז</Run>
    </TextBlock>
</StackPanel>
```

You can see how this appears in Figure 8-4. This new feature makes the development of internationalized applications in Silverlight very straightforward.

FIGURE 8-4 Using characters from special fonts in Silverlight.

The *TextBox* Control

You provide an area for your users to enter text using the *TextBox* control. In its simplest form, the *Text Box* control provides an area that the user can fill with a single line of text. Here's an example:

```
<StackPanel>

  <TextBox />
  <TextBox />

</StackPanel>
```

This is very simply a *StackPanel* that contains two *TextBox* controls. Figure 8-5 shows what this code displays, and I have typed some values in the *TextBox* controls to show you how a user would fill them in in an application.

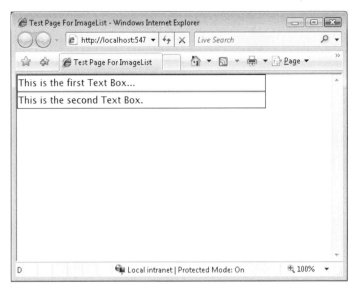

FIGURE 8-5 Simple *TextBox* controls.

To make these *TextBox* controls capable of accepting multiline input, you need to do two things. First, you have to specify a height or place them in a container that gives them the nondefault height. Then, you have to use the *AcceptsReturn* property, set to *True*, to allow them to accept carriage return characters. You can see this in action in Figure 8-6.

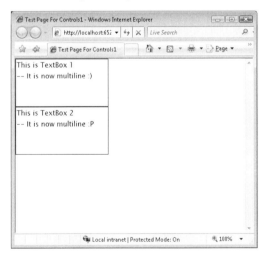

FIGURE 8-6 Amending the *TextBox* controls to accept multiline input from the user.

When you use the *TextBox* like this, the *Text* property returns a string with each line separated by a '\r'.

Whenever the text changes on the *TextBox*, the *TextChanged* event fires. Note that this happens after every keystroke, so if you want to capture all the changes, it might be better to capture the *LostFocus* event and manage the text from there.

Your *TextBox* controls automatically accept Input Method Editor (IME) input for foreign language support. If you have the system keyboards and language support already installed, IME works the same in Silverlight as it does for any HTML control. You can see this in Figure 8-7, where IME languages are actually being mixed in the same *TextBox*—amazing!

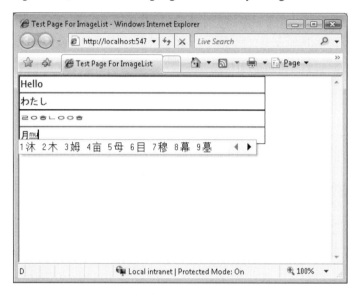

FIGURE 8-7 *TextBox* control with international text input.

In this case, the *Text* property returns a Unicode-encoded string that contains all the characters with '\r' denoting the line separators.

With *TextBox* controls, you can select ranges of *Text*, and you can also configure how the selection appears. You use the *SelectedText* property to set or get the text in the current selection. You can read the start of the current selection with *SelectionStart* and the length with *SelectionEnd*. Whenever the selection changes, the *SelectionChanged* event fires. Take a look at the following example.

First, here is the XAML:

```
<TextBox Height="100" AcceptsReturn="True"

  Text="ABCDEFGHIJKLMNOPQRSTUVWXYZ"
  SelectionChanged="TextBox_SelectionChanged">
</TextBox>
```

This defines the *SelectionChanged* event, which is handled in code by the *TextBox_SelectionChanged* event handler. You can see that here:

```
private void TextBox_SelectionChanged(object sender, RoutedEventArgs e)
{
  TextBox t = sender as TextBox;
  int st = t.SelectionStart;
  int ln = t.SelectionLength;
  string strT = t.SelectedText;
}
```

In this case, the *st* variable is an *int* containing the index of the starting character in the selection (which is zero based), *ln* is the length of the selection, and *strT* is a string containing the selection. So, for example, if you make a selection like the one shown in Figure 8-8, *st* will be 9, *ln* will be 8, and *strT* will be JKLMNOPQ.

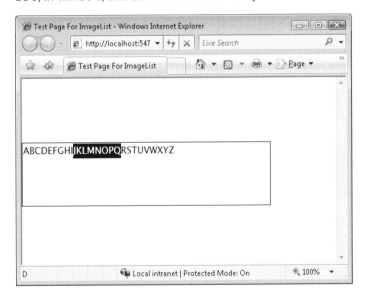

FIGURE 8-8 Selecting a range of text.

You also can control the font that is used in the *TextBox* by using exactly the same method as in the *TextBlock*. For details about how to do this, take a look at the section titled "The *TextBlock* Control" earlier in this chapter.

The *PasswordBox* Control

Related to the *TextBox* control is the *PasswordBox* control. The *PasswordBox* works in an almost identical way in every regard to the *TextBox*. In a *PasswordBox*, you can use the *PasswordChar* property to specify the character to use instead of the typed character to render the keystroke.

So, for example, if you want a *PasswordBox* that renders a # (number sign) whenever the user types a character, you use XAML like this to define it:

```
<PasswordBox PasswordChar="#" x:Name="pw"></PasswordBox>
```

Additionally, you should note that the contents of what the user types are stored in the *Password* property instead of the *Text* property, so when querying for what the user has typed, be sure to use the *Password* property.

Common Properties, Events, and Methods

The previous sections detail many of the basic controls that are available in Silverlight, highlighting their specific properties, methods, and events. However, all or most of these controls share a number of items of common functionality that you need to know about when you begin to develop your Silverlight applications.

Handling Focus

Controls that can receive input expose *GotFocus* and *LostFocus* events. The *GotFocus* and *LostFocus* events fire whenever the user enters or leaves a control, either by selecting it with the mouse pointer or by moving to a control using the Tab key. Both of these events are *bubbling* events, meaning that if the control receives the event but doesn't handle it, the event is passed up to its parent, and it continues to be passed up until it is caught by an event handler.

Handling the Mouse

Silverlight controls expose several mouse events:

- **MouseEnter**   The MouseEnter event fires when the mouse pointer enters the drawing area of a control.

- **MouseLeave**   The MouseLeave event fires when the mouse pointer leaves the drawing area of a control.

- **MouseLeftButtonDown**   The MouseLeftButtonDown event fires when the left button of the mouse is pressed while the pointer is over the control.

- **MouseLeftButtonUp**   The MouseLeftButtonUp event fires when the left button of the mouse is released while the pointer is over the control.

- **MouseMove**   The MouseMove event fires when the mouse pointer moves over the control.

In addition to these events, you might want to use the *captureMouse* and *releaseMouse* methods on a control for maximum control. The *captureMouse* method, when called on a control, causes all mouse events to be directed to that control whether the mouse pointer is in the control's bounds or not. The *releaseMouse* method, as its name suggests, sets event capturing back to normal. These are very useful methods for implementing drag-and-drop operations. Following is an example that achieves this.

Using the Mouse Events for Drag-and-Drop Operations

Following is an XAML document that renders four ellipses on a page. Note that the ellipses all define the same event handlers for their mouse events:

```
<UserControl x:Class="MouseEvents.Page"
  xmlns="http://schemas.microsoft.com/winfx/2006/xaml/presentation"
  xmlns:x="http://schemas.microsoft.com/winfx/2006/xaml"
  FontFamily="Trebuchet MS" FontSize="11"
  Width="400" Height="300">
  <Grid x:Name="LayoutRoot" Background="White">
    <Canvas Width="400" Height="300" Background="Wheat">
      <Ellipse Canvas.Top="0" Fill="Black" Width="20" Height="20"
        MouseLeftButtonDown="Ellipse_MouseLeftButtonDown"
        MouseLeftButtonUp="Ellipse_MouseLeftButtonUp"
        MouseMove="Ellipse_MouseMove" />
      <Ellipse Canvas.Top="40" Fill="Black" Width="20" Height="20"
        MouseLeftButtonDown="Ellipse_MouseLeftButtonDown"
        MouseLeftButtonUp="Ellipse_MouseLeftButtonUp"
        MouseMove="Ellipse_MouseMove" />
      <Ellipse Canvas.Top="80" Fill="Black" Width="20" Height="20"
        MouseLeftButtonDown="Ellipse_MouseLeftButtonDown"
        MouseLeftButtonUp="Ellipse_MouseLeftButtonUp"
        MouseMove="Ellipse_MouseMove" />
      <Ellipse Canvas.Top="120" Fill="Black" Width="20" Height="20"
        MouseLeftButtonDown="Ellipse_MouseLeftButtonDown"
        MouseLeftButtonUp="Ellipse_MouseLeftButtonUp"
        MouseMove="Ellipse_MouseMove" />
    </Canvas>
  </Grid>
</UserControl>
```

Now look at the code-behind for this. First, you need some variables to hold the state of the x and y coordinates of the mouse when you begin dragging, and another variable to indicate whether or not the mouse button is currently being held down.

```
double beginX = 0;
double beginY = 0;
bool isMouseDown = false;
```

When the mouse button is held down over any of the buttons, the *Ellipse_MouseLeftButtonDown* function executes.

```
private void Ellipse_MouseLeftButtonDown(object sender,
        MouseButtonEventArgs e)
{
    Ellipse b = sender as Ellipse;
    beginX = e.GetPosition(this).X;
    beginY = e.GetPosition(this).Y;
    isMouseDown = true;
    b.CaptureMouse();
}
```

Because the sender is a generic object, the first thing you need to do is cast it as an ellipse.
Then, use the *MouseButtonEventArgs* argument to derive the current x and y coordinates and
set them to the beginning values. You want to keep track of when the mouse button is held
down, so set the *isMouseDown* variable to *True*. Finally, you want to capture the mouse events
for this ellipse (whichever one it is) so that, even if the user drags the mouse pointer off this
ellipse, the ellipse will continue to receive the events.

As the user drags the mouse, you want a *MouseMove* event to fire. This is handled by the
Ellipse_MouseMove event handler function. Here it is:

```
private void Ellipse_MouseMove(object sender,
        MouseEventArgs e)
{
    if (isMouseDown)
    {
        Ellipse b = sender as Ellipse;
        double currX = e.GetPosition(this).X;
        double currY = e.GetPosition(this).Y;
        b.SetValue(Canvas.LeftProperty, currX);
        b.SetValue(Canvas.TopProperty, currY);
    }
}
```

This event fires when the mouse pointer moves over an ellipse, regardless of whether the user
is dragging. You are interested in doing something only if the user is dragging, which, by definition, means that the *isMouseDown* variable is *True*. So, in this case, get the current coordinates of the mouse pointer and use them to set the value of the *Top* and *Left* attached
properties of the ellipse. The effect of this is to move the ellipse to the location of the mouse
coordinates, giving you a drag operation.

Finally, when the user releases the mouse button, the *MouseLeftButtonUp* event fires, which is
captured by the *Ellipse_MouseLeftButtonUp* function. Here it is:

```
private void Ellipse_MouseLeftButtonUp(object sender,
        MouseButtonEventArgs e)
{
    Ellipse b = sender as Ellipse;
    isMouseDown = false;
    b.ReleaseMouseCapture();
}
```

This then resets the *isMouseDown* variable and releases the mouse capture from the control that had captured it. The effect is that mouse behavior will have returned to normal, and the ellipse will have moved to the drop location. You can see this in action in Figures 8-9 and 8-10.

Figure 8-9 shows how the application looks in its default state. When the user moves the mouse pointer over any of the ellipses in the application, and then holds down the mouse button and moves the mouse, this causes the ellipse in the application to move, and the user can drag to rearrange the ellipses on the screen. You can see this in Figure 8-10.

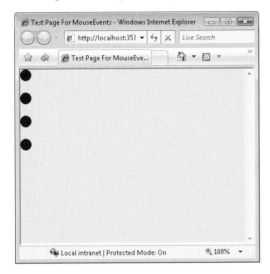

FIGURE 8-9 Drag-and-drop application.

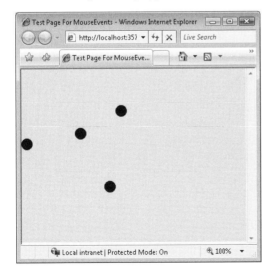

FIGURE 8-10 Dragging and dropping.

In addition to mouse events, keyboard events can fire on many controls. You learn more about these in the next section.

Using the Keyboard

In addition to the *TextBox* control that offers users the ability to input text using the full keyboard, many controls expose the *KeyDown* and *KeyUp* properties that you can use to capture keyboard input. The *KeyDown* property fires whenever an element has focus and a key is pressed on it. Its *Event Handler* function takes a generic sender object and a *KeyEventArgs* object that you can use to extract information about the key that was pressed. This has a *key* property that returns a *Key* object that contains information about the key. This is a platform-independent property, so it is the best choice for you to use in your applications. Another property that the *KeyEventArgs* offers is the *platformKeyCode* property, which you can use with the *key* property to get operating system–specific keys.

Additionally, the *Keyboard.Modifers* event returns a *ModifierKeys* value that you can use to derive whether any modifier key (Alt, Ctrl, Shift, Windows, or Apple) is pressed. Simply assign the return to a *ModifierKeys* value, and check its return value for the string that corresponds to the desired modifier key (for example, Shift).

Summary

This chapter introduces some of the basic Silverlight controls and describes how you can use these core controls to build your Silverlight applications. You looked at the *Button, CheckBox, ComboBox, HyperlinkButton, Image, ListBox, RadioButton, TextBlock, TextBox*, and *PasswordBox* controls. Additionally, you examined some of the common properties, methods, and events that are shared across all controls so that you have a good overview of how to get started using presentation and layout controls in Silverlight.

In the next chapter, you find out about more advanced Silverlight controls and learn how you can use these extended controls to enhance your applications.

Chapter 9
Silverlight Controls: Advanced Controls

Chapter 8, "Silverlight Core Controls," introduces you to the Microsoft Silverlight control set and provides you with a tour through some of the basic controls, such as *TextBox* and *CheckBox*. However, modern, rich, interactive applications (RIAs) tend to require controls that are much more sophisticated, such as data-bound grids, calendars, and more. In this chapter, you learn about how to use these controls in your Silverlight applications. Some of these controls, such as the *DataGrid*, are worthy of a book of their own, so you won't get the full control API here, but you should gain enough knowledge about these advanced controls to understand what is going on when you use them. Then, you can begin experimenting on your own and learn more about how they work.

The *DataGrid* Control

The *DataGrid* control is designed to assist you in displaying data in a row/column format, similar to a spreadsheet. It is a *data*grid, as opposed to just a grid, because it is bindable to a data source. You look at how to display data in more detail in Chapter 12, "Building Connected Applications with Silverlight," but to understand the power of the *DataGrid*, you will also use some of those techniques here.

When you add a *DataGrid* control to your Extensible Application Markup Language (XAML) surface, you end up with XAML like this:

```
<UserControl
  xmlns:data="clr-namespace:System.Windows.Controls;assembly=System.Windows.Controls.Data"
  x:Class="SilverlightApplication1.MainPage"
  xmlns="http://schemas.microsoft.com/winfx/2006/xaml/presentation"
  xmlns:x="http://schemas.microsoft.com/winfx/2006/xaml"
  Width="400" Height="300">
    <Grid x:Name="LayoutRoot" Background="White">
      <data:DataGrid></data:DataGrid>
    </Grid>
</UserControl>
```

This *DataGrid* isn't very functional at the moment, so add two properties to it—a name and *AutoGenerateColumns*, which, when the grid is bound to the *DataGrid*, instruct the grid to generate the required columns for the data automatically. Here's how the *DataGrid* XAML should look after these additions:

```
<data:DataGrid x:Name="GrdHeadline" AutoGenerateColumns="True">
</data:DataGrid>
```

That's all it takes to get a *DataGrid* ready to use bound data. Before you look at more of the properties, methods, and events associated with the control, do a simple data binding. You can bind to an RSS feed at *http://feeds.reuters.com/reuters/oddlyEnoughNews?format=xml*.

Next, add a button to the page, and wire up a *Click* event handler. Add the following code to this to set up a *WebClient* object to read from the URI, and add an event handler to manage the completion of the download:

```
WebClient client = new WebClient();
Uri uri =
   new Uri("http://feeds.reuters.com/reuters/topNews?format=xml");
client.DownloadStringCompleted +=
   new DownloadStringCompletedEventHandler(
        client_DownloadStringCompleted);
client.DownloadStringAsync(uri);
```

Now, after the download of the data is complete, the event handler at *client_DownloadStringCompleted* will fire. In this function, you use a custom class of type *NewsHeadLine*. Here is the code for this class:

```
public class NewsHeadLine
{
  public string strHead { get; set; }
  public string strLine { get; set; }
}
```

Also, the client *_DownloadStringCompleted* uses the System.Xml.Linq libraries, so you need to add a reference to these by right-clicking References and selecting Add Reference. In the .NET tab, the System.Xml.Linq library is listed, as shown in Figure 9-1. Select it, and click OK.

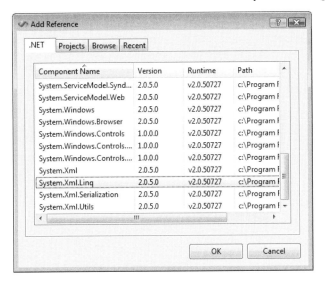

FIGURE 9-1 Adding the System.Xml.Linq reference.

You also need to instruct your code to use this to compile. To do this, you simply need to add this statement at the top of Page.xaml.cs:

```
using System.Xml.Linq;
```

Now, here is the code for the *client_DownloadStringCompleted* event handler:

```
void client_DownloadStringCompleted(
  object sender, DownloadStringCompletedEventArgs e)
{
  XDocument xmlHeadlines = XDocument.Parse(e.Result);
  var headlines = from story in xmlHeadlines.Descendants("item")
                  select new NewsHeadLine
                  {
                     strHead = (string)story.Element("title"),
                     strLine = (string)story.Element("link")
                  };
            Deployment.Current.Dispatcher.BeginInvoke(() =>
              {
                  GrdHeadline.ItemsSource = headlines;
              });
}
```

This code parses the return from the service call (stored in e.Result) into an *XDocument* object. It then uses Linq to select the data from the *XDocument*, creating a collection of headlines. This collection is then set to the *ItemsSource* property of the *DataGrid*. You can see the results in Figure 9-2.

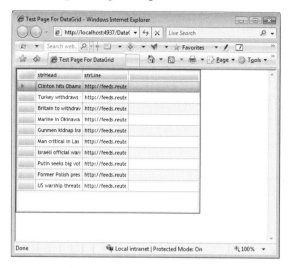

FIGURE 9-2 Sample headline collection created by running the *DataGrid* control.

The *DataGrid* has two selection modes: single, in which only one row at a time may be selected; and multiple, in which several rows may be selected by holding down the Ctrl and/or Shift keys and clicking.

You set these modes using the *SelectionMode* property, which you can set to *DataGridSelectionMode.Single* for single selection and *DataGridSelectionMode.Extended* for multiple selection.

When using single selection mode, the *SelectedItem* mode contains the selection. It is of type *object*, so you need to cast it to the correct type before it can be used. Previously, you filled this grid with items of the *NewsHeadLine* class that you defined.

So, for a single selection, you can get the data from the selection like this:

```
NewsHeadLine theHeadline = GrdHeadline.SelectedItem as NewsHeadLine;
```

When the list is set to allow multiple items, you can use the *SelectedItems* property that returns a list collection. This is very straightforward to manage. Here's the code:

```
string strHead;
string strLink;
System.Collections.IList listOfItems = GrdHeadline.SelectedItems;
foreach(NewsHeadLine newsHead in listOfItems)
{
  strHead = newsHead.strHead;
  strLink = newsHead.strLine;
}
```

In this case, the *SelectedItems* method returns a *System.Collections.IList*. You can then iterate through the list, pulling out each *NewsHeadline* object and getting its data.

When using any kind of grid, and the *DataGrid* is no exception, it is always useful to make your grid more readable with striping—that is, distinguishing alternate rows with different colors or shading. In this case, you can use the *RowBackground* and *AlternatingRowBackground* to set striping for your *DataGrid*. You set these to a brush color with the following code:

```
GrdHeadline.RowBackground =
    new SolidColorBrush(Colors.LightGray);
GrdHeadline.AlternatingRowBackground =
new SolidColorBrush(Colors.Yellow);
```

You can see the effect of this formatting on the output shown in Figure 9-3.

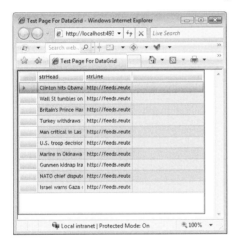

FIGURE 9-3 Using alternating row colors.

You might have noticed that the columns are added in the order that the data is defined in the *NewsHeadLine* class. You aren't limited to having the columns appear in this order, however, and you can override the default setting by using the *DisplayIndex* property. For example, the *DataGrid* has two columns, with the headlines listed in the first column and the links listed in the second. You could flip these around like this:

```
GrdHeadline.Columns[0].DisplayIndex = 1;
GrdHeadline.Columns[1].DisplayIndex = 0;
```

You can further manipulate how the grid renders your data by using a data template. This is XAML that defines how you want the data to be laid out, including binding to specific fields.

For example, the previous output samples had each cell in the grid bound to a particular element in the RSS feed. If you prefer to have two fields from the RSS feed within the same cell, you would achieve this by using a data template. Consider the following XAML:

```
<UserControl
xmlns:my="clr-namespace:System.Windows.Controls;
  assembly=System.Windows.Controls.Data"
x:Class="DataGrid.Page"
  xmlns="http://schemas.microsoft.com/client/2007"
  xmlns:x="http://schemas.microsoft.com/winfx/2006/xaml"
  Width="400" Height="300">

  <Grid x:Name="LayoutRoot" Background="White">
    <my:DataGrid x:Name="GrdHeadline" AutoGenerateColumns="True">
      <my:DataGrid.Columns>
        <my:DataGridTemplateColumn>
          <my:DataGridTemplateColumn.CellTemplate>
            <DataTemplate>
              <StackPanel Orientation="Vertical">
              <TextBlock Text="123"></TextBlock>
              <TextBlock Text="{Binding strHead}"></TextBlock>
              <TextBlock Text="{Binding strPubDate}"></TextBlock>
              </StackPanel>
            </DataTemplate>
          </my:DataGridTemplateColumn.CellTemplate>
        </my:DataGridTemplateColumn>
          <my:DataGridTemplateColumn>
            <my:DataGridTemplateColumn.CellTemplate>
              <DataTemplate>
                <TextBlock Text="{Binding strLine}"></TextBlock>
              </DataTemplate>
            </my:DataGridTemplateColumn.CellTemplate>
          </my:DataGridTemplateColumn>
      </my:DataGrid.Columns>
    </my:DataGrid>
  </Grid>
</UserControl>
```

In this XAML, the *DataGrid* has its columns predefined using *<my:DataGrid.Columns>*. Within this, you can override the default columns template of one field per cell by defining a new *<my:DataGridTemplateColumn.CellTemplate>* for each cell, which will contain the code to define how you want the cell to be rendered.

As you can see, you have defined only two cells, so this grid, regardless of the number of data fields, will have only two columns. The first column, defined by the first cell template, will be a *StackPanel* containing three text fields—a hard-coded "123," the data-bound *strHead* property of the *NewsHeadline* class, and the data-bound *strPubDate* of the *NewsHeadline* class. The *StackPanel* stacks these fields vertically.

The second column, defined by the second cell template, is a simple *TextBlock* that binds to the *strLine* field. You might have noticed that another field, *strPubDate*, that wasn't in the initial class sample is added here, so the class definition and binding code need to be updated. Here's the new class definition:

```
public class NewsHeadLine
    {
        public string strHead { get; set; }
        public string strLine { get; set; }
        public string strDescription { get; set; }
        public string strPubDate { get; set; }
    }
```

And following is the new data binding code that binds the additional fields:

```
void client_DownloadStringCompleted(object sender, DownloadStringCompletedEventArgs e)
{
  XDocument xmlHeadlines = XDocument.Parse(e.Result);
  var headlines = from story in xmlHeadlines.Descendants("item")
                    select new NewsHeadLine
                    {
                      strHead = (string)story.Element("title"),
                      strLine = (string)story.Element("link"),
                      strDescription = (string)story.Element("description"),
                      strPubDate = (string)story.Element("pubDate")
                    };
                Deployment.Current.Dispatcher.BeginInvoke(() =>
                  {
                      GrdHeadline.ItemsSource = headlines;
                  });
}
```

One more quick change you need to make to see the new data: Change the default row height because it is currently capable of showing only one line, which would cause the vertical content in the first cell to be cropped. Also, turn off the automatic column definition because you want to override how the *DataGrid* automatically binds the data. You do this with the following code (put it in the *Page* constructor):

```
GrdHeadline.AutoGenerateColumns = false;
GrdHeadline.RowHeight = 60;
```

Now when you execute this code, you see the *DataGrid* containing the defined column templates shown in Figure 9-4. It's not very pretty, but it does illustrate how you can control the appearance of your output from the *DataGrid* control.

FIGURE 9-4 Using a data template to define how the data is rendered.

The *DataGrid* control has a huge API that deserves a book to describe it in its own right. However, what you've learned about it over the last few pages should give you an appreciation for the flexibility that it provides, and you can use this basic information to take it to the next level as you build your Silverlight applications.

The *Calendar* and *DatePicker* Controls

When you need to select dates for use in your Silverlight applications, you can use the *Calendar* and *DatePicker* controls. The *Calendar* control displays the days in a given month or the months in a given year, and it provides arrow buttons that allow the user to control the current view of month or year by moving to the next or previous month. The *DatePicker* combines this display with a text box in which the user can enter the date according to a format, or the user can access a drop-down list in which to select a specific date.

Look at the *Calendar* control first. It is simple to get started with this control:

```
<UserControl
  xmlns:controls="clr-namespace:System.Windows.Controls;assembly=System.Windows.Controls"
  x:Class="SilverlightApplication2.MainPage"
  xmlns="http://schemas.microsoft.com/winfx/2006/xaml/presentation"
  xmlns:x="http://schemas.microsoft.com/winfx/2006/xaml"
  Width="400" Height="300">
  <Grid x:Name="LayoutRoot" Background="White">
      <controls:Calendar x:Name="cal"></controls:Calendar>
  </Grid>
</UserControl>
```

This code renders the *Calendar* in the default Month view, with the current date highlighted. See Figure 9-5 for an example.

FIGURE 9-5 Using the *Calendar* control.

You use the *DisplayDate* property to set the *month* of the date to display. For example, the following code selects the date January 1, 2009:

```
DateTime d = new DateTime(2009, 1, 1);
cal.DisplayDate = d;
```

This code displays the month of the date you selected, but it does not select the specific day, as shown in Figure 9-6.

When you compare Figure 9-5 and Figure 9-6, you'll notice that there is no day selected on the calendar in Figure 9-6. By setting the display date, the selected date has been nullified, so the *SelectedDate* property is *null*. If you make a selection, this will be set for you (as a *DateTime* type), or you can set it in code by setting the *SelectedDate* property. Here's an example:

```
DateTime s = new DateTime(2009, 1, 31);
cal.SelectedDate = s;
```

FIGURE 9-6 Changing the displayed date.

You can see how this appears in Figure 9-7. Now there is a date—January 31—selected in the calendar that is displayed.

FIGURE 9-7 Using the *SelectedDate* property.

You can specify the range of unselectable dates by using the *BlackoutDates* collection. This collection contains a *CalendarDateRangeCollection* type to which you can add ranges of dates. Any dates falling within these ranges will appear unavailable and thus are unselectable. The *SelectableDateStart* and *SelectableDateEnd* properties can also give you the range of displayable dates. For example, if you want one range to be displayable and another range (usually a subset) to be selectable, you can use these properties to define the appearance of your calendar.

The *DatePicker* combines calendar functionality with a text field. The *Text* property of this field contains whatever the user enters as a date. If the data the user enters cannot be parsed, the *TextParseError* is raised.

Here's the XAML for a DatePicker:

```
<Grid x:Name="LayoutRoot" Background="White">
    <controls:DatePicker x:Name="dp"></controls:DatePicker>
</Grid>
```

When this is rendered, you'll see the text box containing the date, and to the right of the text box, you can see an icon that can be used to show a *Calendar* control for picking the date. When the user selects this icon, the *CalendarOpened* event fires, and when the user dismisses it, the *CalendarClosed* event fires. The *Calendar* and *DatePicker* controls provide you with the basic tools you need to create applications that require input based on dates and that can also display calendar information.

The *RepeatButton* and *ToggleButton* Controls

The *RepeatButton* control provides a button that raises multiple click events when the user holds down the mouse button while the pointer is over the button. The frequency of events fired depends on the *Delay* property, which is specified in milliseconds. For example, consider the following XAML:

```
<RepeatButton x:Name="rpt" Delay="100"
  Content="0" Click="rpt_Click">
</RepeatButton>
```

This defines a *Repeat* button called *rpt* with a delay of 100 milliseconds, which defaults its content to 0. The code to handle the user clicking the button can be found in the *rpt_Click* event handler function. Following is the code for this event handler:

```
private void rpt_Click(object sender, RoutedEventArgs e)
{
  int n = Convert.ToInt16(rpt.Content);
  n++;
  rpt.Content = n.ToString();
}
```

As the user clicks the button, the current value of the *Content* property is retrieved, converted to an integer, incremented, and added back to the value. This causes the caption of the button to be incremented as the user holds down the mouse button over the *RepeatButton*. This can provide a useful type of control for handling multiple repeated actions, such as spinner-type controls, where a button containing an arrow is presented to the user, and as the user holds down the spinner, a value is incremented.

In all other regards, a *RepeatButton* is just a *Button* control, so you can find more details about how to use it in Chapter 8, where the generic *Button* control is introduced.

The *ToggleButton* is a button that, when clicked, remains depressed until you click it again, and then it is returned to its default state. It is effectively a combination of a radio button control and a typical button. The properties associated with a *ToggleButton* control are very similar to those used with radio buttons and generic buttons in that it contains an *IsChecked* property that can be used to derive its current value and an *IsThreeState* property that allows a third state with the value *Null*, which is between the normal and depressed states.

Like the default *Button* control, these are *content* controls, so they can be used to render complex content to create image buttons, video buttons, or whatever you would like for your Silverlight applications.

The *ScrollViewer* Control

The *ScrollViewer* control is a container control for other information; it provides horizontal and/or vertical scroll bars so that the viewer can move the display to see all the information when the dimensions of the content exceed that of the container. The visibility of the scroll bars are set by the *HorizontalScrollBarVisibility* and *VerticalScrollBarVisibility* properties. By default, the vertical scroll bar is displayed and the horizontal is not displayed, regardless of the content. Consider the following XAML example:

```
<UserControl x:Class="sviewer.Page"
    xmlns="http://schemas.microsoft.com/client/2007"
    xmlns:x="http://schemas.microsoft.com/winfx/2006/xaml"
    Width="400" Height="300">
    <Grid x:Name="LayoutRoot" Background="White">
        <ScrollViewer>
            <Image Source="mix08_1280.jpg" Stretch="None" />
        </ScrollViewer>
    </Grid>
</UserControl>
```

In this case, the *ScrollViewer* is the only child control on the 400 × 300 surface, so it will also be 400 × 300. It contains an image, which in this case is 1280 × 1024. You can see the result in Figure 9-8.

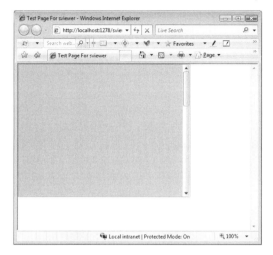

FIGURE 9-8 Using the *ScrollViewer* control.

As you can see, the image shown in Figure 9-8 is gray all along its left side, so all you can see is gray. You cannot scroll to the colorful part of the image that is on the right because there is no horizontal scroll bar.

But if you add *HorizontalScrollBarVisibility="True"* to the *ScrollViewer* definition in XAML, you'll be able to see the rest of the image. Here's the XAML:

```
<ScrollViewer HorizontalScrollBarVisibility="Visible">
  <Image Source="mix08_1280.jpg" Stretch="None" />
</ScrollViewer>
```

And you can see the results in Figure 9-9.

FIGURE 9-9 Using the *ScrollViewer* with horizontal scroll bar.

Tip You can override the visibility of the vertical scroll bar, too. By default, it is visible, but you can turn it off (so that it is not displayed) by changing the *VerticalScrollBarVisibility* to *False*.

The *Slider* Control

With a *Slider* control, the user can select a value from a fixed range by sliding a visual element (called a *thumb*) along a line from the low value in the range to the high value in the range. The value is accessible in the *Value* property, which returns a *Double*.

You can customize the *Slider* control in a number of ways. For example, the *Minimum* and *Maximum* properties are used to determine the minimum and maximum values in the range. If you want to have the user select a value in a range from 0 to 100, set the *Minimum* property to 0 and the *Maximum* property to 100.

Another property associated with the *Slider* control is the *Orientation* property, which is used to determine the direction the user will slide the thumb. It can be set to *Horizontal* or *Vertical*.

The low–high direction of movement of the *Slider* defaults to left–right when the *Orientation* property is set to *Horizontal* and bottom–top when it is set to *Vertical*. You can override these default settings with the *IsDirectionReversed* property, which, when set to *True*, changes the direction of movement of the *Slider*.

In addition to being able to drag the thumb, the user can also click the sliding track in a typical *Slider* control to change the value by a fixed amount. This is determined by the *LargeChange* property, which, when set to a numeric value, increases or decreases the value of the slider by that amount.

Following is an example of a *Slider* control in XAML:

```
<Slider x:Name="sldr" Maximum="100"
Orientation="Vertical"
IsDirectionReversed="True"
LargeChange="10">
</Slider>
```

The *Slider* created here is vertical, with the low value at the top and the high value at the bottom. With this control, the user can select values from 0 through 100 by dragging the thumb, and the user can change the value in increments of 10 by clicking the track.

Summary

In this chapter, you continue to explore the Silverlight control set. You spent a lot of time learning about the *DataGrid* and its associated properties, methods, and events because it is an important control that provides functionality for your applications similar to that of a spreadsheet. The discussion of the *DataGrid* control introduced you to some of the code that Silverlight offers for easy data binding, as well as how to define data templates to use for grid layouts. In addition, you looked through some of the other advanced tools available with Silverlight, including the *Calendar*, *DatePicker*, *ScrollViewer*, and *Slider* controls.

Now, the summary of the base controls available in Silverlight is complete, and in the next chapter, you look at what you need to know to build your own controls.

Chapter 10
Media in Silverlight: Video

Previous chapters introduced you to general controls for building rich interactive Internet applications. In this chapter, you look at video and the options available to you to build video-based applications in Microsoft Silverlight.

First, you learn in some detail about the *MediaElement* control, which provides an API that gives you control over audio and video in your application so that you can build great media applications. You then look into the architecture and implementation of a Silverlight-based client for media that is protected by Digital Rights Management (DRM), including building a sample that will run against content that is hosted and protected on the Internet.

The *MediaElement* Control

One of the most important uses for Silverlight on the Web is to enable cross-platform, next-generation media. To accomplish this, Silverlight supports the *MediaElement* control. In this section, you look at the *MediaElement* in detail and have a chance to work through a use case to build a simple media player that allows for progressive download and playback of videos. In addition, you learn how to paint surfaces with the video brush so that you can add interesting graphical effects. The *MediaElement* control supports the following formats:

Video

- WMV1: Windows Media Video 7

- WMV2: Windows Media Video 8

- WMV3: Windows Media Video 9

- WMVA: Windows Media Video Advanced Profile, non-VC-1

- WMVC1: Windows Media Video Advanced Profile, VC-1

- H.264: Video encoded in the popular H264 format. *Note that this is new in Silverlight 3.*

Audio

- WMA7: Windows Media Audio 7

- WMA8: Windows Media Audio 8

- WMA9: Windows Media Audio 9

- WMA10: Windows Media Audio 10

- MP3: ISO/MPEG Layer 3

- Mono or stereo

- Sampling frequencies from 8 to 48 KHz

- Bit rates from 8 to 320 KBps

- Variable bit rate

In addition to these formats, the *MediaElement* control also supports ASX playlists as well as the HTTP, HTTPS, and MMS protocols.

When it comes to streaming video and/or audio, *MediaElement* supports live and on-demand streaming from a server running Windows Media. If the URI specifies the MMS protocol, streaming is enabled; otherwise, the file is downloaded and played back with progressive download, which involves downloading enough of the file to fill a playback buffer, at which point the buffered video is played back while the rest of the file is downloaded.

If the protocol specified is HTTP or HTTPS, the reverse happens. *MediaElement* tries to progressively download first, and if this fails, the *MediaElement* control attempts to stream the file.

Using the *MediaElement* Control

The *MediaElement* control is easy to get up and running in a basic setting, but it has many advanced features that can provide you with some pretty compelling scenarios when you have learned how to use them. But first walk before you try to run and step through how to do the most common tasks with the *MediaElement*.

Simple Video Playback with the *MediaElement* Control

To get started with the *MediaElement* control, add it to your page and set its *Source* attribute to the URL of the video that you want to play back. Following is an example:

```
<Canvas
  xmlns="http://schemas.microsoft.com/client/2007"
  xmlns:x="http://schemas.microsoft.com/winfx/2006/xaml"
  Background="White"
  >
  <MediaElement Source="balls.wmv"/>
</Canvas>
```

This Extensible Application markup Language (XAML) loads and plays back the media automatically. The *size* of the media is determined by the following rules:

- If the *MediaElement Height* and *Width* properties are specified, the *MediaElement* control uses them.

- If one of the properties is used, the *MediaElement* control stretches the media to maintain the aspect ratio of the video.

- If neither *Height* nor *Width* is set, the *MediaElement* control plays back the video at its default size. If the default size is bigger than the Silverlight control's *allotted* viewing area, the *MediaElement* control crops the video to fit the allotted viewing area.

Here is an example. The balls.wmv video used in this chapter (and available to download from the companion Web site) is a 480 × 360 video. If you instruct the *MediaElement* to show this video and do not set the *Height* and *Width* of the *MediaElement*, the video plays back at 480 × 360. If your Silverlight component is 200 × 200, you will see the upper-left 200 pixels of the video. You can see the portion of the video cropped in this way in Figure 10-1.

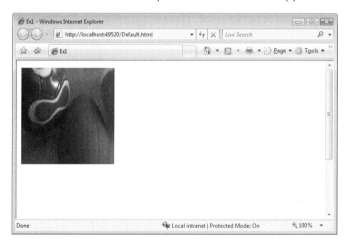

FIGURE 10-1 Video cropped to the size of the Silverlight control.

Controlling the Size of the *MediaElement* Control

As you saw in the previous section, the size of the *MediaElement* is important when determining how the video plays back. If the control does not have its size defined and the video resolution is larger than the dimensions of the Silverlight control, the video is cropped.

To control the height and width of the *MediaElement* itself, you can use its *Height* and *Width* properties. When the control is rendered, the media is stretched (or shrunk) to fit the media control. If the defined size of the media control is larger than the Silverlight control, the media is cropped to the size of the Silverlight control.

Following is an example of the *MediaElement* control set to 200 × 200, and Figure 10-2 shows how the video is rendered as a result:

```
<MediaElement Source="balls.wmv" Height="200" Width="200" />
```

FIGURE 10-2 Video display after sizing the *MediaElement*.

Controlling How the Media Is Stretched

In the preceding example, the video has been stretched to fit the 200 × 200 *MediaElement*. As you can see in Figure 10-2, the video (which, as you recall, has a 480 × 360 pixel native resolution) is stretched to fit the dimensions while maintaining its aspect ratio. This can yield black bars at the top and bottom of the video, giving the video a "letterbox" effect. You can override this behavior using the *Stretch* property of the *MediaElement*. This property can take four different values:

- **None** No stretching takes place. If the *MediaElement* is larger than the video, the video is centered in it. If it is smaller, the center portion of the video is shown. For example, the video is 480 × 360. If the *MediaElement* is 200 × 200 and *Stretch* is set to *None*, the center 200 × 200 area of the video is displayed, as shown in Figure 10-3.

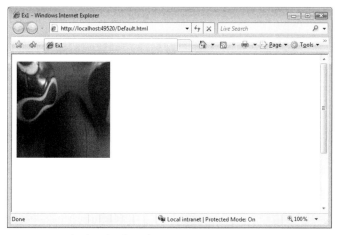

FIGURE 10-3 Setting the *Stretch* property to *None*.

- **Uniform**   This is the default stretching mode, and it maintains the video's aspect ratio and adds bars at the top, bottom, or sides to maintain it.

- **UniformToFill**   This stretches the video, maintaining the aspect ratio but cropping the video to fit the window. So, for example, if the video is wider than it is high (for example, 480 × 360) and is stretched to accommodate a 200 × 200 window, the sides of the video are cropped to fit the allotted viewing window (a smaller square, in this case). You can see how this affects the video display in Figure 10-4. If you compare the image in Figure 10-4 to the same frame of video shown in Figure 10-2, you can see how the image is cropped on both sides.

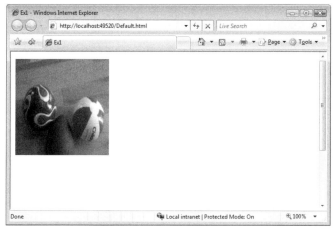

FIGURE 10-4 Using *UniformToFill* stretch mode.

- *Fill*   This stretch mode fills the *MediaElement* with the video, distorting the aspect ratio if necessary. Figure 10-5 shows the video when *Stretch* is set to *Fill*. As you can see in this case, the video has been stretched vertically to fill the paint area.

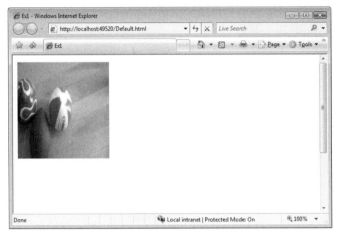

FIGURE 10-5 Using *Stretch* set to *Fill*.

Controlling Video Opacity

You can control the opacity of the *MediaElement* by using the *Opacity* property. This contains a normalized value, with 0 equal to totally invisible, 1 equal to completely visible, and everything in between representing different levels of opacity. The video is rendered with this opacity, and items behind the media element can become visible.

Following is an example of some XAML with a red rectangle and a *MediaElement*. The *MediaElement* is set to 0.5 opacity, which makes the video appear semitransparent. Because the *MediaElement* is rendered second, it is placed higher in the Z-order, and thus it is rendered on top of the rectangle. Figure 10-6 shows the result of this example on the video display.

```
<Rectangle Fill="Red" Height="100" Width="200" />
<MediaElement Source="balls.wmv" Height="200"
        Width="200" Stretch="Fill" Opacity="0.5" />
```

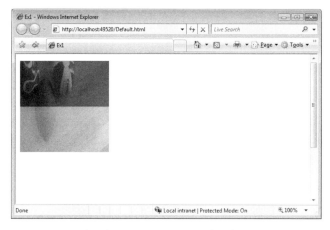

FIGURE 10-6 Using the *Opacity* property with video.

Using Transformations with the *MediaElement* Control

Chapter 5, "XAML Transformation and Animation," describes transformations in detail, but one of the nice things about the *MediaElement* is that you can use it to perform transformations, and the video that you are rendering will also be transformed. This can lead to some very nice effects. For example, the following is a *MediaElement* with a skew transform applied:

```
<MediaElement Source="balls.wmv" Height="200" Width="200" Stretch="Fill" >
    <MediaElement.RenderTransform>
        <SkewTransform AngleX="45"/>
    </MediaElement.RenderTransform>
</MediaElement>
```

You can see how this appears in Figure 10-7.

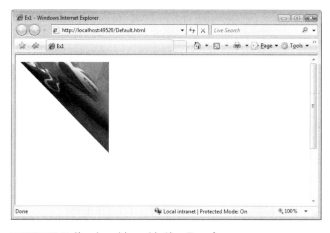

FIGURE 10-7 Skewing video with *SkewTransform*.

Writing Content on Video

With Silverlight, you can place content, including text and graphics, on top of video with ease. You can place it using *ZOrder* properties on user interface (UI) elements, or you can simply place UI elements in the same space as the media element and declare them later in the XAML. (See Chapter 1, "Introducing Silverlight 3," for more information about the UI.) Following is an example of a *MediaElement* that has a *Canvas* containing a rectangle and text block that overlays the video:

```
<MediaElement Source="balls.wmv" Height="200" Width="200" Stretch="Fill" />
<Canvas Canvas.Top="140" Canvas.Left="20">
    <Rectangle Fill="Red" Height="40" Width="160" />
    <TextBlock>Subtitle on Video</TextBlock>
</Canvas>
```

Figure 10-8 shows how this is rendered.

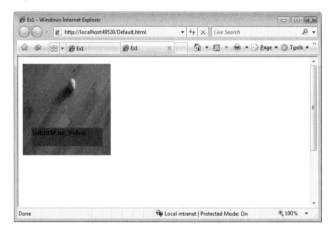

FIGURE 10-8 Rendering content on top of video.

Clipping Media with Geometries

Chapter 4, "Silverlight XAML Basics," introduces you to clipping and geometries. You can also apply these features to a *MediaElement*, where you can define a geometry using shapes or paths and set this to be the clipping geometry for the *MediaElement* you're working with. For example, the following XAML defines an ellipse as the clip region for the *MediaElement*:

```
<MediaElement Source="balls.wmv" Height="200" Width="200" Stretch="Fill" >
    <MediaElement.Clip>
        <EllipseGeometry RadiusX="100" RadiusY="75" Center="100,75"/>
    </MediaElement.Clip>
</MediaElement>
```

You can see the results of this in Figure 10-9.

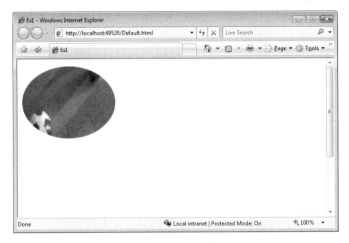

FIGURE 10-9 Clipping media with geometries.

Determining Automatic Playback Behavior

The default behavior for the *MediaElement* after its source is set is to have the media play back automatically. You can control this by using the *AutoPlay* property, which defaults to *true*, but you can override it by setting it to *false*. You can play back the media later using the *AutoPlay Play* method. This and the other methods and events that you can use in programming the *MediaElement* are discussed in the next section.

Controlling Audio

You can use the *MediaElement* control *IsMuted* property to set the audio to accompany the playback or not. This property is a Boolean value, and if you set it to *true*, no audio will be heard.

Additionally, you can control the volume of the audio using the *Volume* property. This is a normalized value with 0 equal to no audio, 1 equal to full volume, and values in between representing the relative volume. So, for example, 0.43 sets the volume to play at 43 percent of its full capacity.

Finally, the balance of the audio can be controlled with the *Balance* property. You can set this property with a value between –1 and +1. A value of –1 causes the audio to be panned all the way to the left—that is, the left speaker plays the audio at 100 percent volume, and the right speaker plays no audio, or plays at 0 percent volume. A value of +1 causes just the opposite to happen—the audio is panned all the way to the right, with the right speaker playing the audio at 100 percent volume. A value of 0 causes the volume to be distributed evenly between the two speakers.

For example, if you set the *Balance* property to a value of 0.8, the right speaker will play the audio at 80 percent volume and the left speaker will play it at 20 percent volume. If you use the value –0.8, the left speaker will play the audio at 80 percent volume and the right speaker will play the audio at 20 percent volume.

Following is some XAML specifying that the audio is not muted, that the master volume is at 50 percent, and that the audio is balanced toward the right speaker:

```
<MediaElement x:Name="vid" Source="balls.wmv" Height="200" Width="200"
    Stretch="Fill" IsMuted="False" Volume="0.5" Balance="0.8" />
```

Programming the *MediaElement*

With the rich programming model of the *MediaElement*, you can control playback with play, stop, and pause methods. You also can respond to the video, capturing the buffering and download progress as well as responding to markers placed in the video. You also can specify events to trap, such as mouse behavior.

Providing Basic Video Controls

The basic video control methods available are *Play*, *Stop*, and *Pause*. When you set the *AutoPlay* property of the *MediaElement* to *false*, these controls are necessary to start playing the video. Even if *AutoPlay* is set to *true* and the video starts playing, you can stop or pause the video using these methods. Following is an example of XAML containing a media element and three simple video playback controls, implemented as *TextBlock* elements:

```
<MediaElement x:Name="vid" Source="balls.wmv" Height="200" Width="200" Stretch="Fill" />
<Canvas Canvas.Top="160">
    <Rectangle Fill="Black" Width="200" Height="24" Opacity="0.7"/>
    <TextBlock Foreground="White" Canvas.Left="20">Play</TextBlock>
    <TextBlock Foreground="White" Canvas.Left="80">Stop</TextBlock>
    <TextBlock Foreground="White" Canvas.Left="140">Pause</TextBlock>
</Canvas>
```

Figure 10-10 shows how the controls appear on the video.

To create the controls, you specify the name of the code function that should run in response to a mouse event using an attribute of the video control element itself. You can find much more detail about handling Silverlight events with JavaScript in Chapter 7, "The Silverlight Browser Bridge." However, in this case, you simply want the video to start, stop, or pause when the user clicks the appropriate text block. You can achieve this by handling the *MouseLeftButtonDown* event, exhibited by the text block, which is hooked to functions that play, pause, or stop the media element.

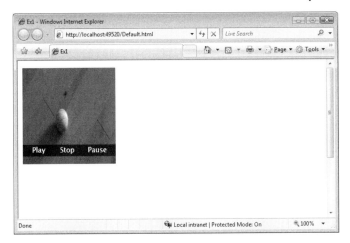

FIGURE 10-10 Adding controls to the video.

In JavaScript, these functions need to be accessible from the page hosting the Silverlight control. So, you can implement them using JavaScript elements on the page or in a .js file that is included on the page using the JavaScript element with its *Src* property set accordingly.

Microsoft Expression Blend 2 provides a pseudo code-behind file for Page.xaml called Page.xaml.js. This is an ideal location in which to implement your JavaScript functionality. If you are using later versions of Expression Blend, you must create the JavaScript manually.

Following is the XAML that defines the same UI that was created in the previous example but with event handler declarations added:

```
<MediaElement x:Name="vid" Source="balls.wmv"
              Height="200" Width="200" Stretch="Fill" />
<Canvas Canvas.Top="160">
    <Rectangle Fill="Black" Width="200" Height="24" Opacity="0.7"/>
    <TextBlock MouseLeftButtonDown="doPlay"
            Foreground="White"
            Canvas.Left="20">Play</TextBlock>
    <TextBlock MouseLeftButtonDown="doStop"
            Foreground="White"
            Canvas.Left="80">Stop</TextBlock>
    <TextBlock MouseLeftButtonDown="doPause"
            Foreground="White"
            Canvas.Left="140">Pause</TextBlock>
</Canvas>
```

Now you can write JavaScript to play, stop, and pause the video. Here's the code:

```
function doPlay(sender, args)
{
  var meVid = sender.findName("vid");
  meVid.Play();
```

```
}

function doStop(sender, args)
{
  var meVid = sender.findName("vid");
  meVid.Stop();
}

function doPause(sender, args)
{
  var meVid = sender.findName("vid");
  meVid.Pause();
}
```

When you define a JavaScript function as an event handler, it should take two parameters. The first, *sender*, is an object that represents the object that raised the event. The second, *args*, contains arguments that are included as part of the event.

Now, in this JavaScript function, you have to get a reference to the *MediaElement* object that you are controlling. You do this using the *findName* method on the sender. Although the sender is the text block that the user clicked, executing its *findName* method will still search through the entire XAML document until it finds an element called *vid* (which you established using the *x:Name* attribute as applied to the *MediaElement* object). If you look back to the XAML, you can see that the *MediaElement* had an *x:Name* value of *vid*, so this should succeed. You are given a reference to the corresponding *MediaElement* object in a JavaScript variable called *meVid*. You can now simply invoke the *Play*, *Stop*, or *Pause* methods on this to control the video.

When using the Microsoft .NET Framework, the process is even simpler—you don't need to use *findName* to access the element, and it's already named *vid*, so your code will look like this:

```
private void doPlay(object sender, MouseButtonEventArgs e)
{
  vid.Play();
}
private void doPause(object sender, MouseButtonEventArgs e)
{
  vid.Pause();
}


private void doStop(object sender, MouseButtonEventArgs e)
{
  vid.Stop();
}
```

Managing Buffering and Download

In progressive video download, the media infrastructure determines how much video it needs to cache before it can start playing back the video. Depending on the bandwidth required to serve the video and the bandwidth available, the media infrastructure creates a buffer to hold enough video so that it can start playing back the video while it is downloading video to the buffer in the background.

When the buffer is 100 percent full, the video begins playing back. Video might pause momentarily as network conditions change and the buffer is refilled. With Silverlight, you can monitor this behavior with the *BufferingProgressChanged* event and the *BufferingProgress* property. You can use these controls to provide the current buffering status to users or to run logic to improve your user experience (UX) as a result of buffering conditions. For example, you might have a poor connection, and buffering might never improve to more than 50 percent. You can trap this value and provide the appropriate feedback to your client.

To manage buffering, hook an event handler to your *MediaElement* that defines a function to handle the *BufferingProgressChanged* event like this:

```
<MediaElement x:Name="vid" Source="balls.wmv" Height="200" Width="200"
        Stretch="Fill" BufferingProgressChanged="doBuff"/>
<TextBlock x:Name="txtBuff"></TextBlock>
```

This specifies that a function called *doBuff* will run whenever the buffering progress changes. This event works hand in hand with the *BufferingProgress* property. The *BufferingProgress* property contains a value from 0 to 1, where 0 is an empty buffer and 1 is a full buffer. The event fires when the buffer changes by 5 percent (that is, 0.05) or more and when it is full.

Following is code that you can use to handle this event firing that provides feedback to your users on the current state of the buffer. First, here's the JavaScript version:

```
function doBuff(sender, args)
{
   var theText = sender.findName("txtBuff");
   var meVid = sender.findName("vid");
   var prog = meVid.BufferingProgress * 100;
   prog = "Buffering % " + prog;
   theText.Text = prog;
}
```

And here's how you would do it if you were using .NET code-behind (with C#):

```
private void doBuff(object sender, RoutedEventArgs e)
{
  double prog = vid.BufferingProgress * 100;
  txtBuff.Text = "Buffering % " + prog;
}
```

You can override the automatic buffer by setting a specific buffer time. So, if you want to control the video-buffering process so that you'll always have a 10-second buffer of video and thereby reduce your risk of paused video while buffers resynchronize in bad network conditions, you can set the *BufferingTime* property. You set this property using a time span. To apply a 10-second buffer, for example, you specify the *BufferingTime* as 0:0:10, as shown in the following example:

```
<MediaElement x:Name="vid" Source="balls.wmv"
     Height="200" Width="200" Stretch="Fill"
     BufferingProgressChanged="doBuff"
     BufferingTime="0:0:10"/>

<TextBlock x:Name="txtBuff"></TextBlock>
<TextBlock x:Name="txtDown"></TextBlock>
```

When progressive download isn't available or supported, the entire video file needs to be downloaded before it can be played back. In this case, you can use the *DownloadProgressChanged* event and *DownloadProgress* property to provide the status of the download. You use these in the same manner as the buffering functions. Following is XAML that defines a *DownloadProgressChanged* event:

```
<MediaElement x:Name="vid" Source="balls.wmv"
     Height="200" Width="200" Stretch="Fill"
     BufferingProgressChanged="doBuff"
     BufferingTime="0:0:10"
     DownloadProgressChanged="doDown"/>

<TextBlock x:Name="txtBuff"></TextBlock>
<TextBlock x:Name="txtDown"></TextBlock>
```

And following is the code for the *doDown* function that defines the event handler—again, first take a look at the JavaScript version:

```
function doDown(sender, args)
{
    var theText = sender.findName("txtDown");
    var meVid = sender.findName("vid");
    var prog = meVid.DownloadProgress * 100;
    prog = "Downloading % " + prog;
    txtDown.Text = prog;
}
```

And here is the .NET version:

```
private void doDown(object sender, RoutedEventArgs e)
{
    double prog = vid.DownloadProgress * 100;
    txtDown.Text = "Downloading % " + prog;

}
```

Managing Current Video State

Silverlight presents a *CurrentState* property and an associated *CurrentStateChanged* event that you can use to respond to changes in state of the media.

The valid states for the *CurrentState* property are as follows:

- **Buffering**   The buffer is less than 100 percent full, so the media is in a paused state while the buffer fills up.

- **Closed**   The media has been closed.

- **Error**   There is a problem downloading, buffering, or playing back the media.

- **Opening**   The media has been found, and buffering or downloading is about to begin.

- **Paused**   The media has been paused.

- **Playing**   The media is being played back.

- **Stopped**   The media has been stopped.

- **Individualizing**   The DRM individualization server is being contacted. This topic is covered later in this chapter.

- **Acquiring License**   Silveright is contacting the DRM license server to get a license to play back protected content. This topic is covered later in this chapter.

Here's how you specify the *CurrentStateChanged* event of the *MediaElement* in XAML:

```
<MediaElement x:Name="vid" Source="balls.wmv" Height="200" Width="200"
    Stretch="Fill" CurrentStateChanged="doState" BufferingTime="0:0:10" />
```

The preceding code specifies a *doState* function to call in response to the changing current state. Following is a sample JavaScript function that runs as a result of this, using the *CurrentState* property of the *MediaElement* in an alert string:

```
function doState(sender, args)
{
   var meVid = sender.findName("vid");
   alert(meVid.CurrentState);
}
```

If you want to do this in C#, there is no alert box, so you could display the content of the *CurrentState* property in the *TextBlock* like this:

```
private void doState(object sender, RoutedEventArgs e)
{
  txtBuff.Text = vid.CurrentState.ToString();
}
```

Managing Playback Position

You can use the *NaturalDuration* and *Position* properties of the media element to control the current playback position status of the media. After the media's *CurrentState* property is set to *Opened*, the *NaturalDuration* property is set. This property reports the length of the video in seconds using the *NaturalDuration.Seconds* property. You can then use code to convert this to hours, minutes, and seconds.

In this example, the *MediaElement* has its *CurrentStateChanged* event wired up to the *doState* function (from the previous example). However, the function now captures the *NaturalDuration* property. The JavaScript version uses the *convertDT* JavaScript helper function to format this as a string. Following is the JavaScript code:

```
function doState(sender, args)
{
    var meVid = sender.findName("vid");
    var txtStat = sender.findName("txtStat");
    var datetime = new Date(0, 0, 0, 0, 0, meVid.naturalDuration.Seconds)
    durationString = convertDT(datetime);
    txtStat.Text = durationString.toString();
}

function convertDT(datetime)
{
    var hours = datetime.getHours();
    var minutes = datetime.getMinutes();
    var seconds = datetime.getSeconds();
    if (seconds < 10) {
        seconds = "0" + seconds;
    }

    if (minutes < 10) {
        minutes = "0" + minutes;
    }

    var durationString;
    if (hours > 0) {
        durationString = hours.toString() + ":" + minutes + ":" + seconds;
    }
    else {
        durationString = minutes + ":" + seconds;
    }
    return durationString;
}
```

This is a great example of how the .NET Framework in Silverlight 3 makes development a lot easier—you can accomplish this in C# with one line of code:

```
txtStat.Text = vid.NaturalDuration.ToString();
```

This would work with XAML that looks something like this:

```
<Canvas x:Name="sample9" Opacity="1">
  <MediaElement x:Name="vid" Source="balls.wmv" Height="200" Width="200"
      Stretch="Fill" CurrentStateChanged="doState"
      BufferingTime="0:0:10" />
  <TextBlock x:Name="txtStat"></TextBlock>
</Canvas>
```

You can report on the current position of the video using the *Position* property. In this example, the position is reported on the status screen when the video is paused. The JavaScript code needed looks something like this:

```
function doPause(sender, args)
{
   var meVid = sender.findName("vid");
   meVid.Pause();
   var txtStat = sender.findName("txtStat");
   var datetime = new Date(0,0,0,0,0, meVid.Position.Seconds);
   positionString = convertDT(datetime);
   txtStat.Text = positionString.toString();
}
```

And, as before, the C# equivalent is even simpler:

```
txtStat.Text = vid.Position.ToString();
```

Using Media Timeline Markers

A timeline marker is a piece of metadata that is associated with a particular point in a media timeline. Markers are usually created and encoded into the media ahead of time using software such as Expression Media, and they are often used to provide chapter stops in video.

Silverlight supports these markers. As it is playing back media, when Silverlight reaches a marker on the timeline, it raises the *MarkerReached* event. You can catch this event and process it to trigger actions upon hitting the mark.

Following is an example of XAML that specifies the event handler for reaching a marker using the *MarkerReached* attribute. It specifies a JavaScript function called *handleMarker* as the event handler:

```
<MediaElement x:Name="vid" Source="balls.wmv" Height="200" Width="200"
MarkerReached="handleMarker" />
```

The arguments raised by this event contain a *marker* object. This object contains a *TimeSpan* object that contains the time of the marker. The previous section, "Managing Playback Position," provides an example showing how to format a *TimeSpan* object into a friendly string. It also contains a *Type* property for the marker, which is a string that is defined by the person performing the encoding. Finally, it contains a *Text* parameter that allows for free-format text and is usually used to describe the parameter. Following is the JavaScript to capture all three and builds a string that is rendered using an alert box:

```
function handleMarker(sender, args)
{
    var strMarkerStatus = args.marker.time.seconds.toString();
    strMarkerStatus += "  :  ";
    strMarkerStatus += args.marker.type;
    strMarkerStatus += "  :  ";
    strMarkerStatus += args.marker.text;
    alert(strMarkerStatus);
}
```

The C# code is very similar; note that the args are in the format *TimeLineMarkerRouted-EventArgs*:

```
private void handleMarker(object sender,
        TimelineMarkerRoutedEventArgs e)
{
  string strMarkerStatus = e.Marker.Time.ToString();
  strMarkerStatus += "  :  ";
  strMarkerStatus += e.Marker.Type;
  strMarkerStatus += "  :  ";
  strMarkerStatus += e.Marker.Text;
}
```

You can see how this looks in Figure 10-11.

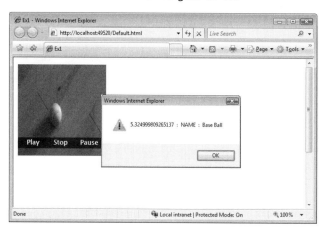

FIGURE 10-11 Capturing timeline markers in Silverlight.

You can also dynamically add timeline markers to your media file using code in Silverlight. You can do this to create chapter stops as a percentage of the length of the file, for example.

Following is an example in which the XAML for the *MediaElement* defines the function *handleOpen* to fire when the media is opened. This inserts a new timeline object into the video at the 10-second position. This element is not permanently stored in the video, and it is lost when the session ends.

```
<MediaElement x:Name="vid" Source="balls.wmv"
    Height="200" Width="200"
    MarkerReached="handleMarker"
    MediaOpened="handleOpened" />
```

The handler should then create a new timeline element in XAML and append it to the *MediaElement* marker collection. This sets up a timeline marker at 10 seconds, with the *Type* set to 'My Temp Marker' and the *Text* set to 'Dynamically Added Marker Marker'.

Here's how it would look if you were building it in JavaScript:

```
function handleOpened(sender, args)
{
   var marker =
   sender.getHost().content.createFromXaml(
      "<TimelineMarker Time='0:0:10'" +
      " Type='My Temp Marker' Text='Dynamically Added Marker Marker' />");
   sender.markers.add(marker);
}
```

And here's how it would look if you were building it in .NET:

```
private void handleOpened(object sender, RoutedEventArgs e)
{
  TimelineMarker t = new TimelineMarker();
  t.Time = new TimeSpan(0, 0, 0, 10);
  t.Type = "My Temp Marker";
  t.Text = "Dynamically Added Marker";
  vid.Markers.Add(t);
}
```

The *MediaElement* markers collection is made up of *TimeLineMarker* objects, so to add a new one, you simply create it and set its *Time*, *Type*, and *Text* properties, and then add it to the collection. Silverlight is smart enough to know when to fire it based on the *Time* you have set, so you do not have to add new markers in time-based order.

Now, when the *MediaElement* reaches the 10-second point on the playback, the alert dialog box shown in Figure 10-12 is raised.

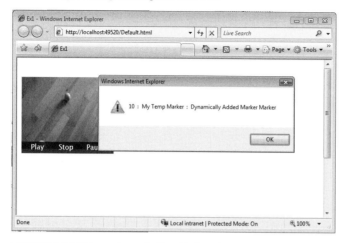

FIGURE 10-12 Using a dynamically added marker.

Painting Video Using the *VideoBrush*

A particularly exciting feature of Silverlight is its ability to paint surfaces with video using a *VideoBrush*. This is a very straightforward process. First, you need a media element that loads the video. This media element should be hidden and should not accept mouse events. You achieve this by setting its opacity to 0 and by setting the *IsHitTestVisible* property to *false*. You also have to name the media element object using the *x:Name* property. Following is an example:

```
<MediaElement x:Name="vid" Source="balls.wmv" Opacity="0" IsHitTestVisible="False" />
```

Now the *VideoBrush* object can be applied to an object in the same way any other brush is used. You need to specify the brush source as the *MediaElement* (which is why it had to be named). You can also specify the *Stretch* property to further control the visual brush effect.

For example, here's a *TextBlock* containing text that has its *Foreground* color painted using a *VideoBrush*:

```
<TextBlock FontFamily="Verdana" FontSize="80"
      FontWeight="Bold" TextWrapping="Wrap"
      Text="Video">
  <TextBlock.Foreground>
      <VideoBrush SourceName="vid"/>
  </TextBlock.Foreground>
</TextBlock>
```

Silverlight renders the text using a *VideoBrush*, and Figure 10-13 shows how this is displayed.

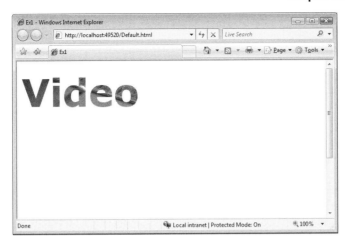

FIGURE 10-13 Using the *VideoBrush* to paint text.

H.264 Video Support

Silverlight 3 adds H.264 decoder support so that the *<MediaElement>* in Silverlight can play back H.264-encoded content. This is an important step for companies that have invested in digitizing their assets using this format and that would like to take advantage of Silverlight for building rich user interfaces.

If you haven't played with H.264 before, you can do so with the full version of Expression Encoder 2, which, with Service Pack 1 added, supports encoding in this format. If you don't have Expression Encoder 2, there's a free encoder at *http://www.h264encoder.com*.

The rest of this section discusses encoding files using Expression Encoder.

With Expression Encoder, you can import files from many different formats. This example uses a MOD file as commonly produced by many camcorders.

Start Expression Encoder and click the Import button. Point it at your file, and you'll see the file being loaded and prepared by Expression Encoder. Before you encode, you can select the encoder profile to use in the Encode tab, as shown in Figure 10-14.

FIGURE 10-14 Expression Encoder video profiles.

You can see that there are two profiles for H.264, *Large* and *Small*. Select the large one.

You can select the range of video that you want to encode (should you want to clip it) by dragging the yellow marker across the timeline immediately under the video window. Right-click, and then click Mark In to clip all before the marker or click Mark Out to clip all after the marker. When ready, click Encode to start the encoder process.

Do note that Expression Encoder 2 SP1 when encoding to H.264 does *not* support Silverlight. This support will be available in a later release.

When the encode is complete, you'll have an H.264-encoded MP4 file. You can then easily play back the file using the Silverlight *MediaElement*.

Here's a simple example. Note that the extension used is .mp4:

```
<UserControl x:Class="Sl3BladH264.Page"
    xmlns="http://schemas.microsoft.com/winfx/2006/xaml/presentation"
    xmlns:x="http://schemas.microsoft.com/winfx/2006/xaml"
    Width="400" Height="300">
    <Grid x:Name="LayoutRoot" Background="White">
        <MediaElement AutoPlay="True" Width="400" Height="400"
            Source="MOVOAC.mp4"></MediaElement>
    </Grid>
</UserControl>
```

You can see an example of this in Figure 10-15.

FIGURE 10-15 Playing back H.264 content.

Protecting Media with Digital Rights Management

Silverlight is compatible with DRM technology, which allows you to protect your video assets. This book doesn't cover how to configure a DRM *server*, details for which are available from Microsoft. As such, consider this section a very light introduction to a complex topic, and one that is focused on how simple it is to build a *client* that accesses protected content.

In this section, you explore how DRM works in Silverlight as well as write some code to build a client that operates against DRM-protected content that is hosted by Microsoft.

How DRM Works in Silverlight

DRM in Silverlight works through a five-step process:

1. The Silverlight client accesses the content through setting the *Source* property of the *MediaElement* as shown earlier.

2. In the case of progressive download, the Silverlight client downloads the content. In the case of streaming, it downloads some of the content, plus the media headers.

3. The Silverlight client sees that the media is protected, and it contacts the *individualization server*. This is a service provided by Microsoft that provides a unique ID to your client so that it can be licensed.

4. Once individualized, the client then contacts the license server to get a license to play back the content.

5. The license server provides the license, and the Silverlight client is able to play back the content.

You can see this process depicted graphically in Figure 10-16.

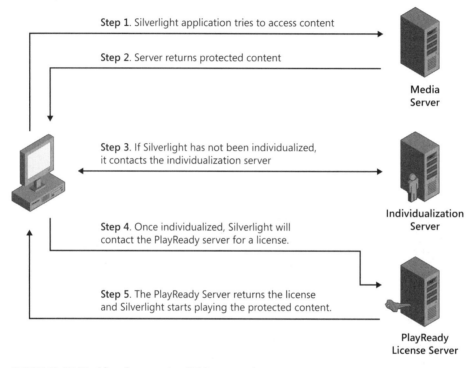

Step 1. Silverlight application tries to access content

Step 2. Server returns protected content

Media Server

Step 3. If Silverlight has not been individualized, it contacts the individualization server

Individualization Server

Step 4. Once individualized, Silverlight will contact the PlayReady server for a license.

Step 5. The PlayReady Server returns the license and Silverlight starts playing the protected content.

PlayReady License Server

FIGURE 10-16 Workflow for accessing DRM-protected content.

Silverlight supports two forms of DRM decryption: the traditional Windows Media Digital Rights Management 10 (WMDRM 10) and PlayReady. Existing content that is encrypted with WMDRM can be played back with Silverlight, but you still need a PlayReady license server. Do also note that if you are using real-time or live media sources and you want to encrypt them, you must use WMDRM 10.

If you are familiar with using PlayReady for DRM protection, it's important to note that Silverlight supports only a *subset* of the PlayReady features:

- Silverlight DRM supports only Windows Media Audio (WMA), Windows Media Video (WMV), and PlayReady-based PlayYourAudio (PYA) and PlayYourVideo (PYV).

- The only license type available to Silverlight is a nonpersistent, play-once license.

- There is no license caching functionality.

Building a Silverlight Client for DRM

Putting together a server with DRM-protected content is beyond the scope of this book. You can build and test a client for the DRM content using Silverlight.

Take a look at this site: *http://web.sldrm.video.msn.com/d1/sldrm.html.* It site hosts a number of instances of a particular video snippet, with a number of different encodings and delivery methods as well as versions that are protected using PlayReady and others that are not protected.

You can see it in Figure 10-17.

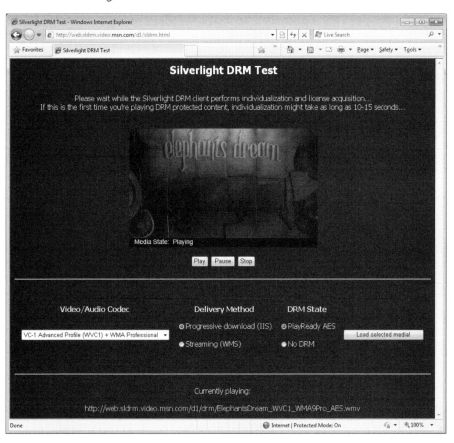

FIGURE 10-17 Sample DRM site.

You can use the drop-down list to select the video and/or audio codec that you want to use, set a delivery method and DRM state, and then load the selected material.

You'll also see the address of the specified material listed at the bottom of the page so that you know the URI of the content of this site and can build your own media clients against it.

Accessing this content from Silverlight is very straightforward—you simply specify the location of the content that you want to play back in the *Source* element of the *MediaElement*, as you saw earlier, or set the *Source* using a URI object in code.

Here's an example of how to do it in C#.

First, define your *MediaElement* control in XAML:

```
<MediaElement x:Name="mel"></MediaElement>
```

Then, in code, set the source using a URI:

```
Uri theUri = new
    Uri("http://web.sldrm.video.msn.com/d1/drm/ElephantsDream_WVC1_WMA9Pro_AES.wmv");

mel.Source = theUri;
mel.Play();
```

This is kept very simple by the fact that content that is encrypted using the PlayReady software development kit (SDK) includes the address of the licensing server in the headers. In this case, the licensing server is at *http://playready.directtaps.net/sl/rightsmanager.asmx*. If you do a trace of your session, you'll see Silverlight connect to the content, read the headers, and then try to direct to the rights manager after individualization.

If your content is *not* protected using PlayReady, but instead by WMDRM, this header will not be present, so you will have to let the *MediaElement* know where to find the license server. You do this using the *LicenseServerUriOverride* property of the *LicenseAcquirer* object on the *MediaElement*.

Here's an example:

```
mel.LicenseAcquirer.LicenseServerUriOverride = new
Uri("http://playready.directtaps.net/sl/rightsmanager.asmx", UriKind.Absolute);
```

Detecting Current State

You can use the *CurrentState* property of the *MediaElement* to detect the current state in the preceding process. *CurrentState* has two possible values as determined by the *MediaElementState* enumeration: *Individualizing* or *AcquiringLicense*, which represent steps 3 and 4 in Figure 10-16.

Thus, you can wire an event handler to the *CurrentStateChanged* property of the *MediaElement* like this:

```
<MediaElement x:Name="mel" CurrentStateChanged="mel_CurrentStateChanged"></MediaElement>
```

And then, you can give status to the user based on the current status like this:

```
private void mel_CurrentStateChanged(object sender, RoutedEventArgs e)
{
    if (mel.CurrentState == MediaElementState.AcquiringLicense)
    {
        // Tell the user that Silverlight is acquiring the license to DRM
    }
    else if(mel.CurrentState == MediaElementState.Individualizing)
    {
        // Tell the user that the process of Individualization is going on
    }
}
```

The *MediaElementState* also contains states for the buffering and playback status of the media. These are covered earlier in this chapter.

User Opt-Out and Error Handling with DRM

The end user can opt out of DRM by disabling the playback of protected content. Users can opt out of playback of protected content by right-clicking Silverlight content and clicking the Configure Silverlight option.

The Playback tab in the Microsoft Silverlight Configuration dialog box is shown in Figure 10-18.

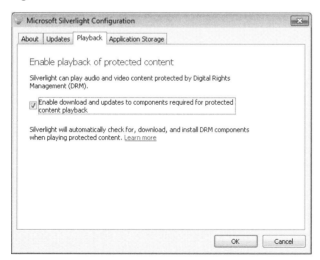

FIGURE 10-18 Silverlight DRM configuration dialog box.

The Enable Download And Updates option in the Playback tab turns on and off the call to request individualization from the individualization servers. If the user clears this option and you attempt to access protected content, the Silverlight media element will throw a new *MediaFailed* event with error code 6008, and the description DRM_E_INDIVIDUALIZATION_DISALLOWED.

Other errors that might occur are described in Table 10-1.

Table 10-1 Errors Users May Encounter When Opening DRM-Protected Media

Error Code / Description	Circumstance
6000 DRM_E_UNABLE_TO_PLAY_PROTECTED_CONTENT	This happens when the *MediaElement* fails to play back the content.
6001 DRM_E_INDIV_DOWNLOAD_FAILURE	This happens when the software from the individualization server has failed to download and run, and thus individualization has failed.
6002 DRM_E_LICENSE_ACQUISITION_FAILURE	This happens when the license acquisition fails. It can also happen if Silverlight cannot access the license server.
6003 DRM_E_INDIV_INSTALL FAILURE	Individualization components failed to install.
6004 DRM_E_SILVERLIGHT_CLIENT_REVOKED	The individualization components are out of date and need to be updated.
6005 DRM_E_INVALID_PROTECTED_FILE_HEADER	Processing of the header of the file failed. This header contains the DRM information, so you cannot proceed. The likely case is that the header was malformed.
6006 DRM_E_LICENSE_PROCESSING_FAILURE	Processing of the license failed. This could be a corruption in downloading the license.
6007 DRM_E_LICENSE_ACQUISITION_SERVICE_SPECIFIC	PlayReady allows for custom errors to be returned. This error is used to handle that.
6008 DRM_E_INDIVIDUALIZATION_DISALLOWED	The user turned off DRM in the configuration settings as discussed previously.

Summary

This chapter takes you on a tour of how to consume media in Silverlight using the *MediaElement* control. You explored how to program against it using the .NET and JavaScript APIs and saw how to set its source and manage the playback of this source. You also looked into managing the states of the *MediaElement*, understanding how buffering works and how you can notify the user of such. You saw how you can use the new H.264 video codec in Silverlight and toured the DRM architecture in Silverlight and how Silverlight can be used to consume protected video.

In the next chapter, you look at other media in Silverlight, including its rich photo management capabilities with DeepZoom and Photosynth.

Chapter 11
Media in Silverlight: Rich Imaging

A core commercial scenario on the Web today is the use of images and rich imaging to provide a great user experience. This is one of the areas in which Microsoft Silverlight is exceptionally strong, providing technologies such as Deep Zoom and Microsoft Live Labs Photosynth. In this chapter, you look at each of these technologies and how to use them in your application. The basic image control for standard imaging support is covered in Chapter 5, "XAML Transformation and Animation."

Deep Zoom with the *MultiScaleImage* Control

Deep Zoom provides you with a new and unique way to manage images in your applications. It is implemented in Extensible Application Markup Language (XAML) by the *MultiScaleImage* element with which, as its name suggests, you can control scale and zoom of your images. Silverlight provides a huge virtual space on which these images can be drawn.

With Deep Zoom, you can provide super-high-resolution images to your users without requiring users to download the full image before they display it. Consider this scenario: You have a very rich image that you want to show, but the image file is 2 gigabytes in size and has a resolution many times larger than the screen resolution. Typically, you would create a Web-friendly lower resolution version that both fits on the screen and is compressed to be much smaller so that Web users can see it. Doing this, of course, causes the image to lose a vast amount of fidelity.

Now, think about how online mapping works. The map effectively is a huge image that has been split into tiles that you can pan around to view the entire map. When you want to view a different part of the map, the mapping software downloads and renders the correct tile. The mapping software provides tiles for when you want to zoom in and out of the map. Deep Zoom works in a similar way. In the scenario with the 2-GB image discussed previously, you can break the image into tiles shown at different zoom levels. The first image you present to users is the low resolution version, which shows a "zoomed-out" state. When users zoom in, Silverlight downloads the correct tiles to render the user's current position in the image at the current particular zoom level. Thus, you can offer users the full fidelity of the image, but they only download the tiles that they need to view the parts of the image that they are looking at.

In addition, with Deep Zoom you can embed an image at one zoom level in an image at another zoom level, providing for many different kinds of special effects. This is best described by example. Look at Figure 11-1, which shows an image of a kid's science project.

FIGURE 11-1 Viewing an image in Deep Zoom.

The image doesn't look too fancy or even very different from a typical photographic image. So, what's all the fuss about Deep Zoom, you might be wondering. In this application, if you rotate the mouse wheel button, you can zoom in or out. Figure 11-2 is another view of this same image, but zoomed out so that the image no longer focuses on the orange. In Figure 11-2, you see the image in relation to the image shown in Figure 11-1: The image in Figure 11-1 looks like a sticker on the orange, but if you zoom in, the smaller image has full fidelity.

If you look closely at the center of the orange in Figure 11-2, you see that the image from Figure 11-1 is embedded in the orange, right at its center. You can zoom out again to see the image shown in Figure 11-3.

In Figure 11-3, the entire image of Figure 11-2 is only a little larger than a pixel in the pupil of the eye, and the entire first image from Figure 11-1 is only a few pixels in size in the second image and can hardly be seen at all in Figure 11-3. It's hard to do the Deep Zoom feature justice by showing you these still images in a book—you really have to see it to believe it. And when you play with it, you will see why the technology is called Deep Zoom: With it, you can arrange pictures so that you can zoom in and out of them very easily by painting them on a giant, scalable canvas.

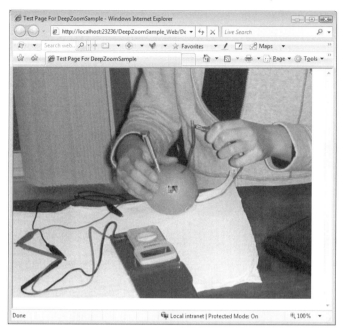

FIGURE 11-2 Zooming out from the original image.

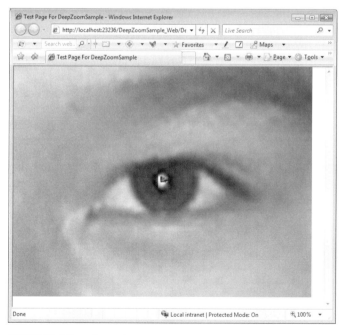

FIGURE 11-3 Zooming out even more.

Using the Deep Zoom Composer

It is fairly simple to create a basic application in which you zoom in and out of images. You simply use the *MultiScaleImage* control and point it at a file that contains metadata about the images. You create the metadata file using Deep Zoom Composer, which you can download from the Microsoft Download Center. You can see Deep Zoom Composer in Figure 11-4.

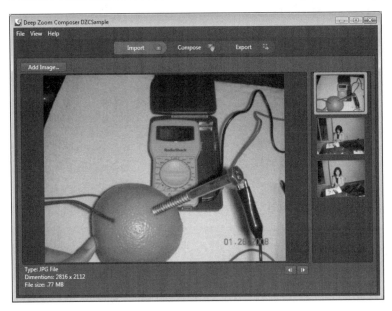

FIGURE 11-4 Deep Zoom Composer.

Deep Zoom Composer follows a simple workflow of *import*, followed by *compose*, and then *export*. So, first you click the Import tab, and then click Add Image to pick an image to use, repeating this step for each picture you want to use. In Figure 11-4, three images are added.

The next step is to compose, which you do using the options in the Compose tab. In this tab, you place an image on the design surface, and then zoom in and out while placing other images. For example, in Figure 11-5, you can see where I placed one image and then zoomed in to the eye.

New images are placed at their default resolution at the Zoom level you selected. In Figure 11-5, you can see where I placed the image in the eye. Later, when you run the application, you would have to zoom directly into the eye to see this image, and it will be tiny until you zoom in further. In Figure 11-6, you see where the image has been placed.

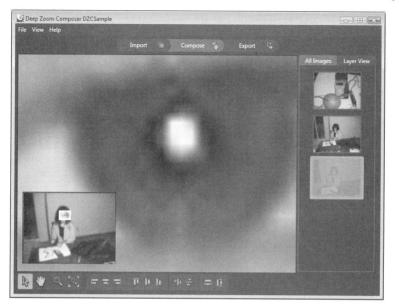

FIGURE 11-5 Composing an image for different zoom levels using Deep Zoom Composer.

FIGURE 11-6 Adding a new image to an image that has been zoomed in.

This simple example shows how you can add to an image another image that appears when you zoom in on the first image. With Deep Zoom, you can build far more complex applications, but for now, this example gives you a good idea of the feature's capabilities.

You are now ready to go to the third step—exporting the details. You can see the Export tab of the Deep Zoom Composer in Figure 11-7.

FIGURE 11-7 Exporting the Deep Zoom metadata.

The Export tab has several options. You can export to the DeepZoomPix service, a free deep zoom based service for photo sharing, or you can export to a project that you can edit and work on. To do this, make sure that the custom tab is selected (as in Figure 11-7), and select the Silverlight Deep Zoom project.

To export the metadata for the images composed in Deep Zoom, you simply need to give the project a name and export it to a specified location. When you have done this, you'll see a dialog box that gives you the option to browse to the project folder. You'll find a GeneratedImages folder within the Web project. Take note of the file called SparseImageSceneGraph.xml, which is a configuration file that defines each image and the location of each image within the other images at the different zoom levels. For example, you can see the scene graph for the two-picture XAML here:

```
<?xml version="1.0"?>
<SceneGraph version="1">
  <AspectRatio>1.33333333333334</AspectRatio>
  <SceneNode>
  <FileName>C:\Code\SLBook\Chapter11\DZCSample
    \source images\DSCN2961.JPG</FileName>
  <x>0</x>
  <y>0</y>
  <Width>1</Width>
  <Height>1</Height>
  <ZOrder>1</ZOrder>
```

```
    </SceneNode>
    <SceneNode>
    <FileName>C:\Code\SLBook\Chapter11\DZCSample
       \source images\DSCN2959.JPG</FileName>
      <x>0.451782754964542</x>
      <y>0.313488814592021</y>
      <Width>0.00099432659277551</Width>
      <Height>0.00099432659277551</Height>
      <ZOrder>2</ZOrder>
    </SceneNode>
</SceneGraph>
```

You can see that this is fairly straightforward XML code. It contains the aspect ratio for the master image (derived from the dimensions of the first image), and then each image becomes a *SceneNode*. The first image is the first *SceneNode*. It is defined as being located at position (0,0), and it is a normalized image—that is, its width and height are set to 1. All other image sizes and locations are then set relative to the first image.

The second image, as you can see, is located at approximately 0.45 on the x-axis and at 0.31 on the y-axis, and it is sized at approximately 0.00099 on x and y relative to the first image. Thus, if you zoom in the first image to approximately 10,000 times the original size, you can view the second image. The Z-order of the second image is 2 (the Z-order of the first image is 1), meaning that it is drawn on top of the first image.

In addition, Deep Zoom Composer slices the image into tiles so that you don't have to load every tile for every zoom level. This provides nice efficiency when you are dealing with large images. When you are zoomed out, you have a small tile, and thus the image will be at a smaller resolution. When you zoom in to the full-resolution version of the image (or beyond), you will see only a portion of the image, and thus you need only download the tiles representing the part of the image that you are viewing, thus saving bandwidth and download time.

The other files to be exported are a set of XML files. These files contain all the details of the tiles and where they are relative to the main image. They are located in the directory that Deep Zoom Composer made, along with a number of other numbered subdirectories containing the images. Because they are XML files, you can open and inspect them.

Building Your First Deep Zoom Project

When you export from Deep Zoom Composer, a Silverlight solution is created for you. You can usually find this in C:\Users\<*yourname*>\Documents\Expression\Deep Zoom Composer Projects\<*yourprojectname*>\Exported Data.

You can open this and edit it in Microsoft Visual Studio.

The Deep Zoom content is rendered using the *MultiScaleImage* control in Page.xaml with its *Source* property set to the location of the XML file that contains the metadata about the composition that you made. In this case, the name of the file will look something like /GeneratedImages/dzc_output.xml. Other attributes of the *MultiScaleImage* allow you to set how it is rendered on the page, for example its width and height.

```
<MultiScaleImage x:Name="msi" Source="/GeneratedImages/dzc_output.xml"/>
```

When you run this application, the *MultiScaleImage* control renders the top element in your composition.

The Visual Studio project created by Deep Zoom Composer generates code for the mouse activity typically associated with the application so that you can pan around or zoom the image. You look at how it does this in the next section.

Using the Mouse and Logical Coordinates in Deep Zoom

The *MultiScaleImage* is just like the other components in Silverlight in that it can declare the functions that should be used to handle events. For example, to pan around the image, you can use the typical mouse events, such as *MouseLeftButtonDown*, *MouseLeftButtonUp*, and *MouseMove*, in a similar manner to drag-and-drop operations on any control. This code is generated for you when you use Deep Zoom Composer.

First, take a look at the XAML for the *MultiScaleImage*:

```
<MultiScaleImage x:Name="msi" Source="/GeneratedImages/dzc_output.xml"/>
```

Next, look at the code behind this in more detail. First, some code is shared across your full application, and it is used for tracking the current state of the mouse and the currently viewed coordinates of the *MultiScaleImage*:

```
double zoom = 1;
bool duringDrag = false;
bool mouseDown = false;
Point lastMouseDownPos = new Point();
Point lastMousePos = new Point();
Point lastMouseViewPort = new Point();
```

Examine what happens when the user clicks the image:

```
this.MouseLeftButtonDown += delegate(object sender, MouseButtonEventArgs e)
{
    lastMouseDownPos = e.GetPosition(msi);
    lastMouseViewPort = msi.ViewportOrigin;

    mouseDown = true;

    msi.CaptureMouse();
};
```

In this example, assume that the user drags the mouse pointer when he or she holds down the mouse button, so the *mouseDown* Boolean can be set to *true*. You also want to know the position of the mouse, which you can store in a *Point*, and the view port position of the mouse, which you can also store in a *Point*. Finally, you want the *MultiScaleImage* to trap all mouse commands, and you can do this by using the *CaptureMouse* method.

When the mouse button is held down, typically users start dragging, and when they do so you want them to be able to pan around the image. Here's the code to achieve this:

```
this.MouseMove += delegate(object sender, MouseEventArgs e)
{
  lastMousePos = e.GetPosition(msi);

  if (duringDrag)
  {
    Point newPoint = lastMouseViewPort;
    newPoint.X += (lastMouseDownPos.X - lastMousePos.X) /
                  msi.ActualWidth * msi.ViewportWidth;
    newPoint.Y += (lastMouseDownPos.Y - lastMousePos.Y) /
                  msi.ActualWidth * msi.ViewportWidth;
    msi.ViewportOrigin = newPoint;
  }
};
```

The *MouseMove* event fires whether the mouse button is held down or not, so you use the *duringDrag* variable to indicate whether the user is dragging by holding down the mouse button. If the user is dragging the mouse pointer, the code in the *if{...}* statement executes.

In this case, you find the new *X,Y* location of the mouse in the *MultiScaleImage* by getting the delta on each coordinate and dividing it by the product of the actual width of the *MultiScaleImage* by its viewport width to give its logical width. Remember that with the *MultiScaleImage*, you can zoom in and out, so the position in the viewport isn't always the same as the position on the screen containing it. This code calculates the position for you. Next, change the current upper left-hand corner of the viewport to the new mouse location. This gives the effect of dragging the image to view a new portion.

Finally, when the user releases the mouse button, you have some house cleaning to do. First, you want to see whether the user was pressing the Shift key to get zooming out functionality in full screen mode when the mouse wheel button is not supported. In addition, you want to release the *bool* functions that are holding the mouse down and mouse dragging states.

```
this.MouseLeftButtonUp += delegate(object sender, MouseButtonEventArgs e)
{
  if (!duringDrag)
  {
    bool shiftDown = (Keyboard.Modifiers & ModifierKeys.Shift) == ModifierKeys.Shift;
    double newzoom = zoom;
```

```
  if (shiftDown)
  {
    newzoom /= 2;
  }
  else
  {
    newzoom *= 2;
  }

  Zoom(newzoom, msi.ElementToLogicalPoint(this.lastMousePos));
}
duringDrag = false;
mouseDown = false;

msi.ReleaseMouseCapture();
};
```

By adding these three simple functions, you enable users to drag the image and pan the view of the image regardless of the zoom level. In the next section, you see how to use the mouse wheel button to zoom in and out of the image and thus reveal the images that are hidden when you are at the outer zoom levels.

Creating the Zoom Functionality Using the Mouse Wheel Button

One problem with building Deep Zoom applications is that the de facto standard control for zooming in and out of an image is the mouse wheel button, but Silverlight and the .NET Framework don't handle events that use the mouse wheel button. You can solve this dilemma in two ways. The first is to use JavaScript rather than C# because the browser can capture rotation of the mouse wheel button and fire an event in response. The second option is to use the browser bridge to Silverlight so that the browser captures the event and then informs .NET that it has done so, after which the code to handle the event is implemented in .NET. Doing this is a lot easier than it sounds, and it is how code that is created by Deep Zoom Composer works.

In the *MouseWheelHelper.cs* class, you can see the following code:

```
HtmlPage.Window.AttachEvent("DOMMouseScroll", this.HandleMouseWheel);
HtmlPage.Window.AttachEvent("onmousewheel", this.HandleMouseWheel);
HtmlPage.Document.AttachEvent("onmousewheel", this.HandleMouseWheel);
```

This code uses the Silverlight browser bridge to attach JavaScript events to .NET events. (The browser bridge is discussed in more detail in Chapter 7, "The Silverlight Browser Bridge.") Whenever any of the specified JavaScript events occur, the *HandleMouseWheel* .NET event fires.

The *HandleMouseWheel* function is as follows:

```
private void HandleMouseWheel(object sender, HtmlEventArgs args)
{
  double delta = 0;
  ScriptObject eventObj = args.EventObject;
  if (eventObj.GetProperty("wheelDelta") != null)
  {
    delta = ((double)eventObj.GetProperty("wheelDelta")) / 120;
    if (HtmlPage.Window.GetProperty("opera") != null)
      delta = -delta;
  }
  else if (eventObj.GetProperty("detail") != null)
  {
    delta = -((double)eventObj.GetProperty("detail")) / 3;
    if (HtmlPage.BrowserInformation.UserAgent.IndexOf("Macintosh") != -1)
      delta = delta * 3;
  }

  if (delta != 0 && this.Moved != null)
  {
    MouseWheelEventArgs wheelArgs = new MouseWheelEventArgs(delta);
    this.Moved(this, wheelArgs);

    if (wheelArgs.Handled)
      args.PreventDefault();
  }
}
```

This function takes an *HtmlEventArgs* object as an argument. The *HtmlEventArgs* object contains an *EventObject* as one of its children. The *EventObject* provides the mouse wheel button metadata, such as *wheelDelta*, which indicates a change in direction resulting from rotation of the mouse wheel button. Different browsers report different values—for example, Opera returns the opposite value of other browsers—so code to handle this issue is used here.

Collections in Deep Zoom

In addition to being able to zoom in and zoom out of an image, you can also build *collections* of images and manipulate them in a zoomable environment.

You might have noticed that when you export images from Deep Zoom Composer, the Create Collection option is available. As its name suggests, this option creates a collection of images. In Figure 11-8, you can see that many images are placed on the design surface. You can export these images as a collection.

When you export images as a collection, as well as the dzc_output.xml file, you also get an XML file for each image, as well as another called SparseImageSceneGraph.xml that contains how each image is placed within the zoom canvas.

In a collection, Silverlight exposes a *SubImages* collection that you can use to manipulate the images. Note that the full set of images is not loaded on page render, so the collection is empty at that point. Instead, make sure that you wire up the *ImageOpenSucceeded* event if you want to manipulate the collection. This event fires when the bin loads and renders correctly.

FIGURE 11-8 Creating a Deep Zoom collection.

Here's the XAML:

```
<MultiScaleImage x:Name="dz"
  Source="/GeneratedImages/dzc_output.xml"
  ImageOpenSucceeded="dz_ImageOpenSucceeded"
  Height="480" Width="640">
</MultiScaleImage>
```

At this point, the *SubImages* collection is populated, and you can use it to manipulate individual images. Here's an example of changing the position of the images:

```
private void dz_ImageOpenSucceeded(object sender, RoutedEventArgs e)
{
  int nImages = dz.SubImages.Count;
  for (int lp = 0; lp < nImages; lp++)
  {
    dz.SubImages[lp].ViewportOrigin = new Point(lp*0.1, lp*0.1);
  }
}
```

As you can see, the process is exactly the same as the one used earlier to manipulate a single image. In the case of collections, each image is manipulated by using *SubImages[lp]*, where *lp* is a loop variable that counts from 0 up to the number of images in the collection. You can see the results in Figure 11-9. Note the difference between this and the original layout, as shown in Figure 11-8.

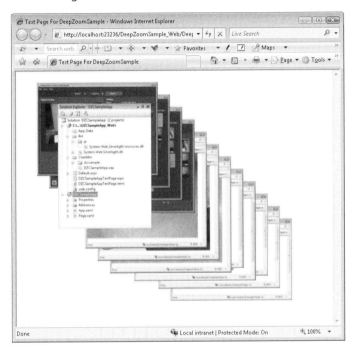

FIGURE 11-9 Laying out an image collection.

With Deep Zoom Composer, you also can stitch pictures together to make them zoomable. You might not have a camera that can create a 2-GB image with a super high resolution, but you can take many pictures of the same scene and stitch them together for the same effect.

Think about it. Say, you have a 4-megapixel camera, so you can take only 4-megapixel shots that, when deep zoomed, will not look as good as images you take with a (for example) 400-megapixel camera.

But what if you could take lots of close-up shots of your subject and then stitch them together? Effectively, you can compose an image with many more megapixels than contained in a single image. A feature of Deep Zoom Composer allows you to do just this.

For example, Figure 11-10 and Figure 11-11 are two of five images I captured of a tall vertical painting I picked up in a Beijing market.

FIGURE 11-10 The top of the painting.

FIGURE 11-11 Another image taken farther down the painting.

With Deep Zoom Composer, you can import images like these and stitch them together. First, start Deep Zoom Composer and import the images.

Then, in the Compose tab, add all the images. You don't have to worry about laying them out. Finally, make sure all the images are selected, right-click one of the images, and then click Create Panoramic Photo. This option is shown in Figure 11-12.

FIGURE 11-12 Creating a panoramic photo in Deep Zoom Composer.

Deep Zoom Composer starts stitching the images together to form a composite image. It's pretty quick. I built this example on a computer with a Windows Experience Index of 3.5, and the process took about 3 seconds to complete.

In most cases, you might find differences in alignment of the images. Deep Zoom Composer provides a Stitching Preview, as shown in Figure 11-13.

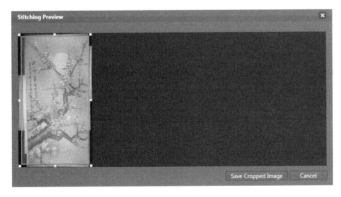

FIGURE 11-13 The preview of the composite stitched image.

In the Stitching Preview, you can choose how to crop your image, and then save it. Deep Zoom Composer adds it to your composition space, and then you can follow the usual workflow to turn this into a Deep Zoom composition.

Creating Photo Scenes Using Photosynth

Photosynth is a technology from Microsoft Research and Microsoft Live Labs that you can use to construct a scene from photographic information about the scene. Probably you've visited many locations where you've taken pictures and then realize that pictures don't do the place justice. For starters, a camera can only take a rectangular image of the scene, not the entire scene, and a flat image can't make the viewer feel immersed in the scene.

With Photosynth, you can effectively stitch together a three-dimensional image of the scene by using a number of flat images. So, imagine you are in the center of a beautiful downtown area and you take pictures of the entire location. When you show these photos to friends, you explain the scene, saying that this building is to the left of the other one in the other picture, and so forth. Photosynth fixes this for you. It works by examining the images for similarities to each other, and then uses this information to estimate the shape of the viewed object in three-dimensional space using the vantage point of each photograph. Photosynth then re-creates the object in 3-D space and maps the images to the appropriate places in space.

Figure 11-14 shows an example synth of images from the Louvre in Paris.

FIGURE 11-14 Synth of images from Paris.

You can download the Photosynth creator and viewer at *http://photosynth.net/learn.aspx*. The images in this chapter don't really do the synths justice. In Figure 11-14, you can see that the main image is brighter than images that are stitched to it on either side. As you pan around, you might feel like you are walking in a 3-D space created by these images.

Photosynth also uses some of the underlying technology of Deep Zoom so that if you have several hundred pictures making up a scene, you don't have to download all of them to view a particular part of the scene.

Creating your own synth scene is very easy. First, you must take some pictures by pointing the camera at an object of interest, and then moving a little bit and taking another photograph from a slightly different vantage point. For example, stand in the center of a room, take a picture, turn a little to the right and take another picture, and so on.

Figures 11-15 and 11-16 show two pictures of a scene that are taken sequentially in this way.

FIGURE 11-15 A picture to add to a synth scene.

FIGURE 11-16 Another picture in the same synth scene.

If you look closely at the figures, you can see that the chair in the first picture is also in the second picture. Photosynth matches these images when creating the synth, recognizing that the second picture is to the right of the first. To create this synth I took about 50 pictures of the whole scene.

Next, download the Photosynth composer software, which also allows you to view synths in your browser. A Silverlight-based player enables users of non-Windows-based operating systems to see the synths, too. (The next section discusses this player in more detail.) However, synth composition is available only to users on Windows-based computers.

You can start Photosynth from the Start menu, or you can click the Start A New Synth button on the Photosynth.net site, as shown in Figure 11-17. You need a Windows Live ID to sign in, and this ID is also used to upload and host your synths.

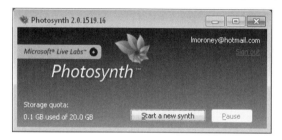

FIGURE 11-17 Starting a new synth.

The Create Synth dialog box appears, as shown in Figure 11-18, and you simply add the photos and provide a name for the synth.

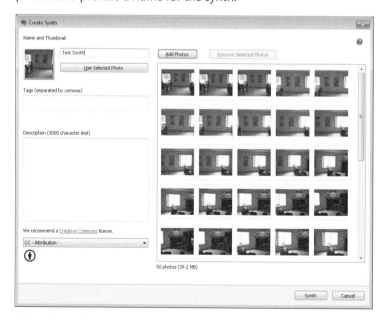

FIGURE 11-18 Creating a synth.

Next, all you have to do is click Synth, and Photosynth does the rest. You can see the finished synth in the browser viewer in Figure 11-19. This figure shows how the images from earlier have been synthesized into a single image in 3-D space. Note that the curvature at the bottom of the screen corresponds to the circle I was turning as I took the pictures.

FIGURE 11-19 The finished synth.

Uploaded synths have a globally unique identifier (GUID). The URL for the synth that I built here is this:

http://photosynth.net/view.aspx?cid=98FF99B1-9B62-408A-9975-3A9F7E68E545

where the value of *cid=* is the GUID. Note the GUID because you will use it with the Silverlight-based viewer. If you create your own synth, you'll get a different GUID. Do note that at this time, all synths are built *online*, so your synth will be viewable by the general public.

Using Photosynth in Silverlight

The Silverlight-based Photosynth player is available at Photosynth.net. To use it, simply substitute the GUID of your synth in this URL. So, to render the synth that I built in the previous section, here's the URL:

http://photosynth.net/silverlight/photosynth.aspx?cid=98FF99B1-9B62-408A-9975-3A9F7E68E545

This URL loads the XAP containing the Photosynth application and uses it to load the synth. You can see this in action on a Mac using Safari in Figure 11-20.

FIGURE 11-20 Using Photosynth on a Mac with Silverlight.

At present, the only way to view your synths is on the Photosynth.net Web site, but be on the lookout for a reusable control. Watch the Photosynth site for more details.

Summary

In this chapter, you looked at the imaging technologies available in Silverlight, including Deep Zoom and Photosynth. With Deep Zoom, you can provide super-high-definition images in bandwidth-constrained environments by providing tile-based download for different pan and zoom levels. You learned how to use a virtual canvas to place one image within a deep-zoomed level of another, effectively nesting them, as well as how to manage collections of images. You used Deep Zoom Composer to create a Silverlight application that provides Deep Zoom functionality to your images and learned a way to stitch multiple lower resolution images together into a single large one that can be zoomed.

Additionally, you took this manipulation process to the third dimension using Photosynth. With Photosynth, you can create a 3-D space out of multiple 2-D images by matching them together based on their contents and interpolating the angle of view of the camera. Photosynth can provide stunning results. You also saw how the Photosynth viewer works cross platform using Silverlight.

Chapter 12
Building Connected Applications with Silverlight

This chapter discusses how to build *connected* applications using Microsoft Silverlight. Silverlight offers a number of data connectivity application programming interfaces (APIs), and you get a good look at how to use them to connect to a hosted service and retrieve its data.

You start with the simplest means of connection in Silverlight, the *WebClient* class, and then delve into how to override the simple functionality using the *HttpWebRequest* and *HttpWebRespose* classes. In addition, you examine connecting to existing Web and Windows Communication Foundation (WCF) services using proxies generated by Microsoft Visual Studio. Finally, in addition to these technologies you look into what it takes to allow for cross-domain access in your Silverlight application using the cross-domain policy files.

To be able to connect to a service, you need a service to connect to, so each technology discussion also involves looking at building a live service that handles your requests and dispatches data back to you.

Building the Data Service

Some of the examples in this chapter demonstrate how to connect to a service that provides financial time series data using a variety of schemes, including XML-over-HTTP from an HTTP-GET request, the same from an HTTP-POST, as well as a Web service and a WCF service that provide this data.

First, start Visual Studio and use it to create a new ASP.NET Web Application project. Call the project PriceHistoryService. You can see this in Figure 12-1.

This creates a standard ASP.NET Web application that contains a Web form called Default.aspx. You will amend this to take in some parameters and return the time series data in a moment, but before doing so, write some helper functions that this and the Web and WCF services that you use later in this chapter can use between them.

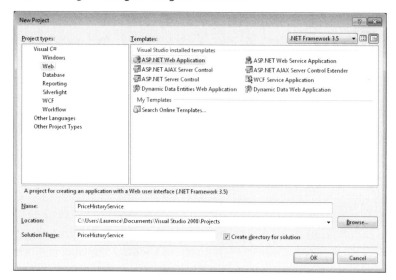

FIGURE 12-1 Creating a new project called PriceHistoryService.

The data that your service exposes to the user is time series data provided by Yahoo.

The Yahoo time series service returns a CSV file containing basic time series data with the following fields: *Date, Opening Price, Closing Price, High, Low, Volume,* and *Adjusted Close.* The API to call it is very simple:

```
http://ichart.finance.yahoo.com/table.csv
```

You can also use the parameters listed in Table 12-1.

TABLE 12-1 **Parameters for Yahoo Time Series Data**

Parameter	Value
s	Stock ticker (that is, MSFT)
a	Start month (0 based, so 0 = January, 11 = December)
b	Start day
c	Start year
d	End month (0 based, so 0 = January, 11 = December)
e	End day
f	End year
g	Always use the letter *d*
ignore	Always use the value *.csv*

To get the time series data for Microsoft (MSFT) from January 1, 2008, to January 1, 2009, you can use the following URL:

http://ichart.finance.yahoo.com/table.csv?s=MSFT&a=0&b=1&c=2008&d=0&e=1&f=2009&g=d&ignore=.csv

Here's a C# function that takes string parameters for ticker, start date, and end date to build this URI:

```csharp
using System.Text;
using System.Xml;
using System.Data;
using System.Net;
using System.IO;
public string BuildYahooURI(string strTicker,
  string strStartDate, string strEndDate)
  {
    string strReturn = "";
    DateTime dStart = Convert.ToDateTime(strStartDate);
    DateTime dEnd = Convert.ToDateTime(strEndDate);

    string sStartDay = dStart.Day.ToString();
    string sStartMonth = (dStart.Month -1).ToString();
    string sStartYear = dStart.Year.ToString();

    string sEndDay = dEnd.Day.ToString();
    string sEndMonth = (dEnd.Month - 1).ToString();
    string sEndYear = dEnd.Year.ToString();

    StringBuilder sYahooURI = new
StringBuilder("http://ichart.finance.yahoo.com/table.csv?s=");
    sYahooURI.Append(strTicker);
    sYahooURI.Append("&a=");
    sYahooURI.Append(sStartMonth);
    sYahooURI.Append("&b=");
    sYahooURI.Append(sStartDay);
    sYahooURI.Append("&c=");
    sYahooURI.Append(sStartYear);
    sYahooURI.Append("&d=");
    sYahooURI.Append(sEndMonth);
    sYahooURI.Append("&e=");
    sYahooURI.Append(sEndDay);
    sYahooURI.Append("&f=");
    sYahooURI.Append(sEndYear);
    sYahooURI.Append("&g=d");
    sYahooURI.Append("&ignore=.csv");

    strReturn = sYahooURI.ToString();
    return strReturn;
}
```

Now that you have the URI for the data, next read the data and use it. In this case, you convert the CSV data to XML. This is a function that can do that:

```
public XmlDocument getXML(string strTicker,
  string strStartDate, string strEndDate)
  {
    XmlDocument xReturn = new XmlDocument();
    DataSet result = new DataSet();
    string sYahooURI = BuildYahooURI(strTicker, strStartDate, strEndDate);
    WebClient wc = new WebClient();
    Stream yData = wc.OpenRead(sYahooURI);
    result = GenerateDataSet(yData);
    StringWriter stringWriter = new StringWriter();
    XmlTextWriter xmlTextwriter = new XmlTextWriter(stringWriter);
    result.WriteXml(xmlTextwriter, XmlWriteMode.IgnoreSchema);
    XmlNode xRoot = xReturn.CreateElement("root");
    xReturn.AppendChild(xRoot);
    xReturn.LoadXml(stringWriter.ToString());

    return xReturn;
}
```

The final helper function you need is the *GenerateDataSet* function that is called in the preceding listing. This takes the comma-separated string returned from the Yahoo data service and turns it into a *DataSet*. This *DataSet* is used later in the Web and WCF services, but for now, it is serialized as XML.

```
public DataSet GenerateDataSet(Stream yData)
    {
        DataSet result = new DataSet();
        StreamReader sRead = new StreamReader(yData);
        string[] columns = sRead.ReadLine().Split(',');
        result.Tables.Add("TimeSeries");
        foreach (string col in columns)
        {
            // Remove spaces from any names
            string thiscol = col.Replace(" ", "");
            // Add the column name
            result.Tables["TimeSeries"].Columns.Add(thiscol);
        }
        string sData = sRead.ReadToEnd();
        string[] rows = sData.Split('\n');

        foreach (string row in rows)
        {
            string[] items = row.Split(',');
            result.Tables["TimeSeries"].Rows.Add(items);

        }
        return result;
    }
```

Put these functions into a class called *HelperFunctions* and add the class to the ASP.NET Web project. Next, add an ASP.NET Web form (ASPX) called GetPriceHistory and edit the ASPX page to remove the HTML markup so that it looks like this:

```
<%@ Page Language="C#" AutoEventWireup="true" CodeBehind="GetPriceHistory.aspx.cs"
Inherits="PriceHistoryService.GetPriceHistory" %>
```

Note You can keep the <!DOCTYPE> declaration at the top of the page.

The nice thing about this is that you can now write code that writes directly to the response buffer and set the response type so that you can write XML over HTTP.

You might notice that this uses the *WebClient* class to manage the communication. This is the *WebClient* that is part of the full Microsoft .NET Framework that ASP.NET uses. In the next section, you look at the *Silverlight WebClient*, which you'll see is strikingly familiar!

So, as the helper functions take strings for the ticker and for the start and end dates, you can make them parameters to the ASPX. You can then pass them to the preceding helper functions to generate XML, which you then write out to the response buffer. In addition to this, set the Multipurpose Internet Mail Extensions (MIME) type to *text/xml* so that any reader can see it as XML and not text.

Here's the code to do that. Remember that *HelperFunctions* is the name of a class containing the functions that build the Yahoo URI, read it, and convert the CSV to XML:

```
HelperFunctions hlp = new HelperFunctions();
protected void Page_Load(object sender, EventArgs e)
{
  string strTicker, strStartDate, strEndDate;

  if(Request.Params["ticker"]!=null)
    strTicker = Request.Params["ticker"].ToString();
  else
    strTicker = "MSFT";

  if(Request.Params["startdate"]!=null)
    strStartDate = Request.Params["startdate"].ToString();
  else
    strStartDate = "1-1-2008";

  if(Request.Params["enddate"]!=null)
    strEndDate = Request.Params["enddate"].ToString();
  else
    strEndDate = "1-1-2009";

  XmlDocument xReturn = hlp.getXML(strTicker, strStartDate, strEndDate);

  Response.ContentType = "text/xml";
  Response.Write(xReturn.OuterXml);

}
```

Remember to make sure that you have all references in place and are using the right system libraries (for example, have *using System.Xml* at the top of your code page).

You now have a simple XML-over-HTTP service that returns time series data. Figure 12-2 shows what the data it returns looks like.

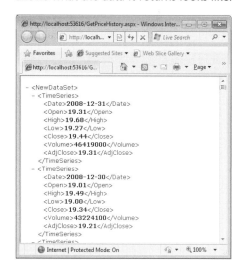

FIGURE 12-2 The XML-over-HTTP service.

In the next section, you see how a Silverlight client can now access this data. Note that the ASP.NET development server is used by this project, and in this session it uses the port 53616 (you can see this in Figure 12-2). This causes some problems when you use Silverlight to access it because Silverlight is subject to cross-domain restrictions when communicating across the network. So, be sure on the Project properties page that you change the project to use the local Internet Information Services (IIS) server.

Using the *WebClient* Class

For basic HTTP connectivity to get information across the Web, such as XML-over-HTTP, the *WebClient* class is perfect. It's simple to use, simple to initialize, and performs well. It also supports basic header manipulation if you need to access the HTTP headers for situations such as using HTTP forms.

In the previous section, you built a service that could be called with the following URL:

http://servername:serverport/GetPriceHistory.aspx?ticker=[ticker]&startdate=[startdate]&enddate=[enddate]

When you run from the local IIS, you can omit the *serverport* parameter.

Create a new Silverlight application using Visual Studio. On the File menu, select New Project. In the New Project dialog box, select the Silverlight Application project template and use it to create a project called PHWebClient.

When the project wizard asks you to host the Silverlight application in a new Web site, do so, and use the default project name.

You can start with a very simple example in which you render the opening prices on the screen. You use the Extensible Application Markup Language (XAML) *ItemsControl* to define an area where items are rendered. In this, you specify a template for how this data is rendered. To keep it simple, just stack *TextBlock* controls vertically using a *StackPanel*.

Here's the XAML:

```
<ItemsControl x:Name="_items">
  <ItemsControl.ItemTemplate>
    <DataTemplate>
      <StackPanel Orientation="Vertical">
        <TextBlock FontWeight="Bold" Text="{Binding open}" />
      </StackPanel>
    </DataTemplate>
  </ItemsControl.ItemTemplate>
</ItemsControl>
```

Note that the *Text* for the *TextBlock* is set to a *Binding*, and this is set to the value called *open*. So, now build the code for the Silverlight client that gets the data and provides the other side of the binding.

Start with a class that represents the time series data. As you might remember, the time series data includes values for the date of a trade, open, close, high, low, volume, and adjusted close. Here's a class that can store these values:

```
public class TimeSeriesData
  {
    public DateTime date { get; set; }
    public double open { get; set; }
    public double close { get; set; }
    public double high { get; set; }
    public double low { get; set; }
    public double volume { get; set; }
    public double adjclose { get; set; }

    public TimeSeriesData(DateTime dteIn, double openIn, double closeIn,
          double highIn, double lowIn, double volumeIn, double adjCloseIn)
    {
      date = dteIn;
      open = openIn;
      close = closeIn;
      high = highIn;
      low = lowIn;
```

```
      volume = volumeIn;
      adjclose = adjCloseIn;
    }

    public TimeSeriesData()
    {
  }
}
```

Nothing special here, just a simple data storage class. So, how do you connect to the price history data service, get the data, and provide the binding? Well, it's pretty simple using the *WebClient* in Silverlight.

The *WebClient* uses an instance of the *System.Net.Uri* class to define the address. So, here's the code to create one of these called *uri*:

```
Uri uri = new
Uri("http://localhost/PriceHistoryService/GetPriceHistory.aspx?ticker=MSFT&startdate=1-1-
2009&enddate=1-10-2009", UriKind.RelativeOrAbsolute);
```

Now, you create an instance of the *WebClient* class and define the function that will be called on the callback when the read from the service is completed:

```
WebClient wc = new WebClient();
wc.OpenReadCompleted += new OpenReadCompletedEventHandler(wc_OpenReadCompleted);
```

Now all you have to do is read the return value from the service call:

```
wc.OpenReadAsync(uri);
```

When the read of the data from the service is complete, the *wc_OpenReadCompleted* function is called. This takes a parameter of the type *OpenReadCompletedEventArgs* called *e*. This argument contains a *Result* property that is a *Stream*. You can read the XML from this stream using a *StreamReader*:

```
StreamReader read = new StreamReader(e.Result);
string strXml = read.ReadToEnd();
```

An *XDocument* class can create an XML document from this string using its *Parse* method. Here's how:

```
XDocument xmlDoc = XDocument.Parse(strXml);
```

Now that you have the data in an *XDocument*, you can use LINQ to create an *IEnumerable* of the *TimeSeriesData* class that you created earlier. Silverlight uses *IEnumerable* classes when data binding, so it is easy to bind once you have it. Here's the LINQ to set it up:

```
IEnumerable<TimeSeriesData> myTimeSeries = from item in xmlDoc.Descendants("TimeSeries")
    select new TimeSeriesData
    {
      open = Convert.ToDouble(item.Element("Open").Value)
      };
```

Note that this code just extracts the *Open* value from the XML. Later examples demonstrate the rest but are omitted here for brevity.

Your visual interface is an *ItemsControl*, and when you set its *ItemsSource* property to an *IEnumerable*, it performs the data binding. However, if this code is run on the *UI Thread* (for example, if you made the client call from the *MainPage* constructor as in this case), you have to use the *Dispatcher* to make the binding occur outside the thread.

Here's how:

```
Dispatcher.BeginInvoke(() => _items.ItemsSource = myTimeSeries);
```

Because this application uses LINQ, remember to add a reference to the System.Xml.Linq DLL using the References folder in your solution, and add a *using* definition for it at the top of your code page. Otherwise, this code will not compile.

So, here it is all put together—the full code-behind on this Silverlight class:

```
using System;
using System.Collections.Generic;
using System.Linq;
using System.Net;
using System.Windows;
using System.Windows.Controls;
using System.Windows.Documents;
using System.Windows.Input;
using System.Windows.Media;
using System.Windows.Media.Animation;
using System.Windows.Shapes;
using System.IO;
using System.Xml;
using System.Xml.Linq;
namespace PHWebClient
{
  public partial class MainPage : UserControl
  {
    public MainPage()
    {
      InitializeComponent();
      WebClient wc = new WebClient();
      Uri uri = new
```

```
Uri("http://localhost/PriceHistoryService/GetPriceHistory.aspx?ticker=MSFT&startdate=1-1-
2009&enddate=1-10-2009", UriKind.RelativeOrAbsolute);
    wc.OpenReadCompleted += new OpenReadCompletedEventHandler(wc_OpenReadCompleted);
    wc.OpenReadAsync(uri);
  }

  void wc_OpenReadCompleted(object sender, OpenReadCompletedEventArgs e)
  {
    StreamReader read = new StreamReader(e.Result);
    string strXml = read.ReadToEnd();
    XDocument xmlDoc = XDocument.Parse(strXml);
    IEnumerable<TimeSeriesData> myTimeSeries = from item in
xmlDoc.Descendants("TimeSeries")
       select new TimeSeriesData
       {
         open = Convert.ToDouble(item.Element("Open").Value)
       };

    Dispatcher.BeginInvoke(() => _items.ItemsSource = myTimeSeries);
  }
 }
}
```

Figure 12-3 shows the output from this code.

FIGURE 12-3 Rendering the data using a *WebClient.*

In this section, you saw how simple it is to connect to a data service that provides XML-over-HTTP and gives you a simple data binding. It provides the foundation for many scenarios, but you can dig a little deeper. Some data services require you to POST values in the HTTP headers using HTTP forms. In the next section, first you see how to build a simple server that accepts HTTP-POST parameters, and then you build a client that consumes them.

Expanding the Service for HTTP-POST

Earlier you created the PriceHistoryService solution that contains the GetPriceHistory.aspx page that was used to give the price history data using the XML-over-HTTP service. You can add to that to create a service that will handle HTTP forms with HTTP-POST variables.Go back to this solution, add a new generic handler (ASHX) to the solution, and call it GetPriceHistoryWithPOST.ashx.

You can see that the code-behind for this gives you a *ProcessRequest* event that takes an *HttpContext* as a parameter. This is everything you need to catch parameters passed in with an HTTP-POST, use them to call the Yahoo service, get the data back, and then format it as XML for the client to process.

Here's the code to achieve this—it's very similar to the ASPX code from earlier in this chapter:

```
public void ProcessRequest(HttpContext context)
{
  HelperFunctions hlp = new HelperFunctions();
  string strTicker;
  string strStartDate;
  string strEndDate;
  if (context.Request.HttpMethod == "POST")
  {
    if (context.Request.Form["ticker"] != null)
      strTicker = context.Request.Form["ticker"].ToString();
    else
      strTicker = "MSFT";

    if (context.Request.Form["startdate"] != null)
      strStartDate = context.Request.Form["startdate"].ToString();
    else
      strStartDate = "1-1-2008";

    if (context.Request.Form["enddate"] != null)
      strEndDate = context.Request.Form["enddate"].ToString();
    else
      strEndDate = "1-1-2009";

    XmlDocument xReturn = hlp.getXML(strTicker, strStartDate, strEndDate);

    context.Response.ContentType = "text/xml";
    context.Response.Write(xReturn.OuterXml);

  }
  else
    {
      context.Response.Write("This must be called with an HTTP-POST with params in the
header");
    }

  }
```

Note that you need to add *using* statements for System.Xml and System.Web.Services at the top of this code to ensure that it compiles.

This code simply checks to see whether an HTTP-POST has been performed, and if it has, it pulls the values for the ticker, start date, and end date parameters from the HTTP-POST form. It then passes these to the *getXML* function in the *HelperFunctions* class, which handles the heavy lifting for you.

The data is then written back on the response stream. If you call this ASHX without an HTTP-POST form, an error text is written back.

Using *HttpWebRequest* and *HttpWebResponse*

HttpWebRequest and *HttpWebResponse* give you fine-grained control over HTTP communications, so you can use these to manage doing an HTTP-POST to the server.

How to use these looks a little convoluted at first, but you'll soon get the hang of it. The flow is like this:

1. Create a new *HttpWebRequest* and initialize it.

2. Get the *Request* stream on an asynchronous callback when the request is ready to go.

3. Once the request is ready to go, write the parameters to it and set up the callback for the response to this request.

4. When the response callback fires, pull the data that you want out of it.

So, to get started, create a new Silverlight project called PHPostClient. Amend the MainPage.xaml file with the *ItemsPresenter* as you did in the *WebClient* project earlier. It should look like this:

```
<UserControl x:Class="PHPostClient.MainPage"
  xmlns="http://schemas.microsoft.com/winfx/2006/xaml/presentation"
  xmlns:x="http://schemas.microsoft.com/winfx/2006/xaml"
  Width="400" Height="300">
  <Grid x:Name="LayoutRoot" Background="White">
    <ItemsControl x:Name="_items">
      <ItemsControl.ItemTemplate>
        <DataTemplate>
          <StackPanel Orientation="Vertical">
            <TextBlock FontWeight="Bold" Text="{Binding open}" />
          </StackPanel>
        </DataTemplate>
      </ItemsControl.ItemTemplate>
    </ItemsControl>
  </Grid>
</UserControl>
```

Next, in its code-behind you manage the communication. So, first, in the *MainPage()* constructor you get everything started. As earlier, make sure that you add a project reference to the System.Xml.Linq DLL, and ensure that you add a *using* statement for System.IO and System.Xml.Linq at the top of your code page.

To set up the *HttpWebRequest*, you need the URI of the service that you are calling:

```
Uri uri = new Uri("http://localhost/PriceHistoryService/GetPriceHistorywithPOST.ashx");
HttpWebRequest request = (HttpWebRequest)HttpWebRequest.Create(uri);
```

You need to specify that this is a POST request on the request object, as well as let the object know that this is an HTTP form, which you specify using the *ContentType* property:

```
request.Method = "POST";
request.ContentType = "application/x-www-form-urlencoded";
```

Finally, you begin the initialization of the request stream. This is performed asynchronously, so you need to specify the callback to handle the next step once the request stream is set up. In this case, your callback is called *RequestProceed*:

```
request.BeginGetRequestStream(new AsyncCallback(RequestProceed), request);
```

The *RequestProceed* callback should take a parameter of type *IASyncResult*. Here's an example in which this parameter is called *asyncResult*:

```
void RequestProceed(IAsyncResult asyncResult)
  {
  }
```

The *HttpRequest* variable isn't global, so there's no context to get it in this function. However, it is stored in the *asyncResult* variable's *AsyncState* property, and you can get a handle on it like this:

```
HttpWebRequest request = (HttpWebRequest)asyncResult.AsyncState;
```

Now that you have it, the next step is to write the data with your parameters into the request so that it can be passed to the service. You do this using a *StreamWriter*, and the stream is available on the request object itself. Here's how to set it up:

```
StreamWriter postDataWriter = new StreamWriter(request.EndGetRequestStream(asyncResult));
```

Writing the parameters is as easy as writing strings to this *StreamWriter*:

```
postDataWriter.Write("ticker=MSFT");
postDataWriter.Write("&startdate=1-1-2009");
postDataWriter.Write("&enddate=1-10-2009");
postDataWriter.Close();
```

You've written out everythinig to the request, so the last thing to do is to start listening to the response. Again, you use a callback. You call the *BeginGetReponse* method of the request and tell it the callback function name:

```
request.BeginGetResponse(new AsyncCallback(ResponseProceed), request);
```

You're almost there! The final step is to catch the response and read the data from it. Your callback is called *ResponseProceed*, and it also takes an *IASyncResult* parameter:

```
void ResponseProceed(IAsyncResult asyncResult)
{}
```

As before, you need to pull the reference to the request out of the *asyncResult*, and additionally you can get the response from the request object. Here's how:

```
HttpWebRequest request = (HttpWebRequest)asyncResult.AsyncState;
HttpWebResponse response = (HttpWebResponse)request.EndGetResponse(asyncResult);
```

Now that you have the response object, you can read the data from it using a *StreamReader*. Here's how:

```
StreamReader responseReader = new StreamReader(response.GetResponseStream());
string responseString = responseReader.ReadToEnd();
```

And now you're back in familiar territory. You have a string of XML data, so you can load it into an *XDocument*, use LINQ to get the data that you want from it into an *IEnumerable*, and bind it to your user interface. Don't forget to add a *TimeSeriesData* class to your project in the same way that you added the *WebClient* project earlier.

```
XDocument xReturn = XDocument.Parse(responseString);
IEnumerable<TimeSeriesData> myTimeSeries = from item in xReturn.Descendants("TimeSeries")
  select new TimeSeriesData
  {
    open = Convert.ToDouble(item.Element("Open").Value)
  };

  Dispatcher.BeginInvoke(() => _items.ItemsSource = myTimeSeries);
```

You can see the results of this code in Figure 12-4.

FIGURE 12-4 Rendering the data returned from the HTTP-POST.

If you think this looks a lot like Figure 12-3, you are right—the visual layer hasn't changed at all, just the plumbing behind it to handle a different communications protocol! In the next section, you look at another methodology for communicating with backend services—SOAP Web services.

Building the SOAP Web Service

In the previous sections, you saw how to build a simple XML-over-HTTP service and an HTTP-POST service that return data to a Silverlight client. Another way of providing a data service is by using a SOAP Web service. You see how to construct and consume one in this section.

First, go back to the PriceHistoryService solution you've been working on and add a new Web service called *PriceHistoryWebService*. Use the extension .asmx for the service.

A Web service is a special type of HTTP-POST service that carries a structured message using the Simple Object Access Protocol (SOAP). Visual Studio handles all the underlying functions for you, so creating a Web service is easy.

In the PriceHistoryWebService.asmx.cs file, you can see a basic Hello World function, which is attributed as a *WebMethod* like this:

```
[WebMethod]
public string HelloWorld()
{
  return "Hello World";

}
```

You can easily create a Web method to return the time series data using the helper functions that you created earlier in the chapter. You simply create a function that takes the three parameters (ticker, start date, and end date) and that uses the *getXML* function on the helper functions to return an *XMLDocument*, which you then pass back to the caller.

Here's the code:

```
[WebMethod]
public XmlDocument getPriceHistoryAsXML(string strTicker, string strStartDate, string
strEndDate)
  {
    XmlDocument xReturn = new XmlDocument();    HelperFunctions hlp = new HelperFunctions();


    xReturn = hlp.getXML(strTicker, strStartDate, strEndDate);
    return xReturn;


  }
```

Executing this code gets you to the test harness for SOAP services, which you can see in Figure 12-5.

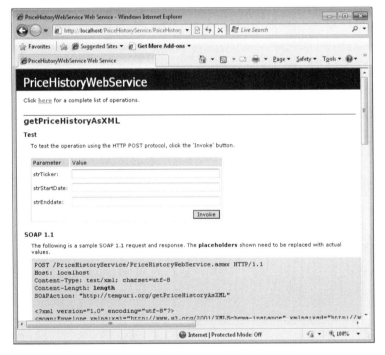

FIGURE 12-5 The Web service test harness.

You can type values for the parameters in this test harness and click Invoke to see the results, or you can click the link at the top of the page to get the address of the Web Services Description Language (WSDL) file that describes this Web service. The address of this WSDL looks something like this:

http://localhost/PriceHistoryService/PriceHistoryWebService.asmx?WSDL

Take note of this address because you need it later to create the proxy class to the Web service that Silverlight uses.

Creating a Web Services Client in Silverlight

Now that you have the Web service and the address of its description in WSDL, you can easily create a client that can consume this Web service.

Create a new Silverlight application and call it PHSoapClient.

Go to the Silverlight project and select References. Right-click and click Add Service Reference. This opens the Add Service Reference dialog box, as shown in Figure 12-6.

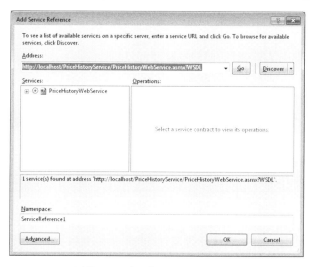

FIGURE 12-6 Adding a Web reference.

Enter the address of the WSDL in the Address box, and click Go. Your service is found and a default namespace (ServiceReference1) is created. Change the name to something a little more friendly, say, PHWebService, and click OK. A proxy class to the Web service is now created for you.

This proxy class contains a SOAP client that can be used to communicate with the service. The client is called *<Service Name>*SoapClient. In this case, you can declare an instance of this class with the following code:

```
PHWebService.PriceHistoryWebServiceSoapClient myClient =
    new PHWebService.PriceHistoryWebServiceSoapClient();
```

Calling the service and getting the data back are as simple as defining the callback function for the return, and then calling the function. The proxy class adds *Async* to the end of the function name, so a service with a Web method called *foo* is callable with *fooAsync*.

Here's the code to set up the callback and to call the Web service for some time series data:

```
myClient.getPriceHistoryAsXMLCompleted +=
  new EventHandler<PHWebClient.PHWebService.getPriceHistoryAsXMLCompletedEventArgs>
  (myClient_getPriceHistoryAsXMLCompleted);
myClient.getPriceHistoryAsXMLAsync("MSFT", "1-1-2009", "1-11-2009");
```

Note that you can use the Tab key on your keyboard to automatically complete the code for these functions.

Your callback will receive a callback containing a parameter called *<Web Method name + Completed Event Args>*. So, in this case, as you call *getPriceHistoryAsXML*, you get a *getpriceHistoryAsXMLCompletedEventArgs* object called *e* returned.

In this case, the XML returned is serialized as a string so that you can load it into an *XDocument* quite easily:

```
XDocument xmlDoc = XDocument.Parse(e.Result.ToString());
```

And now you can use LINQ to create an *IEnumerable* in the same way that you have created the other examples in this chapter. Bind *IEnumerable* to an *ItemsPresenter* as before:

```
IEnumerable<TimeSeriesData> myTimeSeries = from item in xmlDoc.Descendants("TimeSeries")
  select new TimeSeriesData
  {
    open = Convert.ToDouble(item.Element("Open").Value)
  };
  Dispatcher.BeginInvoke(() => _items.ItemsSource = myTimeSeries);
```

As you can see, using a Web service makes for easy communication through an automatically generated proxy class, and Silverlight supports this natively.

Do note, though, that if you try to use classes in your Web service that are not supported by Silverlight, the proxy generation, compilation, or runtime might fail. For example, if your Web service returns a *Dataset*, you'll have problems with the Silverlight proxy.

The next section discusses WCF. With WCF, you can communicate similarly, but in a structured and well-performing way.

Building the WCF Service

Whereas you have been adding to the service project all along, in this case you create a new service. It's sometimes a little tricky to mix up WCF and non-WCF in the same solution, particularly for the configuration files, so keep it simple and create a new WCF service application. In Visual Studio, on the File menu, click New Web Site, and then select WCF Service from the list of available templates. Call your solution PHWCFService.

Before going any further, add an instance of the *TimeSeriesData* class and an instance of the *HelperFunctions* class that you've been using in this chapter.

Because the *TimeSeriesData* class is used between the service and the client, you need to amend it slightly to define the data contract between the server and the client. The data contract allows the proxy generator to generate classes on the client side that replicate what is available on the server side.

```
public class TimeSeriesData
  {
  [DataMember]
    public DateTime date { get; set; }
  [DataMember]
    public double open { get; set; }
  [DataMember]
    public double close { get; set; }
  [DataMember]
    public double high { get; set; }
  [DataMember]
    public double low { get; set; }
  [DataMember]
    public double volume { get; set; }
  [DataMember]
    public double adjclose { get; set; }

  public TimeSeriesData(DateTime dteIn, double openIn, double closeIn,
        double highIn, double lowIn, double volumeIn, double adjCloseIn)
    {
      date = dteIn;
      open = openIn;
      close = closeIn;
      high = highIn;
      low = lowIn;
      volume = volumeIn;
      adjclose = adjCloseIn;
    }

  public TimeSeriesData()
    {
    }
}
```

As you can see, the only difference between this and the earlier *TimeSeriesData* class definition is that you specify the public member variables as data members using the *[DataMember]* attribute.

Next, add a new service to your project. In the Add New Item dialog box, call the service PHService. You'll see that three new files are added to your solution: PHService.svc, PHService.svc.cs, and IPHService.cs.

Start with the IPHService (I for *interface*), and edit it so that it looks like this:

```
using System;
using System.Collections.Generic;
using System.Linq;
using System.Runtime.Serialization;
using System.ServiceModel;
using System.Text;

namespace PHWCFService
{
    // NOTE: If you change the interface name "IPHService" here, you must also update the
    reference to "IPHService" in Web.config.
    [ServiceContract]
    public interface IPHService
    {
        [OperationContract]
        IEnumerable<TimeSeriesData> getTimeSeries(string ticker, string startdate, string
enddate);

    }
}
```

Here, you've defined the interface that your service uses to communicate. Next, you need to
implement it. You do this in PHService.svc.cs.

Here's the code:

```
namespace PHWCFService
{
  public class PHService : IPHService
  {
    HelperFunctions hlp = new HelperFunctions();
    public IEnumerable<TimeSeriesData> getTimeSeries(string ticker, string startdate, string
enddate)
    {
      XmlDocument xmlDoc = hlp.getXML(ticker, startdate, enddate);
      XDocument xDoc = XDocument.Parse(xmlDoc.InnerXml);
      IEnumerable<TimeSeriesData> ret = from item in xDoc.Descendants("TimeSeries")
        select new TimeSeriesData
        {
          adjclose = Convert.ToDouble(item.Element("AdjClose").Value),
          close = Convert.ToDouble(item.Element("Close").Value),
          high = Convert.ToDouble(item.Element("High").Value),
          low = Convert.ToDouble(item.Element("Low").Value),
          open = Convert.ToDouble(item.Element("Open").Value),
          volume = Convert.ToDouble(item.Element("Volume").Value),
          date = Convert.ToDateTime(item.Element("Date").Value)
        };
      return ret;
    }
  }
}
```

By now, this might look familiar! It's part of the magic of the consistency of .NET; your skills in one tier translate to others. Here, you can see that the business logic using XML and LINQ on the server side is identical to using it on the client side!

Before you create the Silverlight client, you have to modify the service configuration to allow Silverlight to use it. WCF supports many binding types for communication, but Silverlight doesn't consume all of them, so you need to change the endpoint configuration to support the binding type. Find the *<system.serviceModel>* section in the Web.config file, and in it you should see your services. The *<service>* tag has a binding attribute. Be sure to change this to *basicHttpBinding* or your Silverlight proxy will fail.

Now that you have configured your service, go ahead and add a Silverlight project to this solution. Call it PHWCFClient.

Now, in the Silverlight project, you can add a reference to the WCF service. Do this by right-clicking the References folder, and clicking Add Service Reference. You can find the service by using the Discover button. Select the service and give it a friendly name such as PHService.

Visual Studio then creates a proxy class for you in your Silverlight project, and this proxy class can talk with the WCF service.

Creating the instance of the client is easy—the friendly name that you used for the service is the namespace of the proxy class, and the proxy class is called *<ServiceName>* with *Client* appended. In this case, the code looks like this:

```
PHService.PHServiceClient myService = new PHService.PHServiceClient();
```

Now, just like in every other example in this chapter, you create the callback function that is invoked when the communication is finished, and you make the call to the service passing it the parameters. Here's the code:

```
myService.getTimeSeriesCompleted +=
  new EventHandler<PHWCFClient.PHService.getTimeSeriesCompletedEventArgs>
  (myService_getTimeSeriesCompleted);
myService.getTimeSeriesAsync("MSFT", "1-1-2009", "1-11-2009");
```

Don't forget that Visual Studio really helps you to type this; press the Tab key when prompted.

In previous examples, you passed XML across the wire, and the XML had to be loaded in an *XDocument* so that you could use LINQ to generate an *IEnumerable* for binding. In this case, if you were looking closely, you can see that the service returns an *IEnumerable* directly. So, now all you have to do to bind to the returned data is to bind to the *Result* property of the event arguments. Here's the full callback:

```
void myService_getTimeSeriesCompleted(object sender,
    PHWCFClient.PHService.getTimeSeriesCompletedEventArgs e)
{
  Dispatcher.BeginInvoke(() => _items.ItemsSource = e.Result);
}
```

And as before, the data binds and shows the close price.

Making Calls Across Domains

In each example in this chapter, you made calls in the same domain, likely *http://localhost*. However, in many instances you need to call data that is on services hosted on other computers. Silverlight uses a policy approach to this, whereby the service being called has to allow Silverlight to call it. It does this by hosting a policy file in its root domain. When Silverlight sees a call to this domain, it first looks for the policy file in the root web. If the policy file isn't there, the call is not made and an error is raised. If the policy file is there, Silverlight parses the file. If a call is disallowed according to the policy, the call is not made and an error is raised. Otherwise, Silverlight attempts the call. This file should be named clientaccesspolicy.xml.

Here's an example of a policy file:

```
<?xml version="1.0" encoding="utf-8" ?>
<access-policy>
  <cross-domain-access>
    <policy>
      <allow-from http-request-headers="*">
        <domain uri="*" />
      </allow-from>
      <grant-to>
        <resource path="/" include-subpaths="true" />
      </grant-to>
    </policy>
  </cross-domain-access>
</access-policy>
```

The *allow-from* nodes define the domains from which calls are allowed. In this case, with the URI set to * you are saying that anyone can call this service. Additionally, in the *grant-to* section, where the resource path and its subpaths are defined, you can specify which resources on the server can be accessed. In the preceding policy file, you are basically saying that anybody can access anything.

Summary

This chapter tours the different methods you can use to connect Silverlight to Web-based services that provide data. It looked at four main methods of connectivity: the *WebClient*, which provides basic functionality; the *HttpWebRequest/HttpWebRespose,* which can be used for more fine-grained control, such as submitting and responding to HTTP form protocols; the standard SOAP Web services approach, where you can use the Web Service Definition file to generate a proxy that allows you to talk to the Web service; and finally, the WCF, which allows you to elegantly and easily move data around.

Chapter 13
Styles and Templates in Silverlight

In the last few chapters, you've learned about many of the controls that are available in Microsoft Silverlight, including how to write your own controls. The Silverlight controls are designed to have a coherent, rich look and feel out of the box, but you might want to tweak the default appearance of controls to fit your own particular design. Fortunately, Silverlight controls are very easy to customize, and Silverlight offers you powerful styling and templating features that you can use to customize the look of your application.

Understanding Styling

To understand styling, look at a simple case in which you use a button in a Silverlight application. Following is the Extensible Application Markup Language (XAML) for a *Button* control:

```
<Canvas Background="LightBlue">
  <Button x:Name="btn" Content="Click Me!" Width="140"></Button>
</Canvas>
```

This code renders a button in the default Silverlight style (which is silver and looks like it is lit from above), and the result looks like the button shown in Figure 13-1.

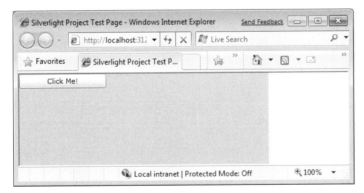

FIGURE 13-1 Basic Silverlight button.

As you saw in Chapter 8, "Silverlight Core Controls," and Chapter 9, "Silverlight Controls: Advanced Controls," many of the controls, including *Button*, are *content* controls, meaning that they can render XAML content. For example, a *Button* control can contain content much more interesting than just a string that says "Click Me!" You can add features to content controls to offer users a richer experience when interacting with the controls.

Say, you want to create an image button—one that includes a graphic. You can do so by using an image as content. Here's an example:

```
<Canvas Background="LightBlue">
<Button Canvas.Left="40" Canvas.Top="40"
 x:Name="btn" Width="60" Height="80">
    <Button.Content>
      <StackPanel Orientation="Vertical">
       <Image Source="icon.jpg"
          Height="48" Width="48">
       </Image>
       <TextBlock Text="Click!"></TextBlock>
      </StackPanel>
    </Button.Content>
   </Button>
</Canvas>
```

You can see how this code is rendered in Figure 13-2.

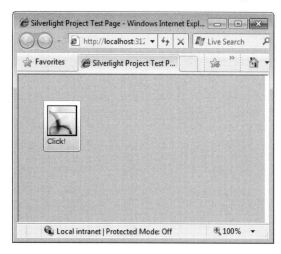

FIGURE 13-2 *Button* using XAML content.

Now, what if you are not happy with the default font and color used for the text on the button, and you want to alter the appearance of the button a bit more? This is quite straightforward in XAML. You can set properties including the font family, size, weight, and so forth to customize the appearance of the button. For example, here's an updated *TextBlock*:

```
<TextBlock Text="Click!" FontFamily="Comic Sans Ms"
Foreground="MediumBlue" FontSize="20">
</TextBlock>
```

You can also add a few other implementations to the button. This is fairly easy to do with XAML because you can copy and paste the first button, and then tweak the location properties of the copies to place them on the page. You can see an example of multiple instances of a button in Figure 13-3.

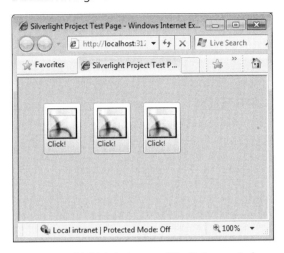

FIGURE 13-3 Multiple instances of the *Button* control.

Although these buttons look nice, and they are very easy to render, when you do it this way, you end up having lots of XAML, and worse, lots of *repeated* XAML—this makes your application harder to inspect, debug, manage, and update, not to mention a lot bigger than it needs to be.

Consider the *TextBlock* controls alone—each one has *FontFamily*, *Foreground*, and *FontSize* properties explicitly declared, even though they are all set to the same value. Consider what happens when you want to change some of this information—you have to go through each control one by one to update them all.

Here is where styles come in handy. The following section discusses moving some of this information into a style.

Creating a Style

You create a style in the *<Resources>* section of your container. You can create one or more styles for which you provide the target type as well as a name for each. For example, to target a *TextBlock* control with a style called *TextBlockStyle*, you can use XAML like this:

```
<Style TargetType="TextBlock" x:Key="TextBlockStyle">
</Style>
```

Note that although you specify the type of control that you want to use, you aren't limited to one style per type. So, just because you are targeting the *TextBlock* with this style doesn't mean that all instances of the *TextBlock* control will use it. You have to configure the style to use on the control itself, and you point the control at the *Key* of the style. Thus, you can have lots of different style definitions aimed at the *TextBlock* control, and each will have different *Key* settings. Then, you pick the style you want to apply to a particular *TextBlock* by setting its *Style* property to a named style. You see how to do this mapping in a moment, but first, consider how you style properties in the *TextBlock*.

You use a *Setter*. A *Setter* is an XAML tag that defines the *Property* that you want to set and the *Value* that you want it to have.

Following is the XAML that you used earlier to set the *Text, FontFamily, Foreground*, and *FontSize* of the *TextBlock*:

```
<TextBlock Text="Click!" FontFamily="Comic Sans Ms"
Foreground="MediumBlue" FontSize="20">
</TextBlock>
```

Now, here is the style that does the same thing:

```
<Style TargetType="TextBlock" x:Key="TextBlockStyle">
  <Setter Property="FontFamily" Value="Comic Sans Ms"></Setter>
  <Setter Property="Text" Value="Click!"></Setter>
  <Setter Property="Foreground" Value="MediumBlue"></Setter>
  <Setter Property="FontSize" Value="20"></Setter>
</Style>
```

You should define this style as a resource on your page. If you look at the root XAML on your page, you can see that it is a *UserControl*. It supports a *<UserControl.Resources>* child. Place the *<Style>* tag in this.

To apply this style to the *TextBlock*, you use the *Style* property, and because the style itself is defined as a resource, you use the *StaticResource* syntax to specify the name of the style:

```
<TextBlock Style="{StaticResource TextBlockStyle}">
</TextBlock>
```

Now you have a single place where you can specify the properties for *TextBlock* controls in the button, making maintenance much simpler and your XAML easier to read and understand.

You can override any properties that a style sets simply by setting properties on the object itself. For example, if you want to override the *Foreground* property that the style sets to *MediumBlue*, it's very easy to do, as shown in this example:

```
<TextBlock Style="{StaticResource TextBlockStyle}"
          Foreground="Black">
</TextBlock>
```

In this case, adding a *Foreground* property setting overrides the style, and the foreground of the *TextBlock* is now set to *Black*.

Also, do note that although the example *TextBlock* is within the image button you've been using, the style isn't limited to this control. You can apply the style to any *TextBlock* on this *Canvas*.

Changing the Style Scope

In the previous example, you created a style on the *Canvas* that contains the controls. By doing so, you limit the scope of the style to that *Canvas* alone. If you have multiple pages in your application, you would have to define styles across each page, which is inefficient.

Fortunately, with Silverlight you can define styles across the application by setting styles in *App.xaml*. Indeed, if you look at the default *App.xaml* file that is set up by the Microsoft Visual Studio template, you can see that the *<Resources>* section has already been defined!

```
<Application xmlns="http://schemas.microsoft.com/client/2007"
  xmlns:x="http://schemas.microsoft.com/winfx/2006/xaml"
  x:Class="SilverlightApplication1.App">
  <Application.Resources>

  </Application.Resources>

</Application>
```

So, now you can place style definitions in this section, and they will be available throughout the application. Here's an example:

```
<Application xmlns="http://schemas.microsoft.com/client/2007"
  xmlns:x="http://schemas.microsoft.com/winfx/2006/xaml"
  x:Class="SilverlightApplication1.App">
  <Application.Resources>
    <Style TargetType="TextBlock" x:Key="TextBlockStyle">
      <Setter Property="FontFamily" Value="Comic Sans Ms"></Setter>
      <Setter Property="Text" Value="Click!"></Setter>
      <Setter Property="Foreground" Value="MediumBlue"></Setter>
      <Setter Property="FontSize" Value="20"></Setter>
    </Style>

  </Application.Resources>
</Application>
```

With this code, you can apply this style to any *TextBlock* in the application. As mentioned earlier, you can override any of the *Style* properties by specifying properties on the control.

Templates

In the previous section, you built an image button by taking advantage of the fact that the *Button* control is a *content* control. Instead of inserting only text in the control, you used XAML that defined a *StackPanel* that contained an *Image* and a *TextBlock*. You then used styles to efficiently set the properties of the *TextBlock* to use consistent settings.

The next logical step, of course, is to set the style of the *entire* control, the *Button* and each of its subcontrols—the *StackPanel, Image*, and *TextBlock*—all in one step. This is where templates become essential tools for customizing the look of your Silverlight applications.

Templates work the same way as styles do: you place them in a *<Resources>* section and use a *Setter* to define them. To create a *Template*, you apply the setter to the *Template* property, and then use *<Setter.Value>* to define the *ControlTemplate* for the specified target.

You can understand better by looking at the code:

```
<Canvas.Resources>
    <Style TargetType="TextBlock" x:Key="TextBlockStyle">
      <Setter Property="FontFamily" Value="Comic Sans Ms"></Setter>
      <Setter Property="Text" Value="Click!"></Setter>
      <Setter Property="Foreground" Value="MediumBlue"></Setter>
      <Setter Property="FontSize" Value="20"></Setter>
    </Style>
    <Style x:Key="ImageButton" TargetType="Button">
      <Setter Property="Template">
        <Setter.Value>
          <ControlTemplate TargetType="Button">
            <Button>
              <Button.Content>
                <StackPanel Orientation="Vertical">
                  <Image Source="icon.jpg" Height="48" Width="48"></Image>
                  <TextBlock Style="{StaticResource TextBlockStyle}"
                          Foreground="Black">
                  </TextBlock>
                </StackPanel>
              </Button.Content>
            </Button>
          </ControlTemplate>
        </Setter.Value>
      </Setter>
    </Style>
  </Canvas.Resources>
```

Here you can see that the style called *ImageButton* is created, and it contains a setter for the *Template* property. The *Template* contains a *ControlTemplate* that defines a *Button* that contains a *StackPanel* with an *Image* and a *TextBlock* in it.

Note that this *TextBlock* can contain a style reference too because the *TextBlock* control in the template has its style set to the *TextBlockStyle* that you created earlier.

Now, to define the buttons, you simplify the XAML even further:

```
<Button x:Name="btn1" Style="{StaticResource ImageButton}"
        Canvas.Top="20" Canvas.Left="20"></Button>

<Button x:Name="btn2" Style="{StaticResource ImageButton}"
        Canvas.Top="20" Canvas.Left="120"></Button>

<Button x:Name="btn3" Style="{StaticResource ImageButton}"
        Canvas.Top="20" Canvas.Left="220"></Button>
```

Each button sets its *Style* to the *ImageButton* resource, which in turn defines the overall template for the control. Figure 13-4 shows the output of this XAML.

FIGURE 13-4 Templated buttons.

The really great thing about templates is that you don't necessarily have to have the specific type of control in the template that you are templating. That probably sounds a little confusing, so take a look at an example to clarify.

In the previous example, you defined a template for a button that contains content that turns it into a simple image button. But to create a button template, you don't actually need a *Button* control. So, if you want image buttons to contain an image and text only and not have the "standard" *Button* control behind them, you can do this very easily. Here's the template:

```
<Style x:Key="ImageButton" TargetType="Button">
    <Setter Property="Template">
      <Setter.Value>
        <ControlTemplate TargetType="Button">
          <StackPanel Orientation="Vertical">
            <Image Source="icon.jpg" Height="48" Width="48"></Image>
            <TextBlock Style="{StaticResource TextBlockStyle}"
                Foreground="Black">
```

```
          </TextBlock>
        </StackPanel>
      </ControlTemplate>
    </Setter.Value>
  </Setter>
</Style>
```

Now, you have a button template (specified by the *TargetType*) that doesn't include a button at all, but Silverlight will treat it as a button, including all relevant properties and events. For example, if you use this buttonless template, when you run the application, you see something similar to what is shown in Figure 13-5.

FIGURE 13-5 Buttonless buttons.

You can see that these are real buttons by writing code against them. For example, they support the full IntelliSense of a *Button* control in Visual Studio, as you can see in Figure 13-6, where the *Click* event is being coded.

```
public Page()
{
    InitializeComponent();
    btn1.Click+=
}                       new RoutedEventHandler(btn1_Click);   (Press TAB to insert)
```

FIGURE 13-6 Coding against your templated buttons.

Because templates are just special styles, you can also use them in *App.xaml* in the same manner as discussed earlier to allow control templates to be used across multiple XAML pages.

Summary

This chapter introduces you to the use of styles and templates, which are very important features in Silverlight because they allow you to centralize and finely tune the look and feel of all your controls. You learned how to define a style and how to bind a control to that style as a *StaticResource*. You then saw how you can set a style to be used across the application using *App.xaml*.

You also learned how you can extend this functionality with templates, which are similar to styles but provide the power to "skin" an entire control. You saw how to define a *ControlTemplate* to create an *ImageButton* control that has all the properties, methods, and events of a *Button* without using a *Button*.

In the next chapter, you look at how your controls can be brought to life with data through data binding and templating.

Chapter 14
Data Binding with Silverlight

In Chapter 12, "Building Connected Applications with Silverlight," you looked at connectivity in Microsoft Silverlight and how you can access services to get data. You saw some simple data binding examples, where you had data in XML and could use LINQ to XML to create bindable objects.

In this chapter, you look at how to build objects of your own and how you can use them in simple binding scenarios. Objects are the building blocks of all data binding in Silverlight, so they can help you understand the more complex binding scenarios.

Creating a Data Object

In Chapter 12, you used a data class for time series data. In this chapter, you build on that class to create a class that is bindable and that raises events that you can use to catch data binding events such as property changes.

Create a new Silverlight project in the usual manner and call it CH14_Sample1.

To this, add a folder called Data and add a new class called *TimeSeriesBoundData* to this folder.

This class implements the *INotifyPropertyChanged* interface whose definition lives in *System.ComponentModel*, so ensure that you have this declaration at the top of your class definition:

```
using System.ComponentModel;
```

Next, you should change your class declaration to ensure that it implements the *INotifyPropertyChanged* interface as discussed:

```
public class TimeSeriesBoundData : INotifyPropertyChanged
```

This class raises an event when a property changes, and you will see shortly how you can capture that event in code. So, the first thing to do in the class is to declare this event:

```
public event PropertyChangedEventHandler PropertyChanged;
```

If you recall from Chapter 12, the data class for time series data had member variables for open, close, high, low, volume, adjusted close, and date. Consider here how to implement these in this class, where changing the value (on a binding or otherwise) causes an event to be raised.

Here's how this looks for the *open* value:

```
private double _open;
      public double open
      {
          get { return _open; }
          set
          {
              _open = value;
              OnPropertyChanged("open");
          }
      }
```

This declares a private member variable called *_open*, which stores the value in the class. The *get* simply returns this value, and the *set* changes it to the value that is being passed in. The *value* variable that you see here is generated for you at run time when something updates the property, whether it is code setting the value or a data binding.

At this point, you want to raise the event that the value has changed, so call *OnPropertyChanged* and pass it the string *open*, indicating that the *open* value has changed.

Look at what this function does:

```
private void OnPropertyChanged(string propertyName)
{
    if (PropertyChanged != null)
    {
        PropertyChangedEventArgs args =
            new PropertyChangedEventArgs(propertyName);
        PropertyChanged(this, args);
    }
}
```

As you can see, this is pretty straightforward. First, it ensures that the *PropertyChanged* event is not *null*, namely, that a *PropertyChanged* event has actually happened. If an event has happened, the function creates a *PropertyChangedEventArgs* (remember that property changes in the Microsoft .NET Framework are usually handled by a function that takes the object and the arguments as parameters) and initializes these arguments with the string that is passed in, which you have defined as the name of the property whose change causes this function to be raised.

That's pretty much all the functionality for this data class. For your convenience, here is the full class with all properties defined:

```
using System;
using System.Net;
using System.Windows;
using System.Windows.Controls;
using System.Windows.Documents;
using System.Windows.Ink;
```

```csharp
using System.Windows.Input;
using System.Windows.Media;
using System.Windows.Media.Animation;
using System.Windows.Shapes;
using System.ComponentModel;

namespace CH14_Sample1.Data
{
    public class TimeSeriesBoundData : INotifyPropertyChanged
    {
        public event PropertyChangedEventHandler PropertyChanged;


        private void OnPropertyChanged(string propertyName)
        {
            if (PropertyChanged != null)
            {
                PropertyChangedEventArgs args = new PropertyChangedEventArgs(propertyName);
                PropertyChanged(this, args);
            }
        }

        private DateTime _date;
        public DateTime date
        {
            get { return _date; }
            set
            {
                _date = value;
                OnPropertyChanged("date");
            }
        }

        private double _open;
        public double open
        {
            get { return _open; }
            set
            {
                _open = value;
                OnPropertyChanged("open");
            }
        }

        private double _close;
        public double close
        {
            get { return _close; }
            set
            {
                _close = value;
                OnPropertyChanged("close");
            }
        }
```

```
private double _high;
public double high
{
    get { return _high; }
    set
    {
        _high = value;
        OnPropertyChanged("high");
    }
}

private double _low;
public double low
{
    get { return _low; }
    set
    {
        _low = value;
        OnPropertyChanged("low");
    }
}

private double _volume;
public double volume
{
    get { return _volume; }
    set
    {
        _volume = value;
        OnPropertyChanged("volume");
    }
}

private double _adjClose;
public double adjClose
{
    get { return _adjClose; }
    set
    {
        _adjClose = value;
        OnPropertyChanged("adjClose");
    }
}
    }
}
```

Now that you have a class that can be bound and that raises events, look at a simple scenario where this class is bound to user interface elements in your Extensible Application Markup Language (XAML).

Binding to the Data Object

The project that you created earlier has a MainPage.xaml class that contains a *UserControl*. Remember that you created the bindable class in the Data folder. If you look closely at the class, you can see that it was placed in a *Data* subnamespace of your main application namespace.

So, whereas your application namespace is *CH14_Sample1*, you can see that the namespace of the bindable class is *CH14_Sample1.Data*.

To use this in the user interface, make sure you create a reference to it in the XAML. At the top of the XAML, make a declaration to the namespace.

It should look like this:

```
xmlns:data ="clr-namespace:CH14_Sample1.Data"
```

Here's the complete *<UserControl>* header definition, including this declaration:

```
<UserControl x:Class="CH14_Sample1.MainPage"
    xmlns="http://schemas.microsoft.com/winfx/2006/xaml/presentation"
    xmlns:x="http://schemas.microsoft.com/winfx/2006/xaml"
    xmlns:data ="clr-namespace:CH14_Sample1.Data"
    Width="400" Height="300">
```

To make a simple data binding, you can add an instance of the *TimeSeriesBoundData* class to your *UserControl* as a resource.

To add a resource to the *UserControl*, you use *<UserControl.Resources>*, like this:

```
<UserControl.Resources>
</UserControl.Resources>
```

Remember that when you added the reference to the *CH14_Sample1.Data* namespace to the *UserControl* headers, you defined the *data* prefix for classes in this namespace. To define an instance of the *TimeSeriesBoundData*, called *TSD*, you use XAML like this:

```
<data:TimeSeriesBoundData x:Key="TSD"></data:TimeSeriesBoundData>
```

So, here's how your XAML looks:

```
    <UserControl.Resources>
        <data:TimeSeriesBoundData x:Key="TSD"></data:TimeSeriesBoundData>
    </UserControl.Resources>
```

Now that you have an instance of a *TimeSeriesBoundData* stored on your page as a resource, it's time to create some bindings to it. You create bindings using a *TextBox* that renders the value of one of the properties of the *TimeSeriesBoundData* as well as allows you to *change* the value. Additionally, you add a *TextBlock* that renders the value of the open data.

First, look at the XAML for the *TextBox*:

```
<TextBox Canvas.Top="0" x:Name="txtInput"
    Text="{Binding Source={StaticResource TSD}, Path=open, Mode=TwoWay}">
</TextBox>
```

You're probably familiar with the *Text* property of the *TextBox* by now. With the *Text* property, you specify the text that should be used to initialize the *TextBox*. In this case, you have a strange value in braces. This value is called a *Binding*. It defines that the location of the *Binding* is the resource called *TSD* that you defined in the *UserControl.Resources* section. It defines that the property that you define to (defined using a *Path*, that is, the path to the desired property) is *open*, and finally that the mode of binding is *TwoWay*, which means that you can read from the binding *and* write to the binding. Thus, with this binding, you can render values from the bound data as well as write values to it.

The *TextBlock* works in a similar way, but because a *TextBlock* doesn't allow you to *input* data, just render it, the binding needs to be only one way. Here's the XAML:

```
<TextBlock Canvas.Top="20" x:Name="txtView"
    Text="{Binding Source={StaticResource TSD}, Path=open, Mode=OneWay}">
</TextBlock>
```

As you can see here, the *Mode* value in the data binding is *OneWay*, but other than that, the declaration is identical to the *TextBox* declaration.

Here's the full XAML for this application:

```
<UserControl x:Class="CH14_Sample1.MainPage"
    xmlns="http://schemas.microsoft.com/winfx/2006/xaml/presentation"
    xmlns:x="http://schemas.microsoft.com/winfx/2006/xaml"
    xmlns:data ="clr-namespace:CH14_Sample1.Data"
    Width="400" Height="300">
    <UserControl.Resources>
        <data:TimeSeriesBoundData x:Key="TSD"></data:TimeSeriesBoundData>
    </UserControl.Resources>
    <Canvas x:Name="LayoutRoot" Background="White">
        <TextBox Canvas.Top="0" x:Name="txtInput"
            Text="{Binding Source={StaticResource TSD}, Path=open, Mode=TwoWay}">
        </TextBox>
        <TextBlock Canvas.Top="20" x:Name="txtView"
            Text="{Binding Source={StaticResource TSD}, Path=open, Mode=OneWay}">
        </TextBlock>
    </Canvas>
</UserControl>
```

When you execute this application, you see a simple UI with a *TextBox* and *TextBlock* as shown in Figure 14-1.

FIGURE 14-1 Basic data-bound UI.

Notice that the *TextBlock* and *TextBox* both contain the value 0. This is because the data was never initialized, and because the *open* value is a double, it's default is 0.

Also notice that typing values in the *TextBox* does nothing. This is because the binding occurs when the *TextBox* changes, and the change event happens when you *leave* the *TextBox* by tabbing out or by moving focus to another part of the UI. Note that this UI has only a *TextBlock*, which cannot receive focus. You must use the Tab key to move out of the *TextBlock* and to see the change on the *TextBlock*.

You can see the results of the data binding in Figure 14-2.

FIGURE 14-2 Seeing the data binding in action.

So, now you've created your first bindable class and can see how to bind it using XAML data binding.

This data binding works well if you type *123*, as you can see in Figure 14-2, but what happens if you use the value *123ABC*? Remember that *open* is a double value, and *123ABC* isn't a double, so when you try to make the change, nothing happens because the value is invalid. In the next section, you look into this issue in more detail and find how you can use a special class for converting the data in the binding to make sure that objects bind cleanly.

Using Conversion in Binding

If you run the example from earlier in this chapter and try to bind an invalid value (such as *123ABC*) by typing it into the *TextBox*, you'll notice that no binding occurs. This is because an error happened during the binding. There's nothing in your code to catch and handle this error, so you see nothing happening right now.

You can see the error in the Output tab in Microsoft Visual Studio. It should look something like this:

```
System.Windows.Data Error: ConvertBack cannot convert value '123abc' (type 'System.String').
BindingExpression: Path='open' DataItem='CH14_Sample1.Data.TimeSeriesBoundData'
(HashCode=35912612); target element is 'System.Windows.Controls.TextBox' (Name='txtInput');
target property is 'Text' (type 'System.String').. System.FormatException: Input string was
not in a correct format.
   at System.Number.StringToNumber(String str, NumberStyles options, NumberBuffer& number,
NumberFormatInfo info, Boolean parseDecimal)
   at System.Number.ParseDouble(String value, NumberStyles options, NumberFormatInfo numfmt)
   at System.Double.Parse(String s, NumberStyles style, NumberFormatInfo info)
   at System.Double.Parse(String s, NumberStyles style, IFormatProvider provider)
   at System.Convert.ToDouble(String value, IFormatProvider provider)
   at System.String.System.IConvertible.ToDouble(IFormatProvider provider)
   at System.Convert.ChangeType(Object value, Type conversionType, IFormatProvider provider)
   at MS.Internal.Data.SystemConvertConverter.Convert(Object o, Type type, Object parameter,
CultureInfo culture)
   at MS.Internal.Data.DynamicValueConverter.Convert(Object value, Type targetType, Object
parameter, CultureInfo culture)
   at System.Windows.Data.BindingExpression.UpdateValue().
```

Now this isn't very user-friendly, so what can you do to handle the error? You can either write lots of code to handle each possible binding error, or you can use the *Converter* functionality that's available as part of the data binding syntax. *Converter* defines a class that is used to clean your data as part of the binding.

Add a new class to the Data folder called *ToDoubleConverter.cs*. This implements the *IValueConverter* interface, which is found in *System.Windows.Data*. Add the following declaration to the top of the class:

```
using System.Windows.Data;
```

To implement the class, you need to amend the class declaration as follows:

```
public class ToDoubleConverter : IValueConverter
```

This interface requires that you implement the *Convert* and *ConvertBack* functions. The former is used when the data is read from the binding, the latter when it is being written to the binding.

So, in both cases, ensure that the value is a double. Note that you don't really need a double in the *Convert* for this sample because the error you encounter occurs when you type a string into the *TextBlock*, causing a *ConvertBack* to be called.

```
public object Convert(object value, Type targetType,
    object parameter, System.Globalization.CultureInfo culture)
        {
            double nReturn = 0.0;
            double.TryParse(value.ToString(), out nReturn);
            return nReturn;
        }

    public object ConvertBack(object value, Type targetType,
    object parameter, System.Globalization.CultureInfo culture)
        {
            double nReturn = 0.0;
            double.TryParse(value.ToString(), out nReturn);
            return nReturn;
        }
```

The conversion is pretty simple—you create a double value containing 0, and then use the *TryParse* functionality in .NET to see whether the string can be parsed into a double. If it can, it is parsed; if it cannot, the value is zero.

Here's the complete *ToDoubleConverter* class:

```
using System;
using System.Net;
using System.Windows;
using System.Windows.Controls;
using System.Windows.Documents;
using System.Windows.Ink;
using System.Windows.Input;
using System.Windows.Media;
using System.Windows.Media.Animation;
using System.Windows.Shapes;
using System.Windows.Data;

namespace CH14_Sample1.Data
{
    public class ToDoubleConverter : IValueConverter
    {

        #region IValueConverter Members

        public object Convert(object value, Type targetType, object parameter,
System.Globalization.CultureInfo culture)
        {
            double nReturn = 0.0;
            double.TryParse(value.ToString(), out nReturn);
            return nReturn;
        }
```

```
        public object ConvertBack(object value, Type targetType, object parameter,
System.Globalization.CultureInfo culture)
        {
            double nReturn = 0.0;
            double.TryParse(value.ToString(), out nReturn);
            return nReturn;
        }

        #endregion
    }
}
```

At this point, you should compile your application and ensure that there are no errors. If you do this, the autocomplete functionality works in Visual Studio for the next step, where you add an instance of the *Converter* class to your application.

Go back to the *<UserControl.Resources>* section in your XAML and add an instance of the *ToDoubleConverter*. Here's how:

```
<data:ToDoubleConverter x:Key="dblConverter"></data:ToDoubleConverter>
```

So, now the *Resources* section looks like this:

```
<UserControl.Resources>
    <data:TimeSeriesBoundData x:Key="TSD"></data:TimeSeriesBoundData>
    <data:ToDoubleConverter x:Key="dblConverter"></data:ToDoubleConverter>
</UserControl.Resources>
```

You can see that this instance of the *Converter* class is called *dblConverter*.

The last step is to implement the converter as part of the binding. The conversion takes place when you type an invalid value (such as *ABC123*) in the *TextBox*, so you need to specify to use this instance as part of the binding.

Here's the new *TextBox* declaration:

```
<TextBox Canvas.Top="0" x:Name="txtInput"
    Text="{Binding Source={StaticResource TSD}, Path=open, Mode=TwoWay,
        Converter={StaticResource dblConverter}}">
</TextBox>
```

Now when you run your application and type an invalid value in the *TextBox*, you'll see that it is converted to 0 and bound correctly.

Catching Property Changed Events

Earlier when you created the bindable class for the time series data, you built the class so that a change on one of the properties raises an event. These events are standard events, so they are pretty easy to catch. Also, you added an instance of the *TimeSeriesBoundData* class to your application as a resource called *TSD*.

Take a look at the constructor for the Silverlight application. The XAML is called MainPage.xaml by default, so you can see that the constructor function is called *MainPage()*.

After the *InitializeComponent()* call in the constructor, add the following code to get a reference to the class instance that is in the resources. Here's how:

```
TimeSeriesBoundData theData = this.Resources["TSD"] as TimeSeriesBoundData;
```

Now that you have this reference, you can specify the event handler for the *PropertyChanged*. In Visual Studio, if you type **theData** and then a period (**.**), you open the shortcut menu for the available properties, methods, and events. Look down the list, and you'll see the *PropertyChanged* event available. Select it, and press the Tab key. Then, type **+=**, and you'll see a tooltip appear with the suggested code. Press Tab to enter this code, and press Tab again to generate the stub for the event handler.

The stub looks something like this:

```
void theData_PropertyChanged(object sender, System.ComponentModel.PropertyChangedEventArgs e)
{}
```

Now, whenever the value of any of the properties changes, this event is fired.

The arguments object, called *e* contains a property called *PropertyName*, which you defined earlier in this chapter. *PropertyName* is a string that contains the name of the property that changed.

You can read this easily like this:

```
string theProperty = e.PropertyName;
```

Now that you have the name of the property that has changed, you can perform any additional processing.

If you run this application and set a breakpoint on the preceding line of code, you can see that *e.PropertyName* will be *open*.

The Binding Language

In this chapter, you can see a number of examples of binding in which a list of values is used in braces to define how the binding can work.

Look at these properties, the various values that they support, and how you can use them:

- **Source**   *Source* defines where the binding occurs. It can be a resource in the XAML, in which case you define it as a *StaticResource*, or another bindable source such as an *IEnumerable*, as discussed in Chapter 12.

- **Path**   *Path* is the identifier of the property that you want to bind to on the source.

- **Mode**   *Mode* defines the binding mode. It can contain the value *OneWay*, in which case it's a read-only binding; *TwoWay*, in which case it's a read and write binding; or *OneTime*, which is a one-off binding that occurs at the first render of the control.

- **Converter**   You use *Converter* when data conversion is needed during a binding. You saw an example of this earlier in the chapter. *Converter* contains the name of an instance of the *Converter* class. It can also use a *ConverterParameter* and *ConverterCulture* for finer-grained handling. These aren't discussed in this book.

Summary

In this chapter, by building a bindable class and a simple application that provides both one-way and two-way data binding, you saw the basics of how data binding works in Silverlight. You also looked at how you can handle errors in the data binding using a *Converter* as well as the binding language that XAML uses to define the binding. The information in this chapter is a foundation on which you can build data-bound applications and understand how data binding works in sophisticated data-bound controls such as the *DataGrid*.

Chapter 15
Using Dynamic Languages in Silverlight

Microsoft Silverlight supports the use of *dynamic* languages, which are defined as programming languages that execute many features at *run time* that other languages, such as C#, execute at *compile* time. Such behaviors include extending objects and definitions, modifying the type system, and more. Dynamic languages are designed to be a simple approach that you can use to execute a run-evaluate-print loop with lots of trial and error as you develop, as opposed to the traditional model of code-compile-test-recompile.

Silverlight supports three of the more popular dynamic languages: Ruby, Python, and Dynamic JavaScript. This book is written to the Silverlight 3 beta specification, which does not include a Microsoft Visual Studio 2008 project template, but the software development kit (SDK) does provide a tool, Chiron.exe, that you can use to work with dynamic languages.

The dynamic language initiative from Microsoft is open source and is available on the CodePlex Web site at *http://www.codeplex.com/sdlsdk*. In this chapter, you explore building some basic applications for Silverlight with dynamic languages. This chapter isn't intended to be a learning tool for the languages themselves, but the programs are fairly straightforward, so you'll be able to figure out what they're doing even if you aren't an expert in the particular language.

This chapter is intended solely as a primer in dynamic languages and how to use them in Silverlight. You spend most of your time in this chapter touring Visual Studio and learning how you can use it to create IronPython, IronRuby, and managed JavaScript applications in Silverlight, as well as how to integrate Chiron.exe into Visual Studio. Later on, you tour the famous Silverlight clock sample and find out how it was implemented in Ruby.

Your First Silverlight IronPython Application

The Chiron tool is easiest to use if you have a specific application directory structure set up for your application. In this section, you learn how to do this step by step.

First, start Visual Studio, and create an *empty* Web site by selecting New Web Site on the File menu. You'll see Empty Web Site as an option in the New Web Site dialog box, as shown in Figure 15-1.

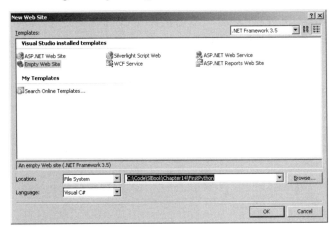

FIGURE 15-1 New Web Site dialog box.

This option creates an empty directory that Visual Studio can access as a Web site. You will use Chiron to run the site, but you will find that creating the pages, code, and so on is easier in Visual Studio.

From the Solution, right-click the project folder, and select Add New Item—this opens the Add New Item dialog box that you can use to create a new HTML page. Select the HTML Page option, and give it the name Default.html. See Figure 15-2.

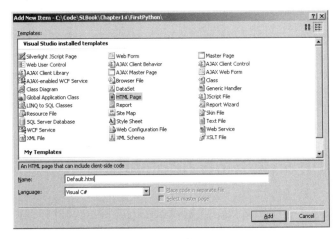

FIGURE 15-2 Add a new item to your site.

This gives you a basic HTML page, which you need to edit to turn into a page that will host the Silverlight application. Following is the code for such a page:

```
<html xmlns="http://www.w3.org/1999/xhtml" >
<head>
  <title>Dynamic Silverlight Test Page </title>
  <style type="text/css">
    html, body {
       height: 100%;
       overflow: auto;
    }
    body {
       padding: 0;
       margin: 0;
    }
    #silverlightControlHost {
       height: 100%;
    }
  </style>
</head>
<body>
  <div id="silverlightControlHost">
   <object data="data:application/x-silverlight-2,"
    type="application/x-silverlight-2"
    width="100%" height="100%">
      <param name="source" value="app.xap"/>
      <param name="background" value="white" />
      <param name="windowless" value="true" />
    </object>
    <iframe style='visibility:hidden;height:0;width:0;border:0px'></iframe>
  </div>
</body>

</html>
```

This uses the *<object>* tag approach to host Silverlight in the page. This is a very simplified example, so it doesn't include the code to provide an install experience if Silverlight isn't present on the system. For more details on how to do this, refer to Chapter 6, "The Silverlight Browser Object."

Note the *source* parameter, which is set to *app.xap*. Chiron will build this for you, as you see in a moment. For it to have this name, your code file must be called app. Do note that Chiron is not compiling the code into the XAP file, it's just putting all the script into this file so that Silverlight can load it.

First, you look at how to build your application with IronPython and an app.py file, and later you see how to create the same functionality with IronRuby and Dynamic JavaScript.

Next, create a directory in your Web site called app. In this, select Add New Item, and then select the XML File template and call the file app.xaml.

Here's some simple Extensible Application Markup Language (XAML) that you can put in this file:

```
<UserControl x:Class="System.Windows.Controls.UserControl"
    xmlns="http://schemas.microsoft.com/winfx/2006/xaml/presentation"
    xmlns:x="http://schemas.microsoft.com/winfx/2006/xaml" >

  <Grid x:Name="layout_root" Background="White">
    <TextBlock x:Name="Message" FontSize="30" />
  </Grid>

</UserControl>
```

This code defines a simple *UserControl* object that contains a *TextBlock* called *txtMessage*. This *TextBlock* contains the text "Hello World,"—note that it ends with a comma. You'll see why in a moment.

Next, add the IronPython code file. Again, right-click the app folder in your Web site, and select Add New Item. In the dialog box, select Text File and call it app.py (py is the extension for Python).

As a quick check, Figure 15-3 shows what your solution should look like at this point.

FIGURE 15-3 Your solution structure.

Now you can edit your Python code file to make it do something more interesting. Here's the code:

```
from System.Windows import Application
from System.Windows.Controls import UserControl

def handleClick(sender, eventArgs):
    sender.Text = sender.Text + " from Python!"
```

```
class App:
    def __init__(self):
        self.scene =
          Application.Current.LoadRootVisual(UserControl(),
                                            "app.xaml")

    def start(self):
        self.scene.txtMessage.MouseLeftButtonUp += handleClick

App().start()
```

If you've been writing Silverlight applications in C# or Microsoft Visual Basic, the syntax will be somewhat familiar to you. For example, the line

```
from System.Windows import Application
```

is equivalent to the C#

```
using System.Windows;
```

and then a reference to the *Application* class in code.

The code then defines a Python class called *App* and sets the *scene* object for this *App* by loading the XAML file that you defined earlier. As part of this class definition, it defines the startup event hander with

```
def start(self):
```

and specifies the code to execute in this handler. This code defines the event handler for the *MouseLeftButtonUp* event on the *TextBlock* control called *txtMessage* that you defined earlier. The event hander is called *handleClick*.

The event handler code is as follows:

```
def handleClick(sender, eventArgs):
    sender.Text = sender.Text + " from Python!"
```

This adds the text "from Python!" to the end of the *Text* property of its sender (which in this case is the *TextBlock*) upon being called.

To run this application, you'll use Chiron. You can configure Visual Studio to start Chiron by right-clicking the project file in Solution Explorer (note that you must use the project file and not the solution file—the project file is usually the first child of the solution) and clicking Property Pages on the shortcut menu.

On the Property Pages, select Start Options, and then select Start External Program. Use the ellipsis button (...) to browse to the location of Chiron.exe, which is in the bin directory of the Dynamic Languages SDK for Silverlight. (You can download the full SDK called AgDLR at *http://www.codeplex.com/sdlsdk*.)

Type **/b** in the Command Line Arguments box, and then enter the location of the Web site in the Working Directory box. Figure 15-4 shows an example of this.

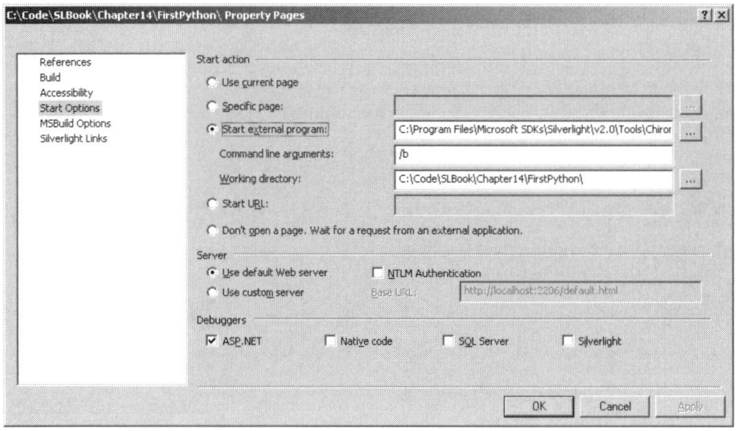

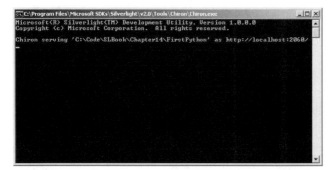

FIGURE 15-4 Configuring Visual Studio to use Chiron.

Now you can execute your dynamic Silverlight application by pressing F5 in Visual Studio. Chiron will start, and you'll see evidence of this in a command prompt window that looks like the one shown in Figure 15-5.

FIGURE 15-5 Chiron being executed by Visual Studio.

This shows you that the application is accessed through *http://localhost:2060*. Visual Studio will also start a browser at this address, which gives you a listing of the files in the Web directory, as you can see in Figure 15-6.

FIGURE 15-6 Chiron directory listing.

Select Default.html to see your dynamic Silverlight application. The "Hello World," message will display in the browser, as shown in Figure 15-7.

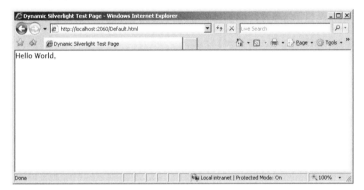

FIGURE 15-7 Your first Silverlight Python application.

Now, if you click the "Hello World," text, the additional message "from Python!" is added to the block, as shown in Figure 15-8.

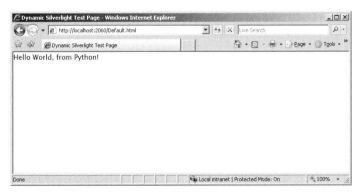

FIGURE 15-8 Dynamic application in action.

Although this is an extremely simple application, it demonstrates how the Dynamic Language Runtime works in Silverlight and how you can configure Visual Studio to use dynamic languages. In the next section, you learn about how you can use IronRuby and managed JavaScript in the same application.

Using Ruby and JavaScript

In the previous section, you stepped through the process used to configure Visual Studio to build dynamic language applications in IronPython. Because the Dynamic Language Runtime also supports Ruby and Dynamic JavaScript, you can use them in the same application, as you'll see in this section.

Using Ruby

To begin the process of using Ruby, first you need to create a project structure, including an HTML file and an XAML file, similar to the one you created for IronPython in the previous section. In this case, in the app folder, instead of an app.py file, you create an app.rb file for your Ruby code. Also make sure that you configure the project settings to start Chiron the same way as you did in the previous example. (Look back at Figure 15-4 for details on how to do this.)

Edit the app.rb so that it contains this IronRuby code:

```
include System::Windows
include System::Windows::Controls

def handleClick(sender, eventArgs)
  sender.text = "Hello World, from Ruby!"
end

class App
  def initialize
      @scene = Application.Current.LoadRootVisual(UserControl.new(),
                                       "app.xaml")
  end

  def start
      @scene.find_name('txtMessage').mouse_left_button_up
      { |sender, args| handleClick(sender, args) }
  end
end
App.new.start
```

As you can see, it is very similar to the example in IronPython. This includes the *System.Windows* and *System.Windows.Controls* namespaces. It then defines a *handleClick* event handler to change the text whenever it is called.

Then, the class called *App* is defined. The class constructor loads the XAML and uses it to initialize the class, and the *Start* event wires up the event handler to the *TextBlock* defined in the XAML and named *txtMessage*.

Now, when you run the application, you get the same results—the *TextBlock* renders "Hello World," and when the user clicks the text, it adds "from Ruby!"

Using Dynamic JavaScript

To use JavaScript, follow the same routine as you did in the previous two examples; that is, create a Web site in Visual Studio, and then add the HTML and XAML files to it. Remember that you also need to configure the project to use Chiron. You can see how to do this by referring to Figure 15-4.

This time, instead of app.py or app.rb files, you add an app.jsx file to the app directory. Edit the contents of the app.jsx file so that it contains the following JavaScript code:

```
Import("System.Windows.Application")
Import("System.Windows.Controls.UserControl")

function handleClick(sender, eventArgs) {
    sender.Text = sender.Text + " from Dynamic JavaScript";
}

function App() {
    this.scene =
      Application.Current.LoadRootVisual(new UserControl(),
                                      "app.xaml")
}

App.prototype.start = function() {
    this.scene.txtMessage.MouseLeftButtonUp += handleClick
}


app = new App
app.start()
```

As you can see, the code is still very familiar. Managed JavaScript uses the *Import* statement to add a reference to the *SystemWindows.Application* and *System.Windows.Controls.UserControl* classes. In JavaScript, the application itself is a function to which you add properties, so the *scene* is a member of the *App* function, and it is defined by loading the XAML. The *MouseLeftButtonUp* event is handled by the *handleClick* function, and this is defined in the *start* function for the application.

The *handleClick*, as in the earlier examples, adds specific text, in this case, "from Dynamic JavaScript", to the string in the *txtMessage TextBlock* that is defined in the XAML.

The results are essentially the same as those for the two previous examples. The application displays a "Hello World" message, and then it is amended with additional text when the user clicks the message.

A More Complex Example

The first Silverlight sample to see the light of day (back when Silverlight was called WPF/E) is the clock example. You can see what it looks like in Figure 15-9.

This is a great sample of a Silverlight application because it demonstrates many of the principles of programming in Silverlight. The clock itself requires no programming to operate—it is all managed by Silverlight animations, and all you need to do is initialize the clock hands to the starting position based on the system time.

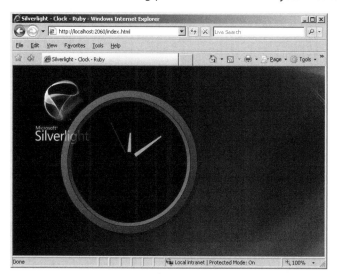

FIGURE 15-9 Silverlight clock.

First, look at the XAML for the clock. Note that this XAML is abbreviated just to show the three clock hands and their animations:

```
<Canvas x:Class="System.Windows.Controls.Canvas"
    xmlns="http://schemas.microsoft.com/client/2007"
    xmlns:x="http://schemas.microsoft.com/winfx/2006/xaml"
    Opacity="0" x:Name="parentCanvas">
```

```xml
<Canvas.Triggers>
    <EventTrigger RoutedEvent="Canvas.Loaded">
        <EventTrigger.Actions>
            <BeginStoryboard>
                <Storyboard>
                    <DoubleAnimation x:Name="hour_animation"
                        Storyboard.TargetName="hourHandTransform"
                        Storyboard.TargetProperty="Angle"
                        From="180" To="540"
                        Duration="12:0:0"
                        RepeatBehavior="Forever"/>
                    <DoubleAnimation x:Name="minute_animation"
                        Storyboard.TargetName="minuteHandTransform"
                        Storyboard.TargetProperty="Angle"
                        From="180" To="540"
                        Duration="1:0:0"
                        RepeatBehavior="Forever"/>
                    <DoubleAnimation x:Name="second_animation"
                        Storyboard.TargetName="secondHandTransform"
                        Storyboard.TargetProperty="Angle"
                        From="180" To="540"
                        Duration="0:1:0"
                        RepeatBehavior="Forever"/>
                </Storyboard>
            </BeginStoryboard>
        </EventTrigger.Actions>
    </EventTrigger>
</Canvas.Triggers>

<!-- Hour hand -->
<Path Data="M -4, 16 l 3 40 3 0 2 -40 z" Fill="white">
    <Path.RenderTransform>
        <TransformGroup>
            <RotateTransform x:Name="hourHandTransform"
                Angle="180"/>
            <TranslateTransform X="150.5" Y="145"/>
        </TransformGroup>
    </Path.RenderTransform>
</Path>

<!-- Minute hand -->
<Path Data="M -4, 16 l 3 70 3 0 2 -70 z" Fill="white">
    <Path.RenderTransform>
        <TransformGroup>
            <RotateTransform x:Name="minuteHandTransform"
                Angle="180"/>
            <TranslateTransform X="150.5" Y="145"/>
        </TransformGroup>
    </Path.RenderTransform>
</Path>

<!-- Second hand -->
<Path Data="M -1, 16 l 0 70 2 0 0 -70 z" Fill="red">
    <Path.RenderTransform>
```

```
        <TransformGroup>
          <RotateTransform x:Name="secondHandTransform"
                  Angle="180"/>
          <TranslateTransform X="150.5" Y="145"/>
        </TransformGroup>
      </Path.RenderTransform>
    </Path>

</Canvas>
```

The XAML begins with the three animations stored within their storyboards. Because you can think of the hands of the clock as lines that rotate, you can see that these are *DoubleAnimation* types that are affecting the angle of the rotation. For more about animation and how it works in XAML, see Chapter 5, "XAML Transformation and Animation."

The point to note in the animations is their names. They are called *hour_animation*, *minute_animation*, and *second_animation*. Remember these when you look at the code. Each animation targets a named transform where the hour, minute, and second target the transforms called *hourHandTransform, minuteHandTransform,* and *secondHandTransform,* respectively. You can see these transforms farther down in the XAML. Each of the hands is implemented as a *Path*, and these paths have transforms associated with them that are called by the names that you saw targeted previously.

So, the animations begin on *Canvas.Loaded* and repeat forever, moving the hands through the 360 degrees of the clock over the appropriate length of time. But how can they be initialized to represent the current time on the clock? That's where your code comes in.

The code for the clock is in two Ruby modules; the first is a helper class that was built by the Silverlight Dynamic Languages team to share across all your Ruby-based applications. It's listed here:

```
include System::Windows
include System::Windows::Controls
include System::Windows::Media

class SilverlightApplication
  def application
    Application.current
  end

  def self.use_xaml(options = {})
    options = {:type => UserControl, :name => "app"}.merge(options)
      Application.current.load_root_visual(
        options[:type].new, "#{options[:name]}.xaml")
  end

  def root
    application.root_visual
  end
```

```
    def method_missing(m)
      root.send(m)
    end
end

class FrameworkElement
  def method_missing(m)
    find_name(m.to_s.to_clr_string)
  end
end
```

This defines a number of helper functions and objects, including the following:

- ***application***   Points to the current application (simply abbreviating *Application.current*)

- ***root***   Points to the root visual, namely, the top-level element in the XAML

- ***method_missing***   Handles the translation of a method name into a *clr* string format to aid in programming

- ***use_xaml***   Manages the loading of the XAML into the Visual Tree

The code for the clock application uses the *root* and *use_xaml* helper functions, so take a look at it:

```
require 'Silverlight'

class Clock < SilverlightApplication
  use_xaml :type => Canvas

  def start
    d = Time.now()
    root.hour_animation.from    = from_angle  d.hour, 1, d.minute/2
    root.hour_animation.to      = to_angle    d.hour
    root.minute_animation.from  = from_angle  d.minute
    root.minute_animation.to    = to_angle    d.minute
    root.second_animation.from  = from_angle  d.second
    root.second_animation.to    = to_angle    d.second
  end

  def from_angle(time, divisor = 5, offset = 0)
    ((time / (12.0 * divisor)) * 360) + offset + 180
  end

  def to_angle(time)
    from_angle(time) + 360
  end
end

Clock.new.start
```

Note that the first line of this code is

```
require 'Silverlight'
```

which means that the Silverlight.rb file must be included because you are going to be deriving the application class from it.

Then, you define a *Clock* class that derives from *SilverlightApplication* (defined in Silverlight.rb) like this:

```
class Clock < SilverlightApplication
```

The *use_xaml* function from *SilverlightApplication* is called, and you specify that the type of XAML you are using is *<Canvas>* based. This is a throwback to Silverlight 1.0, when all XAML had *<Canvas>* as its root.

Next comes the *start* function, which the *use_xaml* function calls after the initialization is completed. It gets the current time using the *Time.now* function, and then uses this to figure out the *from* and *to* values for the three animations. Remember the names of the animations—*hour_animation*, *minute_animation*, and *second_animation*? Now you can see how they are used. In Ruby, you call a function with its name, followed by a space, followed by a comma-separated list of parameters. So, the angle representing the current *hour* is derived by calling the *from_angle* and passing it the appropriate parameters, which in this case are the current hour, 1, and the current minute divided by 2. The reason for dividing the minute by 2 is that the 0-degree case for the transform is actually pointing downward, so we want to offset it by 180 degrees and thus divide the current minute by 2 to "flip" the angle that the *minute* value gives.

You can see the function here:

```
def from_angle(time, divisor = 5, offset = 0)
    ((time / (12.0 * divisor)) * 360) + offset + 180
End
```

Looking back at the code, you can see that the *start* condition simply uses this function to calculate the appropriate transformation angles from which to start animating, and then assigns those to the *from* property of the animation. Similarly, the value that you are animating *to* is 360 degrees plus the current *from* value. Thus, the transformation sweeps the hand through 360 degrees from the starting value over the appropriate time frame (24 hours for the hour hand, 1 hour for the minute hand, and 1 minute for the second hand).

Finally, you start the application by creating a new instance of the *Clock* class and starting it:

```
Clock.new.start
```

Thus, using Ruby, you've created a functional Silverlight application—a working animated clock.

Summary

This chapter introduces you to dynamic languages and how to build a simple *Hello World* application using IronPython, IronRuby, and managed JavaScript. You saw how to configure Visual Studio to work with the Chiron tool that is used to build and manage the running of dynamic applications.

This is just a simple illustration of what is possible, however—enough to get you going and then inspire you to keep experimenting with dynamic languages for yourself.

And with that, this book comes to an end. Before you picked up this book, you might have been curious about Silverlight and what you can do with it. When I wrote this book, I did not want to create an exhaustive and encyclopedic reference, but instead I wanted to present all the great features of Silverlight in an approachable way so that you could select any chapter, work your way through it, and by the end understand what is involved in the technology— and have the confidence to go even further with what you have learned.

I hope you have had as much fun working through these chapters as I had writing them!

Index

Best Practices for Software Engineering

Software Estimation:
Demystifying the Black Art
Steve McConnell
ISBN 9780735605350

Amazon.com's pick for "Best Computer Book of 2006"! Generating accurate software estimates is fairly straight-forward—once you understand the art of creating them. Acclaimed author Steve McConnell demystifies the process—illuminating the practical procedures, formulas, and heuristics you can apply right away.

Code Complete,
Second Edition
Steve McConnell
ISBN 9780735619678

Widely considered one of the best practical guides to programming—fully updated. Drawing from research, academia, and everyday commercial practice, McConnell synthesizes must-know principles and techniques into clear, pragmatic guidance. Rethink your approach—and deliver the highest quality code.

Agile Portfolio Management
Jochen Krebs
ISBN 9780735625679

Agile processes foster better collaboration, innovation, and results. So why limit their use to software projects—when you can transform your entire business? This book illuminates the opportunities—and rewards—of applying agile processes to your overall IT portfolio, with best practices for optimizing results.

Simple Architectures for
Complex Enterprises
Roger Sessions
ISBN 9780735625785

Why do so many IT projects fail? Enterprise consultant Roger Sessions believes complex problems require simple solutions. And in this book, he shows how to make simplicity a core architectural requirement—as critical as performance, reliability, or security—to achieve better, more reliable results for your organization.

The Enterprise and Scrum
Ken Schwaber
ISBN 9780735623378

Extend Scrum's benefits—greater agility, higher-quality products, and lower costs—beyond individual teams to the entire enterprise. Scrum cofounder Ken Schwaber describes proven practices for adopting Scrum principles across your organization, including that all-critical component—managing change.

ALSO SEE

Software Requirements, Second Edition
Karl E. Wiegers
ISBN 9780735618794

More About Software Requirements:
Thorny Issues and Practical Advice
Karl E. Wiegers
ISBN 9780735622678

Software Requirement Patterns
Stephen Withall
ISBN 9780735623989

Agile Project Management with Scrum
Ken Schwaber
ISBN 9780735619937

For C# Developers

Microsoft® Visual C#® 2008 Express Edition: Build a Program Now!
Patrice Pelland
ISBN 9780735625426

Build your own Web browser or other cool application—no programming experience required! Featuring learn-by-doing projects and plenty of examples, this full-color guide is your quick start to creating your first applications for Windows®. DVD includes Express Edition software plus code samples.

Microsoft Visual C# 2008 Step by Step
John Sharp
ISBN 9780735624306

Teach yourself Visual C# 2008—one step at a time. Ideal for developers with fundamental programming skills, this practical tutorial delivers hands-on guidance for creating C# components and Windows–based applications. CD features practice exercises, code samples, and a fully searchable eBook.

Learn Programming Now! Microsoft XNA® Game Studio 2.0
Rob Miles
ISBN 9780735625228

Now you can create your own games for Xbox 360® and Windows—as you learn the underlying skills and concepts for computer programming. Dive right into your first project, adding new tools and tricks to your arsenal as you go. Master the fundamentals of XNA Game Studio and Visual C#—no experience required!

Programming Microsoft Visual C# 2008: The Language
Donis Marshall
ISBN 9780735625402

Get the in-depth reference, best practices, and code you need to master the core language capabilities in Visual C# 2008. Fully updated for Microsoft .NET Framework 3.5, including a detailed exploration of LINQ, this book examines language features in detail—and across the product life cycle.

Windows via C/C++, Fifth Edition
Jeffrey Richter, Christophe Nasarre
ISBN 9780735624245

Jeffrey Richter's classic guide to C++ programming—now fully revised for Windows XP, Windows Vista®, and Windows Server® 2008. Learn to develop more-robust applications with unmanaged C++ code—and apply advanced techniques—with comprehensive guidance and code samples from the experts.

CLR via C#, Second Edition
Jeffrey Richter
ISBN 9780735621633

Dig deep and master the intricacies of the common language runtime (CLR) and the .NET Framework. Written by programming expert Jeffrey Richter, this guide is ideal for developers building any kind of application—ASP.NET, Windows Forms, Microsoft SQL Server®, Web services, console apps—and features extensive C# code samples.

ALSO SEE

Microsoft Visual C# 2005 Step by Step
ISBN 9780735621299

Programming Microsoft Visual C# 2005: The Language
ISBN 9780735621817

Debugging Microsoft .NET 2.0 Applications
ISBN 9780735622029

microsoft.com/mspress

About the Author

 Laurence Moroney is a Senior Technology Evangelist at Microsoft, focusing on Silverlight and User Experience. He has more than a decade of experience in software design and implementation and has authored about a dozen books on topics as varied as the Windows Presentation Foundation, Web Development, Security, and Interoperability. In addition to this, he has written over 150 articles for various print and online media and has spoken on these topics in conferences around the world. Laurence lives in Sammamish, Washington, with his wife Rebecca and his two children.

What do you think of this book?

We want to hear from you!

Your feedback will help us continually improve our books and learning resources for you. To participate in a brief online survey, please visit:

microsoft.com/learning/booksurvey

...and enter this book's ISBN-10 or ISBN-13 number (appears above barcode on back cover). As a thank-you to survey participants in the U.S. and Canada, each month we'll randomly select five respondents to win one of five $100 gift certificates from a leading online merchant. At the conclusion of the survey, you can enter the drawing by providing your e-mail address, which will be used for prize notification only.*

Thank you in advance for your input!

Where to find the ISBN on back cover

Example only. Each book has unique ISBN.

Stay in touch!

To subscribe to the *Microsoft Press® Book Connection Newsletter*—for news on upcoming books, events, and special offers—please visit:

microsoft.com/learning/books/newsletter